More Praise for *EPIC Change*

"As a serial entrepreneur and CEO of a Hi-Tech startup, I thought I 'got' change. I was wrong; Tim Clark has given me a model to harness change into sustainable results."

—**Darren Lee**, CEO, NextPage

"Through a systemic approach, Tim describes the challenges and solutions to all kinds of organizational change to create competitive advantage in a global world."

—**Juan Carlos Linares**, president, DBM Colombia, Bogota, Colombia

"Tim Clark provides an insightful and thought-provoking description of the human dynamics inherent in change, as well as a valuable framework for executives to follow for the health of their organizations. I highly recommend this book to anyone whose responsibilities or interests involve leading others; these concepts are essential for competitiveness in the twenty-first century global economy."

—**Mark Jennings**, managing director, Grey Mountain Partners

"Not only a must-read ... this is a book that deserves study over and over. It is filled with practical, substantive, and complex-made-simple concepts and tools to benefit anyone leading large organizational change. As a change consultant, *EPIC Change* is already influencing the way I approach my work with my clients who are leading change."

—**Marcelino Sanchez**, corporate manager, Enterprise Change Management, Textron, Inc.

"Utah Valley State College has gone through significant change as we have moved to Utah Valley University. We have used Dr. Clark's theory and strategy in moving us successfully to a bright future. His writing and presentations are both academically sound and organizationally practical."

—**Dr. William Sederburg**, president, Utah Valley University

"Only exceptional leaders can see clearly the crisis facing their organizations, coalesce their team, develop the sense of urgency, and communicate the vision and strategy needed to steer the organizations through the crisis. Tim Clark has produced an indispensable, best-in-class, road map for change leaders. Ignore this book at your peril."

—**Joseph A. Cannon**, editor, *Deseret News*

JB JOSSEY-BASS

EPIC CHANGE

How to Lead

Change in the Global Age

Timothy R. Clark

BICENTENNIAL
1807
WILEY
2007
BICENTENNIAL

John Wiley & Sons, Inc.

Published by Jossey-Bass
A Wiley Imprint
989 Market Street, San Francisco, CA 94103-1741   www.josseybass.com

Wiley Bicentennial logo: Richard J. Pacifico

Jossey-Bass books and products are available through most bookstores. To contact Jossey-Bass directly
call our Customer Care Department within the U.S. at 800-956-7739, outside the U.S. at 317-572-3986,
or fax 317-572-4002.

Jossey-Bass also publishes its books in a variety of electronic formats. Some content that appears in
print may not be available in electronic books.

Library of Congress Cataloging-in-Publication Data

Clark, Timothy R., 1964-
  Epic change : how to lead change in the global age / Timothy R. Clark.
    p. cm.
  Includes bibliographical references and index.
  ISBN 978-0-470-18255-0 (cloth)
1. Organizational change—Management. 2. Leadership. I. Title.
  HD58.8.C524 2008
  658.4′092—dc22

                                        2007021303

Printed in the United States of America

FIRST EDITION

HB Printing   10 9 8 7 6 5 4 3 2 1

CONTENTS

To Tracey

EPIC CHANGE

PART ONE

OVERVIEW

Several years ago I left the dreamy spires of Oxford to return to the United States and look for a teaching position. It was my career plan to settle down into an academic post somewhere. But that was not to be. I ultimately found myself on a very different path; I took a job with a large manufacturing organization and stayed for eight years.

During that time, I became a plant manager rather than a tenured professor. Instead of walking the halls of academe in khakis and loafers, I found myself in fire-retardant greens and steel-toed boots with metatarsal shields. When I made the theory-to-practice transition and traded the ivory tower for the shop floor, I could not have imagined the journey ahead. In the end, the company I worked for succumbed to the competitive pressures of international rivals. We shuttered the operations, declared bankruptcy, and liquidated the assets. The crushing reality of our demise appeared in the form of overseas engineers who came on site in legions, disassembled the factory, boxed it up, and shipped it back across the ocean.

I had participated in an archetypal case of global change, felt its impact on a single organization, and struggled in the bloody aftermath. From my cockpit, I witnessed the long arm of macro-economic force tap an organization on the shoulder and say, "You're out of the game!" Emotionally, I was stunned. I had given several years of my professional life to a cause that had ended in failure and loss for several thousand people. Intellectually, I recognized that I had been thrust into a leadership issue of first importance—the imperative to respond to fearsome adaptive challenge. This is the issue that I seized upon and have tried to advance in this book.

In the field of change, we have something of a crisis of leadership today, in part, I believe because the strength of our theory has not kept pace with the magnitude of our challenge. It is ultimately not very helpful to tell leaders that the turbulence, speed, and dislocation of the global age have ushered in a monumentally challenging era. It's equally unproductive to tell leaders that the chief impulse of organizations is to rest, and that without strong leadership organizations slump into intractable and rebellious complacency. So what? Unless there is solid, empirically-based theory and a set of practical tools to help a leader respond to a change imperative, we haven't helped anybody. At the end of the day, leadership will always be an applied discipline.

When confronting an adaptive challenge, leaders need to know where their expenditure of effort should go, how to give them, and why. They need to know the mechanisms that arouse and call forth institutional will. They need to know the levers that will multiply force and bring transforming potential to an organization struggling to survive. These are the urgent questions that have driven my research agenda. Most of the leaders involved in the cases I studied make the same confession: they don't have a well-developed theory about the process and how to proceed. Hence the need to puzzle out the answers.

I understand that practitioners learn from theorists. I was one of them. What I have come to appreciate is how much theorists learn from practitioners. In this book, I have attempted to make some headway in solving the riddle of large-scale organizational change by learning from a spectrum of cases and a stable of practitioners.

In Part One, I want to accomplish two things, First, I want to frame the issue. By this I mean that I want to explain just how central successful change leadership is in the global age. I want to show the immense stakes on the table and the torturous course and lasting consequences of getting it wrong. My second aim is to lay out the discernable patterns of large-scale organizational change from primary research and provide an overview of what I call the EPIC methodology. Once I set the stage with these two tasks, I will present a fuller analysis. I will attempt to explain how leaders can win titanic battles with the competitive forces that prey on their organizations.

CHAPTER ONE

A MORE DANGEROUS CALLING

Everything in life can be summarized in two words: Challenge—Response.
ARNOLD TOYNBEE

Consider the changing physical profile of linemen who play in the National Football League (NFL). In 1976, there wasn't a single player who tipped the scales at over three hundred pounds. Ten years later, there were 18. During the following decade, the number of players in this fleshy category swelled to 289. Fast-forward to the present, and that number has nearly doubled, with no fewer than 570 players on NFL rosters weighing in at not a biscuit under the three-hundred-pound threshold, constituting fully 20 percent of the player population.[1] Yet the beefier trend isn't new. Players have gradually been getting bigger since the early days of the game; for example, the average lineman for the Pittsburgh Steelers weighed 210 pounds in 1946. Beyond the girth, however, what catches the eye is the astonishing acceleration of the trend.

The hardwood is no different from the gridiron. Look at the mobility of labor in the National Basketball Association (NBA). When Larry Bird was a rookie for the Boston Celtics in 1979, there were six international players in the entire league. By 1997, that number had risen to twenty-nine In 2006, there were a striking eighty-two international players from thirty-eight countries on opening-day rosters, with players hailing from such unlikely places

3

as Congo, Latvia, and Turkey. Eight players alone come from Serbia and Montenegro. A record seven international players competed in the NBA finals in 2006, and in 2007 the league's best and second-best players were both international players.[2] Again, we note a curious and almost inexplicable acceleration of the trend.

These examples of accelerating change are more than carnival curiosities; they characterize the global age. They symbolize the storms of our time—a hastening pace, intensifying competition, and a new Darwinian ferocity. There are similar examples in every industry. And it's no different in health care, education, government, and the nonprofit sector. In both scope and magnitude, the adaptive challenges confronting organizations are unprecedented. There is simply less deliverance through incremental change than there used to be. Organizations frequently require transformational change to revive their fortunes in addition to ongoing, steady improvement. One thing is clear: if there is to be no slowing down, no spontaneous return to order, and no new era of stability, the implications for leaders are permanently and profoundly important.

When competitive forces accelerate, it elevates the leadership challenge. It introduces new demands and skill requirements. The compression creates more cognitive complexity and emotional intensity. Without warning, forces may combine at any time to thwart existing plans and with a hard shoulder push you as a leader onto a different path. If you are not prepared to lead in the midst of turbulence, the global age will pin you against the limits of your ability to respond. If you can't perform on the new leadership stage, you eventually will fail upward.

The challenge is to get comfortable with uncertainty, live on the edge of chaos, and sustain competitive advantage in the face of endless dynamism. It has become a universal aspiration to figure out how. Organizations everywhere are clamoring to infuse their leaders with the skills that will combine to produce this aptitude. Take a look at almost any Fortune 500 company's leadership development model and you are likely to find some variation of leading or managing change listed as a core competency. Non-business organizations are moving in the same direction. The Office of Personnel Management (OPM), the United States federal government's Human Resources department, for example, identifies "leading change" as its first "executive core qualification" for federal employees who advance to the executive service.

The demand for guidance and direction with issues of change is also reflected in executive education. If the offerings of topflight business schools are any indication, courses on change are in constant high demand. Open-enrollment courses on the subject have found a permanent place in the curriculum. Here's just a sampling of what the market has to offer:

- University of California Berkeley, Haas School of Business: "Leading Change: Demystifying Uncertainty"
- University of Chicago, Graduate School of Business: "Implementing Innovation and Change"
- Columbia University, Graduate School of Business: "Leading Strategic Growth and Change"
- Duke University, Fuqua School of Business: "Leading Innovation and Change"
- ESEAD (Spain): "Managing Change via Culture Reengineering"
- Harvard and Stanford Schools of Business: "Leading Change and Organizational Renewal"
- INSEAD (France): "Women Leading Change in Global Business"
- Massachusetts Institute of Technology (MIT): "Leading Change in Complex Organizations"
- University of Michigan, Ross School of Business: "Healthcare Leadership and Change"
- Oxford University, Said School of Business (U.K.) and HEC School of Management (France): "Consulting and Coaching for Change"
- University of Pennsylvania, Wharton School of Business: "Leading Organizational Change"
- University of Virginia, Darden School of Business: "Managing Individual and Organizational Change"

Why all of the fuss? Again, no matter how anticipatory or prophetic an organization tries to be, there will be trajectories in markets and technology that no one will predict. When organizations need to break camp, they need leaders who know how.

If an organization initiates change behind a leader who lacks this competency, it has taken an intolerably high risk. Organizations recognize that leading change, especially large-scale change, is unquestionably the most formidable challenge in leadership. Think about the essence of the task: to lead change is nothing less than to summon and redirect institutional will and capacity.

A standard definition of leadership, taught in the nation's colleges and universities, is the ability to influence people to achieve a shared goal. But if we're talking about change leadership, this definition crucially misses the mark. It's a midstream definition that assumes a shared goal. That is seldom the case. Once a goal is identified, the change leader's first order of business is to make it a shared one, something that can be the hardest and most time-consuming part of the process. Until a goal is shared, there is only dormant potential to achieve it, and people won't yet permit you to lead them. The goal will simply be denied or ignored. So my definition of change leadership starts one step back, where goals are made, communicated, and affirmed. The essence of change leadership is to respond to the adaptive cycle (see Figure 1.1).

The rationale behind this book is the overwhelming evidence that too few leaders do change leadership well. No leader can afford to move headlong into a serious change effort without a solid understanding of how to navigate the process. The risk is too great. At the same time, if an organization's very existence is at stake, the leader has to act by responding to the threats, sudden shocks, seismic shifts, and rocking dislocations.

Change leadership: The ability to help an organization respond to adaptive challenge.

Here lies the dilemma: by forcing a response to adaptive challenge and at the same time by increasing the risk of failure, the global age is creating a disorienting encounter for leaders. It's making leadership a more dangerous calling than ever before.

Change in the global age is making leadership a more dangerous calling than ever before.

FIGURE 1.1. THE ADAPTIVE CYCLE.

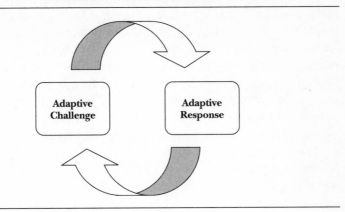

Evidence of Executive Churn

This isn't merely intuitive theorizing. Mounting empirical evidence casts a shaft of confirming light on this thesis. For instance, the casualty rate among chief executives continues to rise. In 2005, there were 129 CEO changes in U.S.-based Fortune 1000 companies, a 126 percent increase in turnover since 2000.[3] In terms of CEO transitions among North American public companies in particular, Liberum Research reports that CEO changes rose 30 percent, from 2,106 in 2005 to 2,733 in 2006. It also reports that management changes in general rose an astonishing 68 percent, from 16,672 in 2005 to 28,058 in 2006.[4] If it isn't out of a breach of character and fiduciary duty (which I address in Chapter Five), leaders usually fail out of an inability to lead change.

In a recent study conducted by the Conference Board, researchers interviewed 540 CEOs and found that "adaptability to change" was their top business challenge.[5] Another study questioned over a thousand board members from business and health care organizations that fired or forced out their chief executives. Respondents reported that the leading cause of failure was "mismanaging change."[6] And a study conducted by Accenture found that three out of four major change efforts fail to meet their original objectives.[7]

In all of this, we acknowledge today's menacing environment. No leader emerges unscathed. No leader is without bumps, bruises, and scar tissue from some degree of navigational error. The leadership success rate has gone down across the board because adaptive challenges come with greater speed. A good measure of that speed is skill obsolescence. Randy MacDonald, senior vice president of human resources at IBM, which employs 330,000 people around the world, estimates that 22 percent of the organization's workforce will have obsolete skills in only three years.[8]

I was more than a bit startled to hear a quartet of prominent leadership scholars recently declare that "superior results over a sustained period of time is the ultimate mark of an authentic leader."[9] My own research comes to a very different conclusion. What I find instead is a pattern in which capable leaders at every level are struggling with unremarkable results and are often checkered with failure. The leader who is able to move through a career with sustained results and uninterrupted success is the rare exception indeed. Often these are the leaders who are either not playing hard enough or gaming the system to select low-risk opportunities that are likely to return professional success. So-called Teflon leaders are more often those who have ridden market waves but successfully avoided down cycles. The vast majority of leaders are struggling with the mantle and millennial requirement to lead change.

LEADERS DON'T GET PAID TO MAINTAIN THE STATUS QUO

Organizations don't outperform their leaders; they reflect them. An organization's ability to adapt and adjust to shifting demands is really

A leader's role is not to maintain the status quo. It is to maintain competitive advantage.

a function of a leader's ability to lead change. In today's convulsing environment, this capacity has become more central and more embedded in the definition of leadership than ever before. It resides at the core because it encapsulates a leader's essential stewardship of keeping an organization viable. Regardless of what other competencies you as a leader may have or what other achievements you may attain, if you can't lead organizational change in response to adaptive challenge, your chance of surviving in a leadership role is dramatically lower than it was just a few years ago.[10] As leadership scholars Ronald Heifetz and Donald Laurie argue, "Getting people to do adaptive work is the mark of leadership in a competitive world."[11] Or, as Kim Clark, the former dean of the Harvard Business School, observes, "Leadership shows up powerfully and in its most relevant context when you're talking about significant change—when you are looking at the way the organization moves through time and how it adapts, grows, reacts, and responds to the stresses and strains and turbulences of life."[12]

The Four Spheres of Leadership Literacy

In the global age, change leadership is more about the authority of knowledge than the authority of position, more about consent than command, more about influence than power. In the knowledge category, there have traditionally been three spheres of leadership literacy that are essential to leading change: personal, organizational, and market. These spheres represent the arenas within which leaders perform their work and accomplish their goals. Mastering these spheres has been important to leadership effectiveness and organizational success. But the global age has added a fourth sphere to this repertoire: awareness and understanding of the global arena. Figure 1.2 illustrates the four literacy requirements with concentric circles.

Personal

Change leadership begins in the inner world in the sphere of personal understanding. Awareness of self is an enabling precondition to personal development. If you're a low self-monitor and carry around a heavily edited version of your own reality, you have fewer bearing points to comprehend your performance. There's a high chance that you will wander without solid and cumulative personal progress. As Warren Bennis, a noted student of leadership, explains, "Leaders, like the rest of us, have all sorts of ways of not looking at themselves, of overlooking shortcomings."[13]

FIGURE 1.2. THE FOUR SPHERES OF LEADERSHIP LITERACY.

This is true, but the most outstanding leaders whom I've worked with are, as a group, far more submissive to the reality of their own strengths and weaknesses than the average person is. Reality has tutored them to seek the unvarnished truth of themselves, accept feedback in the unsparing light of day, and then do something about it. Those who lack personal knowledge are terribly handicapped. As Bennis further observes, "A lack of self-knowledge is the most common, every-day source of leadership failures."[14] It's also the source of a lack of achievement. The late historian Arthur Schlesinger insightfully reminded us that everything that matters in our intellectual and moral life begins with an individual confronting his own mind and conscience in a room by himself. Hence, the first requirement for any leader is to become an intentional self-learner.

ORGANIZATIONAL

Literacy in the organizational realm means grasping the enterprise and understanding from a systems perspective how the organization does what it does in converting inputs into outputs. It assumes that you as the leader understand the fundamental relationships in the system and how they come together to create value. It means that you know how to acquire, develop, and retain talent. It implies that you comprehend your organization's performance operationally, financially, and culturally and that you are fluent in all three of these languages.

Market

The arena of the market is closely related to the arena of the organization. You ultimately can't understand an organization outside its market context. To know the strengths of your assets and the weaknesses of your liabilities in relative terms, you have to know the topography of your market. You've got to be able to spot trends, threats, disruptions, and opportunities. Where is there waste, inefficiency, or unmet need in your market? These are opportunities.

The combination of organizational and market literacy allows you to formulate strategy and decide how you will compete. Phil Rosenzweig, a professor at IMD Business School in Lausanne, Switzerland, explains it this way: "Wise managers approach problems as interlocking probabilities. Their objective is not to find keys to guaranteed success but to improve the odds through a thoughtful consideration of factors." The reason, he explains, is that "the business world is not a place of clear causal relationships."[15]

Global

Keeping an eye on rivals and looking for budding opportunities in your market isn't enough. How can you innovate if your thinking is confined to your existing market? You can only emulate the competition, which will consign you, as the venture capitalist and former Apple computer marketer, Guy Kawasaki, puts it, to "duke it out on the same curve."[16] Increasingly you must look outside your existing playing field with a wide lens.

Once considered the outer limits, the global arena represents the new literacy requirement: you must keep your eyebrows raised to macrolevel trends going on in the world regardless of how distant, remote, or removed they may seem. Leaders are now obliged to scale their awareness and push out traditional boundaries because what's distant, remote, or removed today can threaten your competitiveness tomorrow—for example:

- In the span of fifteen years, the personal savings rate of Americans, meaning the percentage of after-tax income that the average American spends, fell precipitously from 5.2 percent to a negative 1 percent in 2006, representing the lowest rate since 1933 during the Great Depression.[17]
- In the span of eight years, the wind power industry has increased 500 percent, now producing 11,600 megawatts, or enough to power 2.5 million homes.[18]
- In the span of six years, Wikipedia has created an online encyclopedia through the mass collaboration of 300,000 volunteers, who have created and edited more than 5.3 million entries in over a hundred languages.[19]
- In the span of four years, the number of students in the United States being homeschooled has increased dramatically from 1.1 to 2 million.[20]
- In the span of two years, BATS, an electronic trading network, has become the third-largest stock market in the United States, behind the New York Stock Exchange and NASDAQ.[21]
- In the span of one year, circulation among the nation's fifty largest newspapers has plummeted 3.2 percent.[22]

Because markets can rise and fall with breathtaking speed, situational awareness is no longer a matter of knowing the market. Your strengths today—brand, market dominance, technological superiority, customer loyalty, or something else—often provide nothing but false comfort. The ability to sense and anticipate disruptive forces requires a distant early warning system that must reach into the global context. It doesn't mean that you need international experience and a foreign posting. Rather, it's an operating framework, a paradigm, and a cognitive requirement. It's also a healthy antidote to success-induced complacency, which overtakes leaders when they are doing well. Jim Owens, the CEO of heavy equipment maker Caterpillar, warns, "Almost all good companies make their worse mistakes in the best of times."[23]

Ram Charan, the noted strategist, observes that "only by looking out far over the horizon and taking into account developing trends that may not seem directly relevant now can you really do the kind of analysis necessary to prepare for rapid change and new opportunities." He goes on to say that "you need to spread the net wide, then do the mental processing to identify the underly-ing patterns."[24] Global literacy has become the new requirement because it's often too late to respond when new forces and trends enter your market. Ironically, a recent CEO casualty warned, "Don't get calcified or you'll miss entire trends and you'll get passed over."[25]

You must now take an extra step to broaden your perspective, to move past the confines of market knowledge in order to see bottom-up trends.[26] Your biggest vulnerability is probably not visible in your own market. Without global literacy, you may not see the signs of early warning. The sheer speed of external change demands that you look out into the offing.

As globalization redefines what it means to be in a constant state of readiness, global literacy can help you respond to the inevitable adaptive challenge. It can help you stay on the offen-sive. You may not always act preemptively, but your ability to respond will certainly be more effective if you're informed of global movements.

There are several areas in which leaders should cultivate a basic and ongoing awareness of macrotrends, including areas such as technology, demographics, business and economics, education, health and health care, politics and public policy, and the envi-ronment and natural resources. A high level of external awareness makes you more vigilant and ready for change because you're less likely to be surprised by it. But the awareness has another benefit: when you constantly scan the competitive landscape and make a habit of trying to understand trends and movements, you become better able to respond to the unexpected.

EXAMPLES OF CHANGE

Today's globalizing environment is a constant threat to successful leadership and organizational performance. It doesn't happen immediately, but change on the outside eventually calls forth change on the inside. More than ever before, it's critical to see trends in the distance, allowing you time and space to prepare for their arrival and impact. Let's review some examples of change in the areas I mentioned.

Technology

- The cost of a gigabyte of computer memory dropped from $10 million in 1956 to $7,700 in 1990, to $13.30 in 2000, to $1.00 in 2006.[27]
- In 2000, Japan, Korea, and China accounted for 13 percent of all patents filed with the World Intellectual Property Organization. In 2005, that percentage climbed to 21, or one in five.[28]
- The cost of a high-definition video camera in 1984 was $585,000. Today it's under $6,000.[29]
- The computational capability of an Intel processor, as measured in instructions per second, was 60,000 in 1971. In 2005, it was 10.8 billion.[30]
- An estimated 200,000 open source programs are being developed by programmers around the world today.[31]

Demographics

- Sales of white bread in the United States fell from $2.3 billion in 2001 to $2 billion in 2005. During the same time period, tortilla sales rose from $811 million to $1 billion.[32]
- By the year 2010, one in every three workers in the U.S. labor force will be people of color.[33]
- The percentage of people working as independent contractors and on-call workers increased from 7.9 to 9.1 percent between 2001 and 2005, a rise of 2.1 million.[34]
- One in eight couples who married in 2005 in the United States met online.[35]
- The population of Russia is declining at the rate of 100 people every hour. The current population of 144 million is projected to drop to between 80 and 100 million by the year 2050.[36]

Business and Economics

- In 1976, Americans drank 1.6 gallons of bottled water on average. In 2006, the average had soared to 28.3 gallons.[37]
- Total world cross-border trade as a percentage of global gross domestic product was 18 percent in 1990. It is estimated to be 30 percent by 2030.[38]

- Offshoring employment will grow from 1.5 million jobs in 2003 to 4.1 million in 2008.[39]
- In 2001, the United States accounted for 36 percent of the world's initial public offering activity in dollars. By 2005, that percentage had plunged to 24 percent.[40]
- Internet advertising rose 29 percent to $18 billion in 2006 over the prior year, whereas television advertising rose only 4 percent, to $147 billion.[41]
- Foreign money finances 32 percent of U.S. domestic debt today, up from just 7 percent in 1995.[42]

Education

- More than half of the Ph.D.s being awarded in the United States in science and engineering are going to students from China, India, Korea, and Taiwan.[43]
- Only eighteen out of one hundred high school freshmen in the United States will graduate on time, enroll directly in college, and earn an associate degree in three years or a bachelor's degree in six years.[44]
- The average tuition at a private, nonprofit college in the United States has risen 81 percent, or more than double the rate of inflation, over the past seven years.[45]
- Math performance among American fifteen-year-olds has slipped to twenty-eighth among industrialized nations.[46]
- Three million students are currently pursuing college degrees online in the United States.[47]

Health and Health Care

- AIDS is the fourth leading cause of death in the world and accounts for 2.8 million deaths each year. Researchers estimate that it will become the third leading killer and that 120 million people could die from AIDS in the next twenty-five years.[48]
- In the past five years, seventy-nine medical devices, such as stents, defibrillators, and artificial joints, have been removed from the market due to potentially fatal side effects.[49]
- The overall cost of health care in the United States doubled from 1993 to 2004, from roughly $70 to $140 billion.[50]

- The number of total knee replacement surgeries is projected to soar 600 percent, from 38,300 procedures performed in 2005 to 268,200 in 2030.[51]
- Small and medium-size hospitals are outsourcing the reading of CAT scans to doctors in India and Australia.[52]

Politics and Public Policy

- Cybercrime is the FBI's third-highest priority behind terrorism and counterintelligence.[53]
- China and India have eased the tensions that once characterized their relationship. Bilateral trade grew from $200 million in the 1990s to $20 billion in 2005.[54]
- In 2005, an estimated $300 billion in bribes was paid out in Russia compared to $30 billion in 2001.[55]
- The total value of imported goods covered by antidumping laws increased from $8 billion between 1984 and 1993 to $14 billion between 1994 and 2003.[56]
- Economic freedom has steadily increased throughout the world during the past decade.[57]

Environment and Natural Resources

- Scientists estimate that 90 percent of fish and shellfish species that are fished from the sea could be depleted by the year 2048.[58]
- From 2003 to 2006, the percentage of the total U.S. corn harvest used to produce biofuels rose to from 12 to 16 percent.[59]
- The United States accounts for only 5 percent of the world's population but 25 percent of global carbon dioxide emissions.[60]
- Global wind capacity increased 24 percent to 59,084 megawatts from 2004 to 2005, a growth trend that is expected to accelerate.[61]
- Global wood consumption has increased by 63 percent since 1961.[62]

ACCELERATION

Less than twenty years ago, Charles Handy, the British management scholar, remarked that "circumstances do combine occasionally to discomfort the advocates of the status quo."[63] Change has long since overtaken those words and rendered them obsolete. Circumstances now combine continuously to overthrow the advocates of the status quo. The acceleration of external change has become the central theme of our time. For example, 5 million new subscribers sign up for wireless services every month in India.[64] That's the kind of acceleration that I'm talking about. Consider what these notable business leaders and thinkers have said about the speed of change:

"An analysis of the history of technology shows that technological change is exponential, contrary to the common-sense 'intuitive linear' view. So we won't experience 100 years of progress in the 21st century—it will be more like 20,000 years of progress (at today's rate)."—Ray Kurzweil, noted scientist and futurist.[65]

"American business is in the midst of the greatest transformation since the industrialization and massive growth at the turn of the 20th century."—Robert J. Samuelson, editor, *Newsweek*.[66]

"Are today's toughest jobs really any more demanding than yesterday's? After all, people like to believe they live in the most challenging times ever, but isn't that just egotism? In fact, strong evidence says the hardest jobs now really may be in a class by themselves. That's because the world is going through a genuine epochal transformation on the scale of the industrial revolution 200 years ago."—Geoffrey Colvin, editor, *Fortune Magazine*.[67]

"The twenty-first century will be about velocity: the speed of business and the speed of change."—Bill Gates.[68]

"The marketplace we're now living in is the most dynamic, competitive, global economy in recorded history."—Louis Gerstner, former chairman of IBM.[69]

"Everyone senses that business conditions are different from those of a few years ago, yet few grasp just how fundamental the changes are and how swiftly they are overtaking businesses of all kinds. The business environment has changed by an order of magnitude."—Larry Bossidy, former chairman of Honeywell, and Ram Charan, noted consultant and strategist.[70]

PROFOUNDLY PERSONAL

The leadership challenge has not always been one of perform or perish. Just a few years ago, it was possible to hide in the bowels of an organization, and battalions of managers did. They nestled into their organizations and lived out sheltered professional lives in cocoons of job security and uninterrupted routine, courtesy of stable markets. In some industries, managers went for years without truly being tested because incremental change kept them unmolested in the absence of serious market discontinuity.

I still witness leaders who manage to survive only because they don't visibly fail. Leaders in this category typically project the appearance of

Every leader in the global age will see combat.

success through rhetorical careers: they talk and represent accomplishment while nothing really substantive happens. They like to tinker at the margins while the real focus is maintaining status by running a compromise machine and taking a so-called course of moderation and consensus.[71] Leaders in this category are content to believe that a busy schedule suggests a life full of purpose. But this cohort too represents a dwindling population: leaders everywhere face market upheaval, rapid obsolescence, and short strategy cycles. Every leader in the global age will and should expect to see heavy combat.

In every sector, whether business, health care, government, education, or nonprofit, there's a steady stream of adaptive challenges that is antagonistic and inhospitable to comfort-seeking managers. External change sets in motion a train of consequences that arrives at the doorstep of every leader. Eventually it looks you in the eye and challenges your individual capacity to respond. It will most likely expose and exploit your weaknesses if you're not prepared.

No more vivid and unfortunate example can be found than that of pilloried Michael C. Brown, the former director of the Federal Emergency Management Association at the time Hurricane Katrina hit New Orleans. Under his leadership, the agency was unable to demonstrate strong emergency management in coordinating work among federal, state, and municipal agencies. As the nation's top emergency manager, Mr. Brown directed his field staff to put in place a pet evacuation plan no fewer than ten days after the storm hit. He led a shipwrecked response that forced his ouster. Clearly the impact of external change is ultimately and profoundly personal.[72]

As Mark Vamos, the former editor of *Fast Company* magazine, concludes, "I suspect that it's harder than ever to be a good leader now. Businesses today face unprecedented disruption and an extraordinary lack of certainty."[73] The result of the new challenge is a pronounced leadership gap in many organizations. It's not uncommon to see leaders first unprepared, then overwhelmed, and finally defeated in their efforts to respond to external change.[74] The irony is that while many things will become obsolete, the ability to lead change will only become more important.[75] As Louis Gerstner, the former chairman of IBM, states, "The best leaders are change agents, constantly driving their institutions to adapt and advance faster than their competitors do."[76]

Change leadership has become a gateway competency to both survival and success in the global age. But acquiring this competency is easier said than done. Change leadership is a broadly encompassing skill set, or integrated competency, that combines analytical, strategic, and emotional skills. For example, an analytical skill is to understand the limitations of your organization's competitive advantage and recognize from a distance when its position is being threatened. A strategic skill is figuring out what you're going to do about it. And an emotional skill is dealing with the ambiguity of the situation and winning the hearts and minds of your people to respond to the situation. In change leadership, all of these skills must come together.

The Research

What prompted me to conduct the research for this book is the new context of change leadership and the evidence that few leaders are well prepared to succeed in it. In the global age, there are more opportunities for success yet a higher probability of failure, which translates into a lower tolerance for error. Abraham Lincoln observed in his Second Annual Address to Congress that "the dogmas of the quiet past are inadequate to the stormy present."[77] Given the ongoing acceleration of change in the external environment, Lincoln's observation is once again fitting. A new stormy present has brought new challenges to change leadership, and leaders need new tools to confront and overcome them.

As a consultant, adviser, and researcher, I've worked with a variety of organizations. In the private sector, I've worked with some of the world's best-known multinational corporations as well as a number of small and midsized concerns. I've worked in education, government, health care, and nonprofits. The types of adaptive challenges vary by sector, but the fundamental nature of the change imperatives that leaders face is very much the same across the board.

To provide a broad, empirical base of research that would yield useful findings for leaders at every level, I analyzed fifty-three change initiatives taken from archetypal categories of organizational change. The cases ranged widely in scope, magnitude, and duration. (The research appendix at the end of the book lists the categories.) I conducted in-depth qualitative interviews with both the leaders responsible for leading the change initiatives and other employees involved in the effort at various levels of the organizations. In total, I conducted more than three hundred interviews to deconstruct the cases in an attempt to understand the factors that contributed to both success and failure. As Peter Senge explains, "The bottom line of systems thinking is leverage."[78] Hence, my ultimate quest was to locate the points of greatest leverage available to change leaders.

The research yielded six remarkably consistent patterns for successful change, which I explain in the next chapter. The central finding is what I term the *power curve of change*, which explains the patternlike way in which organizations perform work and absorb stress during any change process. In response to the demands of the power curve, I have developed an approach to help leaders master the process of moving successfully up and down the power curve. That approach, called the EPIC methodology, explains from a systems-level perspective what drives successful change from stage to stage, including how change gets started, sustains momentum, and achieves lasting success. It's an applied approach that takes practical lessons out of primary research findings and the world of theory. The methodology has been field-tested with extraordinary success in a variety of organizations.

ORGANIZATION OF THE BOOK

The book is organized into five parts. Part One, the overview, encompasses this introductory chapter followed by a second chapter in which I introduce the EPIC methodology. In Chapter Two, I also explain the six patterns of successful change based on my research, beginning with a discussion of each of the EPIC stages: evaluation, preparation, implementation, and consolidation. I discuss the link between competitive advantage and change, as well as the dual nature of leadership to perform both operational and change work. The last part of the chapter describes the concept of organizational energy, the power curve, and the EPIC methodology that is built around it. Finally, I discuss which sources of energy a leader must activate in each EPIC stage and how to replenish energy in moving along the power curve. The remaining four parts of the book correspond to the four EPIC stages and the specific energy sources associated with each one.

Part Two addresses the first EPIC stage, evaluation. In Chapter Three, I introduce the first energy source of agility, which is an organization's initial state of change readiness. I discuss the difference between natural and conditioned agility; the intellectual, emotional, and physical dimensions of agility; and what you as a leader can do to increase agility in your organization.

The four chapters in Part Three discuss the four energy sources that must become operative during the second EPIC stage, preparation. We first consider urgency. I explain that urgency can be natural or conditioned and that natural urgency varies depending on whether an adaptive challenge is an opportunity, threat, or crisis. I discuss ways to increase urgency by appealing to both reason and emotion. Finally, I acknowledge that urgency is vital to ignite or catalyze change, yet it's never sufficient as an energy source. In Chapter Five, I address the next energy source, credibility. I explain how credibility functions as a source of energy and how it can make up for a lack of urgency when there isn't enough. I discuss the four gauges of credibility, which represent the key elements that elicit trust and what you can do personally to qualify for each one. You will also have a chance to take a short credibility self-assessment to see where you stand in terms of your own credibility.

In Chapter Six, I address the energy source of a coalition. I look at the applied process of putting a coalition together based on identifying the people needed to support change in order to overcome active and visible resistance as well as passive and invisible resistance. I walk you through a process and provide tools for building a coalition. The final chapter in Part Three addresses the last energy source of the preparation stage, vision. I introduce the concept of high fidelity and its requirements of clarity, relevance, and memory and provide a tool for you to build your own message. At the end of the chapter is a template to guide you through the questions and information sequence of creating a high-fidelity vision.

Part Four considers the third EPIC stage of implementation. In Chapter Eight, I explain how early results represent the critical energy source for this stage, why it can't be replaced with another energy source, and what you as a leader have to focus on in order to generate early results and sustain momentum during what is often the most difficult and challenging part of the change process. I deal with understanding risk and resistance from a motivation standpoint. Although I acknowledge the importance of using sound planning and management principles and practices, my purpose is not to teach the discipline of project management. Rather, I focus on using concepts to help identify motivational risks and sources of potential resistance that might create opposition to change. In Chapter Eight, I introduce tools and a process for identifying potential resistance, especially the resistance that results from small changes that have the potential to explode into strong and broad-based organizational resistance. Using the gain/impact matrix, I talk about how change can be classified depending on its strategic gain and personal impact. Finally, I suggest several ways of avoiding changes that appear to be dangerous based on their disruptive potential.

In Part Five, I address the final EPIC stage of consolidation. I explain what consolidation means and how it is achieved. I address the seventh primary energy source of sustained results, which is necessary for any major change initiative to take root and become a lasting part of the organization. I discuss the difference between consolidation and critical mass, as well as several other pitfalls that tempt leaders to step away from the point of action too soon. I then discuss the three layers of change (structural, behavioral, and cultural) that occur during the consolidation process. I conclude the chapter by exploring the reasons leaders often take their hands off the steering wheel after initial success but before change has progressed to the point of consolidation. Finally, I discuss the applied process of achieving consolidation. This is accomplished through a continuous process of evaluating the progress of change and identifying the elements of resistance that need to be starved and the elements of energy that need to be fed. I conclude with a short chapter in which I raise two final questions. First, does leadership style matter? And second, if culture is both friend and foe in organizational change, what should we do about it?

Conclusion

Change is harrowing, yet it can be supremely rewarding. It is planned deprivation with only potential gratification. It holds out uncertain rewards. It's a risk though not always a choice. It can be directed but not controlled. It implies a redistribution of power, resources, comforts, advantages, opportunities, and so forth. Nobody knows who is going to have to give up what. People don't like that very much; they want guarantees. But organizations thrust into the crucible of change can't hold out that promise. All the organization can do is place bets on leaders and strategies.

Many of the leaders I work with report the same exhilarating experience when they lead change successfully. They talk about ridding their organizations of hindering politics and debilitating lethargy, bringing to the surface capacities that simply do not emerge outside crisis, and creating the most penetrating level of self-awareness they have ever experienced. They talk about a profoundly deep level of satisfaction in professional life. Eventually they reflect on the fact that change has created new value and competitive advantage in their organizations. Before they get too excited, they realize that this is what they're called to do—again and again.

Summary

Key Points

- Change in the global age is making leadership a more dangerous calling than in the past. Global forces are creating relentless market disruption, shorter strategy cycles, and rapid obsolescence. This tumult creates a stream of adaptive challenges for the leader and increases the risk of personal and organizational failure.
- The fundamental challenge of a change leader is to summon and redirect institutional will and capacity. Furthermore, the basic role of any leader is to maintain competitive advantage, not the status quo.
- The accelerating pace of change has created a global literacy requirement for leaders. Leaders must scale their awareness to the global arena in order to understand macrolevel trends regardless of how distant, remote, or removed they may seem because those trends can threaten competitiveness at any time.
- External change will expose and exploit the leader who is not prepared to face adaptive challenge.
- The ability to lead change becomes more important as the speed and scope of external change increase.
- The EPIC methodology is a systems-level approach to leading change based on the concept of creating and replenishing organizational energy along the power curve. The stages of the change process are evaluation, preparation, implementation, and consolidation.

CHAPTER TWO

THE EPIC METHODOLOGY

*My interest is in the future because I am going to
spend the rest of my life there.*
CHARLES KETTERING

Change can be mystifying. We can't deny its complexity. It's not simple, linear, tidy, or mechanistic, and there is virtually nothing elegant about leading it. As a rule, it's dynamic, messy, iterative, unpredictable, and fraught with ambiguities. Some change efforts that appear to be blessed with every chance of success nevertheless fail. Others succeed when it seemed they were destined to fail. Understanding why can be confusing when the reasons for success or failure seem hidden from view. In most cases, numerous factors, both inside and outside the organization, interact in ways that are difficult to track and analyze. Nevertheless, until we can find patterns and principles in the apparent disorder, we are no better off.

The problem is that our current tool set is inadequate. Most leaders approach change initiatives with the classical tools they learned from the discipline of project management. But they soon find themselves overwhelmed by the untidy and often unpredictable nature of the change process. As a recent Accenture study finds, "While traditional project management methods and tools are helpful (and rapidly improving), they are not enough, because they presume stable and predictable outcomes, such as a linear progression of tasks within phases."[1] More often than not, change won't behave that way.

THE SIX PATTERNS OF SUCCESSFUL ORGANIZATIONAL CHANGE

From my research of more than fifty cases of large-scale change, I have isolated six remarkably consistent patterns that characterize the successful cases and form the basis of the EPIC methodology:

1. Change requires leaders and organizations to perform more work and absorb more stress.
2. There are four common stages to a successful change process.
3. The discretionary efforts of people drive change from stage to stage.
4. Leaders provide the energy to fuel the discretionary efforts of people.
5. During the change process, organizations consume energy to perform additional work and absorb additional stress according to a predictable pattern called the power curve of change.
6. There are seven primary energy sources in the change process. Each is essential in a specific EPIC stage.

PATTERN 1: CHANGE REQUIRES MORE WORK AND CREATES MORE STRESS

This first pattern may seem like a penetrating glimpse into the obvious, yet I am continually amazed at how leaders try to deny this fundamental principle. Some leaders try to muscle change through by sheer force of will. Others make it a covert action and try to smuggle it into the organization and keep it a secret. Still others, in an attempt to allay people's fear and forestall their resistance, pretend that change really isn't change, that it's simply an extension of the status quo. None of these subterfuges works. Change may be big or small, simple or complex, short or long. But in all cases, it carries the requirement of extra work and stress. The only question is how much. A distinction that helps determine how much extra work and stress might be involved with a proposed change is based on whether a change is a performance change or a compliance change.

Performance-based change involves more work and stress than compliance-based change does because it requires people and organizations to behave, work, and perform at a higher level or standard. When an organization restructures a department, creates a new product line, acquires another company, or outsources a function, it expects either better or lower-cost performance. Performance-based change tends to have a direct and often heavy impact on people.

Compliance-based change is a bit different. It requires people to accept or comply with something that is new but does not require performance at a higher level or standard. Often compliance-based change is not directly felt or seen. If it is, it tends to be a change in policiy or procedure. For example, a new policy to change the paid-time-off policy doesn't require higher performance, but it does require compliance. Modifying the accounts receivable module in an enterprise system may provide badly needed reporting capability for the accounting and finance department, but the change itself may not create a large direct work and stress requirement on people.

In either case, change inevitably creates a new work and stress requirement. This means that an organization must be prepared to meet that requirement, which is in addition to the normal baseline requirements of running day-to-day operations. It is critical that leaders not only acknowledge the scarcity of resources such as time, capital, and technology but also recognize and factor in the incremental work and stress that accompany any proposed change. A first-layer analysis for the change leader is to assess his or her ability to fulfill the new work and stress requirement based on the current allocation of the physical, mental, and emotional resources of the people who would likely be involved.

PATTERN 2: THE STAGES OF A SUCCESSFUL CHANGE PROCESS

Regardless of the nature, scope, duration, or complexity of a particular change initiative, successful change follows a sequence of four common stages, which form the acronym EPIC:

Evaluation

Preparation

Implementation

Consolidation

The stages may vary in length, and they may overlap, combine, or repeat, depending on the way an organization and its leaders approach change and the challenges that come along the way. But for successful change, a leader must navigate carefully and systematically through each of the four EPIC stages as a set of deliberate management steps. In cases of failed change, leaders routinely slight, ignore, or try to skip the stages. For example, one CEO made a decision to install a new customer relationship management system. He selected the system from a vendor with whom he had outstanding credit and conducted no further analysis. As it turned out, it wasn't the right system for his business. The system was finally abandoned after eighteen painful months and a failed implementation.

The four EPIC stages are distinct from each other based on the amount of work performed and stress absorbed in each one. Think about the dictionary definition of *work*, which is mental, emotional, and physical exertion. With the concept and definition of work in mind, the stages become easier to understand.

Evaluation

The first stage of successful change, evaluation, requires the least amount of work and absorption of stress. During evaluation, the leader continually evaluates competitive reality, internal performance, and alternatives for change as the rest of the organization maintains its current systems. Successful leaders are always evaluating change or leading change or doing both.

Unless an organization is already in the throes of change, it's usually in a state of relative equilibrium. I say "relative" because there's no such thing as true, or absolute, equilibrium in any organization—a condition in which the internal elements of strategy, structure, processes, and systems are stable.

Every organization is destabilized to some degree all of the time. But organizations typically go through cycles of punctuated equilibrium depending on the cycle of market continuity and discontinuity in which they operate.[2] Other markets are so dynamic that they are in chaotic disequilibrium. Regardless of the pattern of speed and disruption of the cycle, when things change in a market and new competitive threats appear, you as the leader have to respond. When things are more settled, you have the opportunity to return to a pattern of scanning market realities and monitoring the competitive landscape.[3] Organizations not pursuing major change should be in the mode of evaluating change. It's clearly the common pattern of successful organizations and the mind-set of the most effective leaders.

Preparation

In the second EPIC stage, preparation, the organization must perform additional work and absorb additional stress than it did during evaluation. Even a slight shift in the allocation of resources signals the preparation stage and represents the organization's initial break from the inertia and equilibrium of the status quo.

During the preparation stage, the task is to analyze alternative paths for change through experimentation, modeling, testing, and trialing options. For example, a large hotel brand can try out new client incentives in a test market before rolling them out to the broader market. But some changes can't be tested in advance, such as the sell-off of a product line or business unit. The pattern of successful change illustrates that leaders test and experiment with options whenever possible before they make a final decision to pursue a particular change alternative. Once a path is chosen, further preparation includes the normal activities of organizing, budgeting, and scheduling. Once the planning is complete, the third stage, implementation, begins.

Implementation

During implementation, the organization exerts itself at the highest level to perform the largest quantity of additional work and absorb the highest level of additional stress required during the change process. During implementation, the organization attempts to achieve desired results by executing the tasks that were planned during preparation. Implementation can be a long march and the most grueling and challenging part of the journey. As Rosabeth Moss Kanter explains it, during implementation, change often looks like "failure in the middle."[4] It's the stage when the organization is most severely taxed and when results can be suspended for long periods of time. Accordingly, it is also the stage when resistance is usually the strongest.

Consolidation

The last EPIC stage of consolidation occurs when change becomes strong and lasting. This happens as a consequence of sustained results over time. When change consolidates, the motivation generated becomes gradually and permanently stronger than the resistance and inertia that oppose it. In other words, there is now more energy pushing change than resisting it. Critical mass, a concept borrowed from physics, defines the beginning of the consolidation process. It is the point at which a process that has begun is able to run on increasingly less energy, almost as if it were self-sustaining.

PATTERN 3: THE DISCRETIONARY EFFORTS OF PEOPLE DRIVE CHANGE

To understand the second pattern, let's step back and consider the many factors that affect the success or failure of change. Some of the factors are what we consider hard or technical.[5] On the other side are factors that we might consider soft or human.[6] The hard or technical side also corresponds closely with the definition of management, which is to maintain systems and control resources, whereas the human side aligns more closely with the definition of leadership, which is to influence people and create something new.

Obviously factors in both categories are important for successful change, but let's think about the technical side first.[7] Here's a list of factors on the technical side of change:

- Capital
- Knowledge
- Process
- Strategy
- Structure
- Systems
- Technology
- Time

Along with these technical factors is a whole set of classical tools and techniques and a discipline that's grown up around it called project management. Managing the technical side has mostly to do with planning, budgeting, scheduling, tracking, and coordinating the completion of tasks. The skillful management of the technical side is of course critical to any change project.

Now let's look at the human side. There are several factors that a leader is likely to confront on this side as well:

- Ambiguity
- Attention
- Attitude
- Commitment
- Communication
- Confidence
- Culture
- Effort
- Energy
- Engagement
- Enthusiasm
- Fear
- Morale
- Resistance
- Uncertainty

Having briefly considered both sides, and reflecting on your own experience, which side is the tougher leadership challenge? I've asked this question in interviews with more than three hundred leaders and managers in organizations across industry, functional area, and from the bottom to the top of the house. The consensus view is that the human side of the equation is far and away the bigger challenge and where the ultimate leadership test is found. Other prominent studies agree.[8]

For example, when the U.S. government set out to create the Department of Homeland Security, it commissioned a study to understand not only the magnitude of the challenge but also what aspects of the change process would be most difficult. It came to the following conclusion: "At the center of any serious change management initiative are the people—people define the organization's culture, drive its performance, and embody its knowledge base. Experience shows that failure to adequately address—and often even consider—a wide variety of people and cultural issues is at the heart of unsuccessful transformations."[9]

Capgemini, one of the most respected consulting firms, states its point of view this way: "When major transformation efforts fail, the most likely reason is insufficient attention to people."[10] Finally, change expert David Nadler summarizes it nicely: "Organizational change, when you get right down to it, boils down to persuading massive numbers of people to stop doing what they've been doing for years and to start doing something they probably don't want to do—at least not at first."[11]

Let's break it down a little further. The underlying principle is simple, yet it bears repeating because too many leaders neglect it. Technical factors consist of inanimate and inert resources. Conversely, human factors deal with people, thoughts, feelings, and behavior. The difference couldn't be more fundamental, which is, of course, what accounts for the different degrees of difficulty associated with managing each of them. The inherent difference means that based on experience and expertise, you can control the technical side to a large extent. But on the human side, you are far more limited—to the point that we can't use the word *control* because people are free-willed beings and because organizations are organisms consisting of free-willed beings. You can only influence people. After completing one of the most remarkable corporate transformations in the past five years, Ravi Kant, the managing director of Tata Motors in India, the world's fifth-largest manufacturer of medium and heavy trucks, underscores the point: "I certainly learned that the wisest approach is not to give orders but to sell new ideas internally."[12] Figure 2.1 illustrates the difference between the two sides of the equation.

The inescapable conclusion is that people drive the change process from stage to stage through their discretionary efforts. I use the word *discretionary* quite deliberately because a person's decision to support change is a choice. Leaders can increase the potency of their influence by setting up positive and negative incentives, but the members of an organization are the ones who ultimately decide to grant or withhold their efforts. You may

FIGURE 2.1. CONTROL RESOURCES, INFLUENCE PEOPLE.

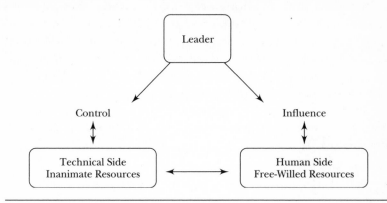

argue that complying with change is part of the normal course of business, part of a person's role and responsibility, and a condition of employment. Leaders do in fact use formal authority, fear, intimidation, and punishment to influence behavior and force change through. But the old compact between employer and employee—security for loyalty—has changed so drastically in recent years that traditional approaches have become far less effective. Leaders may still exert enormous pressure through negative means, but they can't compel change. A forced march never works because people retain the ability to revoke their efforts at any time. Alas, the idea that leaders control the efforts of their people has never been more illusory.[13] Consider that at any given time, only one in four workers across organizations is actively engaged, that is, emotionally committed to the organization. The rest are either not engaged (55 percent) or actively disengaged (19 percent).[14] This is the situation all leaders encounter when they embark on any kind of change agenda. They can usually expect to start from a deficit position.

In the end, this analysis allows us to reach what is perhaps a very useful definition of *leadership:* it's the business of delivering outcomes (often economic) based on human factors through social processes. Indeed, we will see that it is the effective use of social, cultural, and emotional processes that in the end defines successful change leadership.

The typical pattern among organizations is that they are good at managing the technical side of change, which mainly consists of traditional project management, but poor at leading the human side, which mainly consists of sustaining the engagement and efforts of people. Ultimately organizational change is dependent on the human side for a successful outcome.

Table 2.1 illustrates the technical and human sides of change that must be both managed and led, controlled and influenced, simultaneously.

PATTERN 4: LEADERS PROVIDE THE ENERGY

Albert Einstein said, "Everything should be made as simple as possible, but not simpler." Let's apply this principle and reduce change to what we might call the level of irreducible complexity, meaning that it can't get any simpler. Organizations attempt

TABLE 2.1. THE TECHNICAL AND HUMAN SIDES OF CHANGE.

Technical Side	Human Side
Project management	Change management/leadership
Inanimate resources	Free-willed resources
Capital	Ambiguity
Knowledge	Attention
Process	Attitude
Strategy	Commitment
Structure	Communication
Systems	Confidence
Technology	Culture
Time	Effort
	Energy
	Engagement
	Enthusiasm
	Fear
	Morale
	Resistance
	Uncertainty

change in many ways and at many levels. Some change initiatives are big and complex; others are small and simple. Regardless of the change, the process begins with people, time, resources, and a plan. Your job as a leader is to direct these assets in a way that will bring about a successful outcome. How will you do this? How will you motivate people and get them to support change?

Understanding what energy is and how it works inside an organization is vital to understanding organizational change at any level. The most fundamental scientific definition of energy is the *capacity to perform work and cause change*. You can't smuggle change into your organization because it represents work, and that work requires both people and their discretionary efforts. Without energy, there is no change. Energy is what's in the black box that makes change go. If you have ever been part of a major change initiative, you learned firsthand and by observation that it requires large amounts of energy to fuel the efforts of people involved in the process.[15] If the discretionary efforts of people drive change (pattern 3), then we can define energy as any source of motivation that will bring that discretionary effort forward.

As former Harvard professor John Kotter explains, "Motivation and inspiration energize people, not by pushing them in the right direction as control mechanisms, but by satisfying basic human needs for achievement, a sense of belonging, a feeling of control over one's life and the ability to live up to one's ideals."[16] Thus, the capacity of an organization to perform change work is based directly on the motivation of people to offer discretionary effort.

Energy: The capacity to perform work and absorb stress through sources of motivation that influence discretionary effort.

To take it a step further, the central mechanism of successful change is based on an ongoing exchange between the leader and the led. Because the change process requires energy to sustain it, it becomes the leader's job to create and replenish energy throughout the change process. In the successful cases of change that I analyzed, leaders, without exception, were able to maintain a continuous exchange of energy for effort. If the leader has no energy to offer, there will be no exchange of effort because people don't give effort for free; they give it only in exchange for sources of energy.

It's also true that leaders may have reserves of goodwill and credibility that can sustain effort for some time beyond the replenishment of new energy, but when these reserves are depleted, the exchange stops. At some point in the change process, achieving momentum through tangible results will start to generate its own energy to fuel the process. This takes the full burden off the leader as the source of supply. But until you arrive at that point, the change process will likely dip into a failure pattern if you can't provide energy for people to convert into effort.

How does this relate to the hard-management side? Unfortunately, regardless of how beautifully equipped your change initiative may be with technical resources, a change effort without enough energy supplied by leadership will nearly always fail. No amount of hard or technical resources can compensate for a lack of energy. A McKinsey study concludes, "Whatever a company's potential, transformation is doomed to fail unless change leaders can release and orchestrate the energy within the organization."[17] Remember that only free-willed individuals have the ability to perform work and accomplish change. Success, then, is ultimately dependent on the willingness of people to apply effort to change. So in order to truly lead, you must be able to motivate people to dip continuously into their collective store of skills, knowledge, and expertise and give freely.

To summarize, the principle of exchange holds that it is the leader's job to constantly meter the flow of energy inside the organization and replenish that energy through an ongoing exchange of energy for the discretionary efforts of people.[18] Change requires the ongoing exchange of energy for effort between the leader and the led (Figure 2.2). You can't control human effort; you can only influence it through your ability to exchange energy. Change flourishes on the basis of the transactions of energy for effort. If you have no energy to provide, you can't expect the exchange to take place.

But can't you force or mandate change and not worry so much about whether people support it? Won't they eventually get used

FIGURE 2.2.   THE PRINCIPLE OF EXCHANGE.

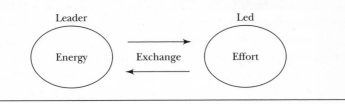

to it? And don't people have to move through the stages of awareness, understanding, acceptance, and commitment at their own
pace anyway? Don't they have to take time to mourn their loss as
they leave the status quo? The answer is that you can press people
into service. In the short term, you'll often get results. In the
long term, you'll suffer the consequences. The reason this is often
unclear is that most leaders don't stay in one position long enough
to live with the long-term consequences of their decisions. Many
managers are off to a new assignment after two or three years.
With a longer-term perspective, it becomes abundantly clear that
attempts to muscle change through fail miserably in the long run.
Leaders face a profound dichotomy: they have to tackle adaptive
challenges head on but also have to be collaborative. They can't
rush into change or will find themselves alone. At the same time,
they can't wait for consensus because it will either take too long
or may never come at all.

Leaders need people to support change before those people
cross a threshold of conviction. We know that people often contribute generous amounts of discretionary effort well before this
point, and we need that to happen. But they don't give that effort
for free. Somewhere there was an exchange, even if it was in the
past. For example, people often support change initially simply
out of loyalty to a person they trust.

As a leader, you're responsible to provide energy to sustain the
process, and there are many ways to generate energy. Anything
that creates motivation to support change falls into the category
of an energy source. Consider this simple example. At a large
consumer products organization, the CEO announced a major

cost-cutting initiative to trim 20 percent from the operating and capital budgets. A month after the announcement, the director of information technology (IT) noticed that requests for new computer hardware had spiked as an immediate response to the belt-tightening measure. Employees flooded her with requests, hoping they could squeeze in last-minute orders before every-body got serious with cost cutting. During the next executive meeting, the IT director said nothing about the clamor for hard-ware. Instead, she brought her laptop computer to the meeting, explained that it was not the latest and fastest machine, and then she mentioned that she had canceled her order for a new one. During the next month, not a single request came to her desk for computer hardware of any kind. Her simple announcement in the meeting supplied significant energy to employees, which they readily converted to improved cost performance.

A related point is that it's also your job to manage and regulate the consumption of energy so that it doesn't outstrip what's available. Some leaders take on too much change at once because they haven't developed an intuitive sense about pacing and spacing. When there's too much change going on, people run ragged, resources get strained, and time runs out. Like individuals, organizations can buckle under the weight of too much change. No one can take an organization to the level of maximum exertion and keep it there. Change is a taxing activity that must include a renewal cycle. Organizations that do it well resemble a tailback that punctuates periods of rest with moments of maximum exertion. The underlying principle is that change represents a process. Every process requires energy for its operation. Change is certainly no exception.

Pattern 5: The Power Curve of Change

During the change process, organizations must perform additional work and absorb additional stress. They need more energy to do it, and they consume that energy according to a common and repeated pattern. What this means is that the energy consumption pattern is very similar regardless of the size or type of change. The pattern shows that organizations consume energy roughly equal to the amount of work performed and stress absorbed in each stage.

Table 2.2.   Energy and the EPIC Stages.

Stage 1: Evaluation	Stage 2: Preparation	Stage 3: Implementation	Stage 4: Consolidation
Energy consumption is low and relatively stable based on ongoing operations and the evaluation of competitive reality, internal performance, and options for change.	Energy consumption increases gradually to supply a gradual increase in work performed and stress absorbed during preparation for change.	Energy consumption increases sharply to supply a significant increase in work performed and stress absorbed during the implementation of change.	Energy consumption decreases gradually to supply a gradual decrease in work performed and stress absorbed as change takes hold and produces its own energy for change during consolidation.

Energy consumption is a mirror reflection of the amount and rigor of the work performed. Table 2.2 provides a brief definition of each of the four EPIC stages based on the amount of energy they typically consume.

In the first stage of evaluation, the organization is usually in a state of relative equilibrium. The organization is humming along, performing work, and consuming energy in a more or less stable and steady pattern, represented by a flat line on the power curve depicted in Figure 2.3.

During the second stage of preparation, energy consumption increases gradually because the organization has given itself more work to perform and stress to absorb. It is analyzing and experimenting with options, making a decision, and planning for implementation. This is the line with a gradual slope on the power curve.

FIGURE 2.3. THE POWER CURVE OF CHANGE.

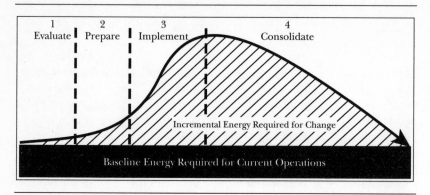

During implementation, energy consumption shifts dramatically, reflecting a significant increase in work requirement and stress load. For most change initiatives, implementation represents the steep climb, the long, hard slog, and consequently, the period of maximum exertion. This is when leaders push their organizations to the limit to achieve the desired results. I depict this stage with a steep upward-sloping line on the power curve. It culminates with the point of critical mass at the top of the curve, which means that the energy required for a process starts to decrease, indicating the beginning of the final stage of consolidation. When change reaches critical mass, the work and energy requirements crest and then start to drop, indicated by a gradual decline in the slope of the power curve.

Figure 2.3 depicts the power curve as it runs, left to right, through the four EPIC stages. It reflects the amount of incremental work performed in each stage, which is equal to the amount of energy consumed based on different work requirements and stress loads associated with each one. Below the curve is a bar that represents the ongoing, or baseline, energy required to maintain current operations. Of course, the exact pattern of the power curve is not the same every time. Depending on the particular change, it may be steeper, flatter, or longer. If it's a major change, for example, the implementation and consolidation stages might last several years. The important point to remember is that the sequence of the stages and the general pattern of work performed, stress absorbed, and energy consumed will hold true across industry, functional area, and type of change.

With the power curve in full view, the leader's job comes into sharp relief. If you've been charged to lead change, it becomes your job to ensure that there is sufficient energy to perform the additional work, absorb the additional stress, and pass through the EPIC stages along the power curve.[19] If you are unable to generate and replenish enough energy to exchange for the discretionary efforts of employees to sustain the process from stage to stage, the change effort will begin to falter.

The power curve shows the path and terrain of the change journey before you begin. It also allows you to anticipate the different energy requirements that you will be responsible to supply along the way. As a practical matter, you will need one more layer of information: you will need to understand where to find the sources of energy and how to release them to your people. This brings us to the sixth and final pattern.

PATTERN 6: THE SEVEN PRIMARY ENERGY SOURCES IN THE CHANGE PROCESS

Remember that energy is the capacity to perform work and absorb stress through sources of motivation that influence discretionary effort. Think about your own experience. We have all been through change in organizations. Sometimes we're motivated to pitch in and help make it happen; sometimes we don't have strong feelings one way or the other, so we sort of sit on the fence. Finally, there are times when we have little or no motivation to support change. In fact, we may be strongly opposed to it, which may lead us to resist the effort. Almost all of us at one time or another have been in the positions of strong support, strong opposition, or something in between. Certainly people think, feel, and behave differently. We perceive and understand information differently. We have different interests, intentions, and motives. But in spite of these differences, the sources of motivation that we respond to as human beings are by and large the same.

Successful change overwhelmingly relies on the same sources of energy in the same sequence to elicit the efforts of people.

The pattern is unmistakably consistent. Seven energy sources are responsible for providing the vast majority of energy in any change effort and for moving the change process along the power curve:

1. Agility
2. Urgency
3. Credibility
4. Coalition
5. Vision
6. Early Results
7. Sustained Results

The pattern goes a step further. Not only do these seven sources of energy fuel successful change, but they do it for the most part in a certain sequence. In other words, the energy sources don't all work at the same time and in the same way. They're not of equivalent value throughout the process. Which energy sources have the biggest impact largely depends on the EPIC stage. For example, sustained results don't fuel change at first because you're either evaluating or preparing for change, and it's normally not possible to generate sustained results from the beginning. Similarly, urgency tends to wane as an energy source over time and usually doesn't propel change forward if you have just been through an arduous implementation stage. So to a large extent, there's a natural sequence to when and how energy sources become activated and contribute to the change process.

Energy sources, once activated, continue supplying energy throughout the change process. They have cumulative impact, but the critical pattern is one of replenishment in which new sources need to be exchanged to keep change moving. It is also important to point out that in spite of the pattern and sequence of energy sources, change is still messy, which means that the EPIC stages will vary and the sources of energy will fuel change a little bit differently in each case. This empirical pattern is enormously important for its practical value. Not only do we know the stages of the change process and the energy requirements, but we also know where to look to supply those energy requirements. We know which energy sources to focus on and in what order. Once energy is replenished in one stage, it becomes the cue to move to the next stage.

THE EPIC METHODOLOGY

Now let's string the pearls. The six patterns put together reveal a methodology that leaders can apply to change at all levels of an organization. The methodology is based on the six patterns of successful change. Successful change occurs when leaders apply this methodology in order to move the process successfully along the power curve.

Table 2.3 summarizes the methodology. The first row outlines the EPIC stages that you must follow in step fashion: evaluate, prepare, implement, consolidate. The second row explains your role as a leader, which is to create energy in step one and replenish it in steps two, three, four, and five according to the work and energy requirements of each stage. The third row shows the seven sources of energy. The stage in which a particular energy source is most critical and must become operative is in bold.

Each stage is a little different. During the evaluation stage, your job as leader is to supply energy for the ongoing evaluation of competitive reality. You're also storing up energy against a time in the future when you embark on change and need generous amounts of discretionary effort from your people. During the preparation step, your job is to ignite the change process from what is often a condition of relative organizational stability and supply a gradual increase in energy consumption to fuel the additional work during that stage. During implementation, your job is to replenish energy to supply a significant increase in work and energy consumption to supply the high level of exertion that you are requiring from your organization. Finally, during consolidation, you must again replenish energy to supply a gradual decrease in work and energy consumption as the organization settles into a new reality.

CONCLUSION

I have explained the six patterns of successful change. In doing so, I have discussed the difference between the technical and human sides of change. I pointed out that the human side is where the tough challenges lie. In leading change, leaders fail more often out of their inability to influence people than in their inability to control resources. Most change failures are failures in motivation rather than failures in ability. I introduced the concept of energy as the capacity to perform work and absorb stress through sources of motivation that influence discretionary effort. I defined the leader's role as one of sustaining the organization's capacity to perform work and absorb stress throughout the change

TABLE 2.3. THE EPIC METHODOLOGY.

EPIC Stage	1: Evaluate	2: Prepare	3: Implement	4: Consolidate
The Leader's Role	Equilibrium step: Supply energy for the ongoing evaluation of competitive reality, internal performance, and change alternatives.	Ignition step: Replenish energy to supply a gradual increase in work performed and stress absorbed during preparation.	Refueling step: Replenish energy to supply a significant increase in work performed and stress absorbed during implementation.	Refueling step: Replenish energy to supply a gradual decrease in work performed and stress absorbed during consolidation.
Energy Sources	**1. Agility**	1. Agility **2. Urgency** **3. Credibility** **4. Coalition** **5. Vision**	1. Agility 2. Urgency 3. Credibility 4. Coalition 5. Vision **6. Early Results**	1. Agility 2. Urgency 3. Credibility 4. Coalition 5. Vision 6. Early Results **7. Sustained Results**

process by harnessing the discretionary efforts of people through the exchange of energy. The power curve illustrates the pattern in which organizations perform work and consume energy during the change process. Finally, I discussed the seven sources of energy that drive successful change and the sequence in which they typically replenish energy to the process.

What I have not discussed is how you as a leader can tap into and use each of the seven energy sources to replenish energy. In the final analysis, your ability to do this will equal your ability to lead change. Because leading change is an applied leadership discipline, it won't matter how well you understand the EPIC methodology intellectually. In the end, impact and value will come only from your ability to apply the methodology effectively to actual change initiatives. Accordingly, the remaining chapters explore how to tap into the seven sources of energy, with a chapter devoted to each one.

Summary

Key Points

- Pattern 1: Change inevitably creates a new work and stress requirement. This means that an organization must be prepared to meet that requirement, which is in addition to the normal baseline requirements of running day-to-day operations.
- Pattern 2: Regardless of the nature, scope, duration, or complexity of a particular change initiative, successful change moves through four EPIC stages: evaluation, preparation, implementation, and consolidation. The stages are based on the type and amount of work performed and the level of stress absorbed in each one.
  - During evaluation, the organization evaluates competitive reality, its own internal performance, and alternatives for change and then makes a decision to pursue change. This stage requires the least amount of additional work and organizational exertion.
  - During preparation, an organization tests options for change, selects one, and creates an implementation plan. Tactically, the stage includes creating structure, defining roles and

responsibilities, budgeting resources, scheduling tasks, and identifying milestones. An organization gradually moves up the power curve during preparation because it has to exert itself more as it performs incrementally more work and absorbs incrementally more stress.

- During implementation, the organization begins the process of executing the change plan, consuming resources, and exerting itself at significantly higher levels. Implementation involves performing the highest quantity of additional work and absorbing the highest levels of additional stress to accomplish the organization's change goals.
- During consolidation, the organization achieves results that start to reduce the energy required to sustain the change process. As results become sustained, the energy requirements continue to fall until the organization regains equilibrium and change becomes a lasting part of the organization.
- Pattern 3: The discretionary efforts of people drive change from stage to stage. Leaders can control inanimate resources, but they can only influence human beings as free-willed resources. The members of an organization ultimately decide to grant or withhold their discretionary efforts during change.
- Pattern 4: Leaders provide the energy to exchange for the discretionary efforts of people. Energy is defined as the capacity to perform work and absorb stress through sources of motivation that influence discretionary effort. It is the leader's job to create and replenish energy through the EPIC stages of change.
- Pattern 5: Organizations perform work and absorb stress according to a predictable pattern during the change process. This pattern is called the power curve. Energy consumption is low and stable during evaluation, rises gradually during preparation, rises sharply during implementation, and then declines gradually during consolidation.
- Pattern 6: There are seven primary energy sources in the change process: agility, urgency, credibility, coalition, vision, early results, and sustained results. Each source is essential in a specific EPIC stage. The leader must understand the sequence of the energy sources and activate each one at the appropriate time. The energy

sources also have a cumulative effect throughout the change process.

- The EPIC methodology outlines the sequential process of creating and replenishing energy up and down the power curve. It explains which sources of energy must be activated in each stage in order to sustain the exchange between energy and discretionary effort.

PART TWO

EVALUATE

Before he made the decision to transform Intel from a memory chip maker to the leading producer of microprocessors in the world, Andy Grove, the former chairman of Intel, spent most of his time evaluating competitive reality and his options for responding to evolving threats. "I believe that the prime responsibility of a manager," he says, "is to guard constantly against other people's attacks and to inculcate this guardian attitude in the people under his or her management."[1]

The first stage of change is evaluation, which should be the normal operating mode of a leader. It's a state of relative equilibrium. Leaders who aren't engaged in change should be engaged in evaluation. In order to maintain competitiveness and fulfill the institutional mission of an organization, every leader has a responsibility to continuously evaluate three things: competitive reality, internal performance, and alternatives for change.

High-quality evaluation requires literacy in the four spheres discussed in Chapter One. It also requires an emotional willingness and discipline to confront reality. Beyond maintaining current operations, the additional energy needed for evaluation is usually minimal, as reflected by the nearly flat portion of the power curve. This makes it nonthreatening and nondisruptive to most people most of the time. In the figure shown here, the arrow indicates the evaluation stage of change.

THE EQUILIBRIUM OF EVALUATION.

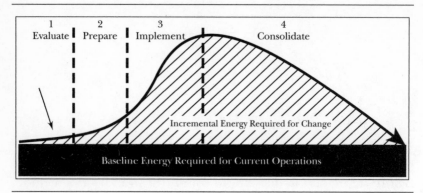

Evaluation is both formal and informal. It includes formal activities such as strategic planning, competitive benchmarking, internal auditing, and market research. But it more often includes the simple things we do every day to keep track of our own performance, the market, and the competition, such as reviewing internal operations and financial results; reading market reports; talking to customers; attending industry conferences; reading trade journals, magazines, and newspapers; and discussing ideas for improvement and innovation with colleagues. Sometimes these evaluating activities seem insignificant. But they shape thinking and, ultimately, crucial decisions to pursue change and how. If you don't continuously evaluate, you risk being uninformed, an intolerably high risk. "Make the wrong bets and the world's bumps will work against you."[2]

CHAPTER THREE

EVALUATE WITH AGILITY

It's not the strongest species that survive, nor the most intelligent, but the ones most responsive to change.
CHARLES DARWIN

EVALUATE WITH AGILITY.

EPIC	1	2	3	4
Stage	**Evaluate**	**Prepare**	**Implement**	**Consolidate**
The Leader's Role	**Equilibrium step** Supply energy for the ongoing evaluation of competitive reality, internal performance, and change alternatives.	**Ignition step** Replenish energy to supply a gradual increase in work performed and stress absorbed during preparation.	**Refueling step** Replenish energy to supply a significant increase in work performed and stress absorbed during implementation.	**Refueling step** Replenish energy to supply a gradual decrease in work performed and stress absorbed during consolidation.
Energy Sources	**1. Agility**	1. Agility **2. Urgency** **3. Credibility** **4. Coalition** **5. Vision**	1. Agility 2. Urgency 3. Credibility 4. Coalition 5. Vision **6. Early Results**	1. Agility 2. Urgency 3. Credibility 4. Coalition 5. Vision 6. Early Results **7. Sustained Results**

Oxford University is a renowned institution. It is also a curiously unique organization. As the oldest university in the English-speaking world, it traces its origins to the eleventh century. Not surprisingly, that long past has lingered.

Several years ago, as a new doctoral student there, I went to the renowned Bodleian Library for the first time. I needed a book—not a rare or old book but a recently published book that any university library would have. I had no idea how to commence a search, so I asked a librarian to help me. She pointed me to massive card catalog drawers and instructed me to make a manual search. After a few minutes, I found the appropriate reference card and presented it to her at the counter. She chided me for taking the card out of the drawer and instructed me to transcribe the title and reference number on a small piece of paper, which she gave me. I did so and returned with the paper in hand, expecting that she would direct me to the stacks where I would find the book. She informed me that I needed to submit my book request form to another desk in another room to another librarian and that I should come back in three days when my book would be available.

I dutifully returned to the library three days later to find my book retrieved from the stacks. I took the book to the counter to check it out, whereupon I was informed that policy did not permit books to be removed from the library. I was shown a reading room and told that I could read the book in that room only and that I was prohibited from taking the book to other parts of the library.

I soon determined that I didn't need that particular book. Indeed, I determined that I didn't need that particular library. Despite its medieval past—or perhaps because of it—the Bodleian was neither effective nor efficient in responding to my needs as a customer. I learned firsthand that institutions that have been around for a long time often have feet of clay compared to their younger rivals. Rather than drawing strength from the past, the past may sap strength from the present. As one noted change expert has observed, "Small and/or young organizations (like puppies or kittens) inherit agility as a birthright."[1]

Agility is the main source of continuous energy during evaluation. It refers to the ability to respond quickly and effectively to an adaptive challenge.[2]

Agility is a state of initial change readiness, docility, and preparation. It's an organization's latent mobilizing capacity when it begins the change process. It results from the

> *Agility: The ability to respond quickly and effectively to an adaptive challenge.*

act of evaluating, which is the continuous assessment of competitive reality, internal performance, and the refinement of strategy.[3] The reason agility is the first energy source is that it represents a resource on hand. It's the stored energy that exists within the organization. For example, if your extended family shows up unexpectedly from out of town and it's a half an hour before dinner, there's no time to go to the store. You have to go to the cupboards and pantry and use what you have to make the best possible meal. That's what agility is: it represents what you have on hand.

In every organization, the time comes when you must begin the change process. When that time comes, you have to rely on the agility on hand. If you have continuously cultivated agility, you will have created an adaptive system, which means that an organization is "stable enough to persist, yet flexible enough to quickly discover new solutions when a new problem arises."[4] This is the goal.

As an organizational trait, agility includes several other characteristics that we often use to describe both people and organizations, such as:

- Flexibility
- Elasticity
- Resiliency
- Recoverability
- Buoyancy
- Durability
- Improvisation
- Creativity

Agility is both individual and organizational. For example, there can be no organizational agility if there are no agile individuals within the organization. This means thinking about agility on both a personal and organization level. But first we need to make an important distinction between natural and conditioned agility.

NATURAL AND CONDITIONED AGILITY

Natural agility results from characteristics that define an organization. Some characteristics promote agility, and others do the opposite. For example, in addition to age, the size of an organization has a bearing on its level of natural agility. When A. G. Lafley took the helm at Procter & Gamble, not only did he take on leadership for a corporation with a 163-year-old storied past, but he also took responsibility to lead more than 100,000 people. Clearly a bigger organization is likely to have less natural agility.

The real question is whether you can do anything about the level of agility you inherit. The answer is undoubtedly yes. Through deliberate means, you have the opportunity to increase both your own agility and the agility of your organization. With proper conditioning, you can move your organization from its heels to its toes.

Why is this so important? Organizations on their heels aren't prepared to meet the challenge and rigors of change. When they start the change process, the risk is much higher that they will fail. They're simply not in shape and not balanced properly to respond. As I work with organizations of various sizes, histories, and track records, I consistently observe that agility not only gives an organization more ability to respond to adaptive challenge, but it also gives it a greater desire. This principle applies to other fields of endeavor. Well-trained athletes want to compete. Accomplished musicians want to perform. Similarly, agile leaders and organizations are more willing and able to respond to adaptive challenge. When it comes to major change especially, organizations rarely, if ever, build up enough natural agility to make the journey. Unfortunately, most organizations that put themselves on courses of rigorous change have little, if any, prior conditioning. They resemble a mountain climber who attempts to scale a high peak without prior preparation. As Larry Bossidy and Ram Charan state, "No matter how observant their leaders are, businesses can't change unless they are conditioned to do so."[5]

THREE DIMENSIONS OF PERSONAL AGILITY

How important is personal agility? If you're not agile as a leader, you'll have a hard time conditioning others to higher levels of agility. It's not like coaching a sports team in which you can be out of shape as a coach and win a championship. You have to be a player-coach, that is, a coach who also plays and is in shape to play. The second answer to the question is that agility is vital to your personal performance and success. If you lack agility, you will have a hard time responding to the most pressing challenges you face as a leader. If you're highly agile, there's a higher chance that you'll succeed in meeting those challenges.

In their study of executive derailment, the Center for Creative Leadership found that the "ability to change or adapt during a transition" is the number one success factor.[6] What can you do to increase your personal agility? First, consider that there are three primary categories of personal agility: intellectual, emotional, and physical. Each is overlapping and connected to the other two.[7]

In my interviews with more than three hundred managers at all levels and in many organizations, I asked them to define agility. The results fell out into the three categories just mentioned. We fleshed them out even more and identified some interesting dimensions to each one. Here's what I found:

Intellectual Agility

- Breadth and depth of relevant knowledge
- Critical and analytical thinking skills
- Creativeness, innovativeness, curiosity, resourcefulness, and cognitive flexibility
- Continuous learning, acquisition of new behaviors and skills[8]
- Intellectual courage to confront reality and avoid denial[9]

Emotional Agility

- Emotional energy, strength, and competitiveness
- Emotional control under stress
- Adaptability and flexibility

- Optimism, confidence, and self-esteem
- Tolerance for ambiguity, uncertainty, and surprise
- Commitment and passion under conditions of adversity and opposition
- Discipline and the ability to delay gratification
- Motivation to meet challenge
- Ability to work without recognition or credit

Physical Agility

- Physical capacity for maximum output
- Physical capacity for output over time, endurance, and stamina
- Ability to concentrate
- Tolerance for mundane and tedious work

INTELLECTUAL AGILITY

We pursue change based on competitive advantage. Unless we're like the Bodleian Library and can double as a museum, we have to keep moving to stay competitive. If we didn't have to worry about maintaining competitive advantage, we wouldn't concern ourselves with change. We could cherish the past and be single-path dependent, and it wouldn't matter because there would be no need for course correction.

Organizations in the past could go for long spells with no real threat to their competitive advantage. For example, U.S. Steel was the first billion-dollar company in the world. For several decades, it had no viable threats from overseas. Even with the ups and downs of the business cycle and domestic competition, the organization and its leaders went for years on autopilot, demonstrating an unwillingness to embrace innovation, a decision that for a time was rewarded with handsome profits.

One of my personal mentors explained it firsthand. He said, "I hired in at U.S. Steel in 1951. We were the 400-pound gorilla, the biggest company in the world. We lumbered from point to point. It was a placid time. No sharp turns. No bold strokes. Radical change wasn't even a part of the business vocabulary back then. We made incremental changes. We had some domestic competition, but virtually no threats from overseas. We posted profits during a long period of unbroken success."

Those days are gone: U.S. Steel now produces less than 10 percent of the nation's steel compared to nearly 70 percent in 1901. My mentor traveled across plain and prairie where the landscape was flat and wide open. The terrain is different today. Now we traverse a mountainous, treacherous expanse. Today we have to be prepared to initiate change at any time to sustain the competitive advantage we have, achieve the competitive advantage we never had, or regain the competitive advantage we lost.

The basis of intellectual agility is to understand the nature of competitive advantage and use it as the lens through which to evaluate the terrain of the competitive landscape. Leaders who don't have this lens are not as inclined to evaluate because they may not see the need. They are more likely to be inwardly focused and therefore surprised by and late to react to competitive threats. In a nutshell, the concept of competitive strategy is quite simple: all organizations must seek and achieve competitive advantage to stay viable. There are only two paths to gaining that advantage. One is to become a low-cost provider of your product, which means that your product is not differentiated and is therefore a commodity. The other option is to create a product that provides more value than that of the competition because it is different in a meaningful way. This is the high-value or differentiated path to competitive advantage. Think about the high-value path for a minute. Theoretically there are limitless ways to add value to products and services on dimensions of value such as quality, speed, comprehensiveness, innovativeness, durability, comfort, convenience, availability, consistency, variety, responsiveness, flexibility, reliability, accuracy, emotional connectedness, artistic appeal, and scalability. As consumers, we enjoy them, discuss them, and worry about them every day—for example:

"How long will this artificial knee last?"

"I thought these tires were rated for fifty thousand miles."

"Why doesn't this customer relationship management system allow me to work online?"

"Don't they understand medium-well? This steak is barely cooked."

"I don't care that you have 97 percent on-time delivery. Will you guarantee that I won't be in the other 3 percent?"

"Her first book was great. What happened?"

"They used to stock size 14 shoes. Don't you have them anymore?"

The marketplace tends to reward these paths and penalizes other paths that lie somewhere in between.[10] It all comes down to the value proposition. Figure 3.1 shows the two simple paths of competitive advantage.

Because there are inherent trade-offs between high-value and low-cost strategies, you have to make a choice between one or the other. Nevertheless, there are rare cases in which a strategy combines both paths.[11] Tabasco Sauce, for instance, is a versatile 125-year-old sauce made from red peppers, vinegar, and salt and aged in oak barrels. Through a proprietary process, the company produces 700,000 bottles a day that are shipped to 160 countries and used in salads, mixed drinks, omelets, and meat loaf. The product combines a low price point, distinctive taste, and enormous versatility. But a Tabasco-like advantage is the rare exception because usually there aren't such high barriers to entry to duplicate a product or service.

A basic understanding of competitive advantage increases agility. It works against the human tendency to deny reality when it's not attractive. From an intellectual standpoint, you're more likely to understand and embrace the reasons for change if those reasons are based on an analysis of competitive advantage. When you constantly evaluate competitiveness, you naturally develop a

FIGURE 3.1. THE TWO PATHS OF COMPETITIVE ADVANTAGE.

set of instincts about when to pursue change based on opportunity or threat. Furthermore, when change is supported by a solid rationale based on trying to achieve, maintain, or regain competitive advantage and the facts are clear that your advantage is at risk, that understanding alone diffuses resistance. Finally, knowing what brings competitive advantage and understanding the principle in the context of a dynamic and ever-changing marketplace helps you embrace the inevitable fact that no matter what competitive advantage you enjoy today, it won't last.

Sometimes the need for change is strategically obvious. When your cost structure is way out of line with that of the competition, you know you've got to do something. When the performance, quality, and value of your product lag behind, it's time to act. At other times, the need for change isn't apparent. Regardless of whether conditions tap you on the shoulder and tell you it's time to change, the mere fact that you have internalized the concept of competitive advantage will foster the intellectual agility to match the speed of change. In many industries, all you have to do is stand still for a month or two, and the forces of commoditization will erase your distinctiveness and deliver you to commodity hell. No product, service, or organization is safe despite the fact that it might enjoy distinctiveness or a low-cost position today. As Jeffrey Immelt, the CEO of General Electric, points out, "Virtually every product and service in today's markets are in danger of being commoditized."[12] The underlying truth about strategy is that competitive advantage goes away. It's a perishable commodity with a shelf life that's bound to expire. You never know how long your advantage will last and when obsolescence will come, but you can be certain that it will come. You can squeeze growth out of existing products and services for only so long before you have to search out new ways to move the revenue needle. The underlying principle is that the more dynamic the industry is, the shorter the competitive advantage. From the moment you gain competitive advantage, it begins to melt like ice.[13] It's always been true that competitive advantage is temporary. It's just more temporary in the global age. Consider that only thirteen of the Forbes 100 from 1917 even exist today.

What this calls for is a new kind of intellectual agility to match the hypercompetitive environment—a mentality that assumes and

anticipates the continuous loss of competitive advantage.[14] Peter
Drucker aptly referred to this idea as "planned abandonment."

Planned abandonment can become a deeply set paradigm and
cultural trait that defines the way we
see and play the competitive game. It
means thinking, planning, and acting
ahead of your current strategy cycle.

> *Planned abandonment: A
> mentality that assumes and
> anticipates the continuous loss
> of competitive advantage.*

It means being in a constant state of readiness. It's the mind-set
behind agility and an acknowledgment of ongoing change. It's
what lies behind the capacity to evolve.[15]

The idea that we should plan to abandon things is quite new.
Throughout history, few people have had the opportunity to live
through major inflection points in technology or movements in
capital, information, and labor. So the whole idea of planned abandonment really is foreign and counterintuitive to many people.
Remember the famous words of Charles Duell, the commissioner
of patents, who in 1899 said, "Everything that can be invented has
been invented." Then there was the surprising statement in 1942
by Thomas J. Watson, president of IBM: "I think there is a world
market for about five computers."

The problem is that many leaders who come from less dynamic
environments are used to longer strategy cycles. But those who see
abandonment as normal and expected have themselves gained
a form of competitive advantage because they work in harmony
with, rather in opposition to, the macroforces that constantly
buffet their organizations. To embrace a planned abandonment
mentality means that you view your competitive advantage like ice:
you acknowledge that every organization will slowly collapse if it
doesn't adapt. Every business model eventually leads to unsustain-
able growth. To remain distinctive, low cost, or both means that
you constantly adjust to adaptive challenges and opportunities.
You have to be willing to give up the way you do things today
and figure out how to do them better tomorrow. You have to be
looking to find the next advantage to give your organization a new
platform for growth.

Keep in mind that a planned abandonment mentality needs
to be appropriate for your organization and industry. If it's not,
you may not see where and how fast the ice is melting. If you're

too late, you may not have time to experiment and test options for a response. You'll be forced to respond without much preparation and hope you choose the right response. So how do you develop the right planned abandonment mentality? How do you calibrate yourself to the right degree with your organization and your industry? It's actually quite simple. The key is to assess the competitive cycles of specific elements of your organization.

I call it an ice-melting assessment.'' Here's how it works. Exhibit 3.1 shows seven elements of an organization along the left-hand column. For each one, ask yourself the two questions

EXHIBIT 3.1. ICE-MELTING ASSESSMENT.

Element	When Did This Last Change?	When and How Do You Expect It to Change Again?
1. Institutional mission, vision, and values		
2. Major strategies		
3. Products and services		
4. Structure or roles and responsibilities		
5. Major processes and systems		
6. Major policies and procedures		
7. Major tools, equipment, and technology		

listed at the top of the second and third columns. Let's take the first one as an example. Considering the institutional mission, vision, and values of your organization, when did these last change? Second, when and how do you expect them to change again? As you ask the questions, consider them in the context of your team, department, functional area, business unit, or the entire organization.

When I have leaders complete this exercise, they are often amazed at how much change is going on and the frequency with which different elements in the organization change. The sheer magnitude of the churn in most organizations is more than most people expect to find. But until we sit down and force ourselves to go through the discipline of doing the assessment, we never come face-to-face with the reality of the changing environment. We seldom appreciate how much we are already engaged in planned abandonment. Formally doing the exercise will help you adopt the proper planned abandonment mentality.

Many leaders are surprised at what they find. It's not uncommon to identify recent or current changes for every element. It's not that we're unaware of the changes going on; it's more that we haven't fully and systematically considered what the organization and its parts are collectively doing to try to maintain competitive advantage. Yet it's vital that you stay on top of your organization's adaptive activities. The imperative is to monitor outside trends by paying attention to a variety of data sources to help you sense market change early. Staying informed about recent, current, and future change is a good baseline measure of intellectual agility.[16]

EMOTIONAL AGILITY

The late August Wilson's play *The Piano Lesson* tells the story of a brother and sister who struggle over what to do with the family piano that is now theirs after their parents pass away. The brother wants to sell the piano to buy land and build a new life, while his sister wants to hold on to it as a family heirloom. The sibling feud illustrates the conflict that we often face when we have to make a decision about leaving the legacy of the past or holding on to it. Even in business, emotions enter in. We don't make and carry out important decisions based solely on logic and dispassionate analysis. The biggest and toughest decisions are usually the most emotional ones to make.

Understanding the strength of your organization's competitive position isn't enough. You can have a lot of intellectual agility and yet be a staunch resister of change. It depends on your emotional preparation. In almost every case of major change, some of the brightest people with the most developed sense of strategy resist the effort, even when they agree with it in principle, because they're not emotionally prepared for the process that will follow. You may even have been one of those people.

To have emotional agility is to understand, accept, and commit to the dual nature of leadership. As a leader, you have a paradoxical role to play in your organization. You must simultaneously preserve and disturb the status quo. You have to stabilize and destabilize, build up and tear down, protect and disrupt. It's all part of your role because that's what maintaining competitive advantage requires.[17]

In practical terms, you have to develop a certain ambidexterity in your skill set in order to do both. It's not easy because there's a natural and dynamic tension between the two sides. The preservation side of your role is more conservative and traditional, while the disturbing side of your role is more rebellious and entrepreneurial. One side has vested interests in the status quo, and the other side may be motivated to overthrow those interests.[18]

Operational and Change Work

A useful way to think about your role is to think in terms of two different kinds of work. When you're maintaining the status quo, you're doing operational work. When you're disrupting the status quo, you're doing change work.[19] You must perform both kinds of work as if you operate in two different spheres of activity. The challenge is that each type of work creates barriers for the other.[20] It's hard to change what you've worked so hard to put in place, but that's what change work can require.

Consider the example of Ann who is a purchasing manager. Ann spends most of her time assigning purchase orders, approving and managing vendors, drafting purchasing agreements, and helping department managers fill out capital budget request forms. This is her normal operational work, the tasks she performs every day. Then her boss calls her in one day and says, "We need to reduce the total cost of our purchases by 5 percent. To do this, I want you to reduce our list of vendors by 50 percent and enter into more favorable long-term contracts with those who are left. I need you to put a team together and get to work." Now she has to shift to change work.

The best way to understand why both are necessary is based on the concept of value. When you're maintaining the status quo, with its culture, processes, systems, structures, and tools, you're doing it to create value. The "current system" is what produces value today. But based on the concept of competitive advantage and the expectation that you will one day abandon the current system, you also devote part of your time to figuring out how the organization is going to create value tomorrow. It's your job to create value today and, at the same time, plan to create value tomorrow.

Operational work: Work performed now to execute the current strategy using current culture, systems, processes, structures, and tools in order to create value today.

Change work: Work performed now to prepare to execute future strategy by changing or reconfiguring some aspect of current culture, systems, processes, structures, or tools in order to meet an adaptive challenge and create value tomorrow.

Figure 3.2 shows a change continuum that ranges from no change at the far left to major change at the far right. Think for a moment about what you do in your role

FIGURE 3.2.   OPERATIONAL VERSUS CHANGE WORK.

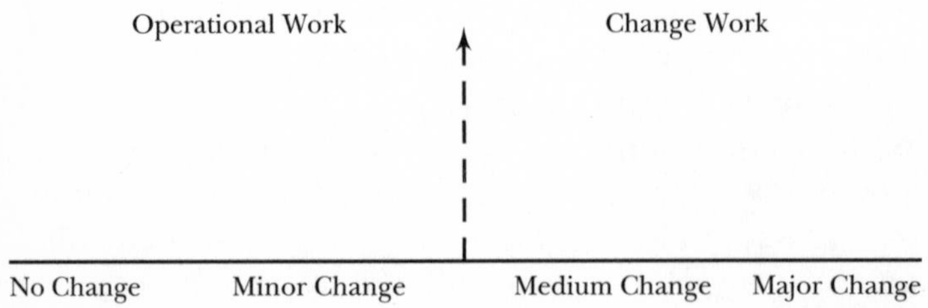

Operational Work		Change Work	
No Change	Minor Change	Medium Change	Major Change

as a leader as it relates to change. If you're like most other leaders, you work across the entire continuum—from no change to major change and everything in between. In reality, there's no clear line of demarcation between the two spheres; it is more of a gradual shift as minor change gives way to medium change. Somewhere in that transition comes the crossover.

Examples of operational work are tasks and activities that are normal, routine, and expected as part of the job. They make use of current strategy, culture, systems, processes, structures, and tools—for example:

- A purchasing manager processes a purchase requisition.
- An orthopedic surgeon performs a routine hip replacement.
- An accountant balances the books.
- A design engineer produces drawings for a new high-pressure valve.
- A human resource generalist provides orientation to new employees.
- A contract manager holds a quarterly review with a major vendor.
- An in-house lawyer draws up a contract for a new acquisition.
- A network administrator brings a server back online after replacing a crashed hard drive.

When people know how to do the work, are familiar with it, and know that it's an expected part of the job, they usually respond willingly and comfortably.

Now let's talk about change work. Examples of change work are things that are not normal, routine, or expected. They don't make use of current strategy, culture, systems, processes, structures, and tools—for example:

- A purchasing manager is asked to speed up the approval process for purchase requests.
- An orthopedic surgeon performs a second hip replacement on an older patient in poor health and with lots of scar tissue.
- An accountant is asked to value a company in an industry that she doesn't understand.
- A design engineer is asked to use a new type of computer-aided design software.

- A human resource generalist is asked to create a succession planning system for an organization that doesn't have one.
- A contract manager is told to improve the contract review process to increase accountability.
- An in-house lawyer has to build a legal defense strategy for a patent infringement case that has just been filed against the company.
- A network administrator is told that his job is being eliminated because the organization is going to outsource the entire IT function.

How do people generally respond when asked to engage in change work? They're uncertain, upset, nervous, anxious, fearful, timid, resistant, suspicious, and scared.

The Psychology of Work

Organizations create value through the strategy, culture, systems, processes, structures, technology, and other assets they have today. This status quo is preserved through operational work. Essentially it means maintaining things the way they are, which offers continuity, comfort, and predictability.[21] Within the scope of operational work, we make adjustments, modifications, and refinements. When we tweak things a little bit here and there, people generally tolerate the small changes without getting emotional. They usually perform operational work without special preparation because they understand why it is needed, how to do it, and what the consequences will be. It's considered within the range of normal expectation. This is understandable because the status quo exerts a strong gravitational pull on an organization—homeostasis—to keep it as it is. People protect it because it represents their comfort zone.[22] So any change beyond a minor one has to fight the forces of the status quo.[23] People understand and expect that you're going to make adjustments, but once you go beyond minor change, you cross over to change work.

It's one thing to talk about modifying a procedure, tweaking a process, upgrading a piece of equipment, or revising a policy. It is quite another to part ways with the past and create a new reality. Both approaches deal with change; the difference is in the degree of change. Major change doesn't carry the past forward; it casts it aside.

Once you engage people in change work, the entire psychology of work changes.

As Figure 3.2 shows, at some point on the continuum, there is an invisible point (represented by the dotted line) beyond which if you as the leader cross, people will see and respond differently. This is the line that separates operational work from change work. Change work is categorically different from operational work in two important respects: it requires different competencies of the leader and is most often performed in an environment of increased fear, stress, uncertainty, and complexity.[24] Think of examples of both kinds of work. How do people generally respond to change work versus operational work? What I observe across organizations is that once you cross over to engage people in change work, the entire psychology of work changes. There are several reasons for this:

- Operational work is understood and expected. Change work is not.
- People are normally prepared to perform operational work. They are normally unprepared to perform change work.
- Operational work is low risk. Change work is high risk.
- Operational work generally supports current responsibilities and routines. Change work often threatens these.
- Operational work provides high security. Change work provides low security.
- Operational work tends to require existing behavior and skills. Change work tends to require new behavior and new skills.
- Operational work preserves current roles. Change work has a tendency to create role ambiguity.
- Operational work tends to preserve the current distribution of power. Change work tends to redistribute power.
- Operational work normally leads to a predictable outcome. Change work is much more likely to lead to an unpredictable outcome.

You can see the challenge. Operational work is a fundamentally different activity from change work. The people whom you lead approach and think about the two differently. As a leader, you have to do so as well. The moment you cross over into change work, you enter a realm of much greater challenge and risk.

Senior leadership at a medical instruments company decided to redesign the supply chain. When a senior operations manager heard that one of the company executives was coming to his building to talk to him about it, he threatened to call security and have the executive escorted out of the building. Of course, this is an extreme example, but it gives a clear view of dynamics. The man was so worried that the supply chain initiative would threaten his role in the organization that he took extreme measures. Because human beings are for the most part gradualists by nature, when people are confronted with change work they often:

- Resist.
- Argue against the change from every available angle.
- Are less concerned whether the change is the right thing if they feel personally threatened.
- Test the resolve and commitment of those proposing change.

So what does all of this mean? It means that leaders have to embrace the dual nature of their role. This is an emotional and psychological transition more than an intellectual one. Much of it comes only through the experience of doing change work and helping others do it. Unfortunately, many managers never make the transition into change work, and it becomes a limiting factor in their career development. A common pattern is that a leader becomes competent in operational work but is unable to fully accept the responsibility to perform change work. It's not surprising that this is the case because change work is a daunting emotional challenge. In addition to intellectual skills, it requires an unflinching willingness to confront reality and an unwavering determination to do something about it, even when it's painful. Agility calls for emotional strength and courage. Much of the time, the emotional dimension of agility separates those who advance from those who don't.

PHYSICAL AGILITY

The third dimension of agility is physical. The turbulence of the global environment has created some new physical demands for leaders. The first pattern is that leaders have to shift more frequently between operational and change work. The average leader has more change initiatives that he or she is responsible to lead than in the past because of the shortened shelf life of competitive advantage. The daily pattern of individual work has changed because the ratio of operational-to-change work is shifting more toward change work. It's not uncommon for some leaders to toggle between operational and change work several times in the course of a single day.

The second trend is related to the first. Although leaders are working on more change initiatives than in the past, no one has relieved them of their operational work responsibilities. In fact, some leaders refer to operational work as their "day job." The reality is that change work seldom takes the place of operational work, so it must be done in addition to regular operational duties. The trend is that the overall load placed on the average leader is more demanding than in the past because the change work component constitutes a bigger chunk of incremental work.

Personal Work Patterns

To assess your own work patterns, use Exhibit 3.2. List the activities you perform in each category of change in the "Examples" column. Estimate the percentage of time you spend in each category. List some examples of activities in each category. Then combine the time you spend performing no change and minor change work, and medium and major change work to get a total estimate for the percentage of time you spend doing operational and change work. Rate the importance of each category of work to your overall job by assigning each a score on a scale from 1 to 5, with 1 being of low importance and 5 being of high importance to the organization.

In my interviews with managers in various organizations, I asked them to complete this assessment and then asked them follow-up questions. I identified the following patterns:

EXHIBIT 3.2. PERSONAL WORK PATTERN ASSESSMENT.

Change Category	Examples	Percentage of Time	Importance to the Organization (1 = low importance to 5 = high importance)
Operational work			
A. No change			
B. Minor change			
Total operational work (A + B)			
Change work			
C. Medium change			
D. Major change			
Total change work (C + D)			

Pattern 1: Frontline managers spend more time doing operational work than change work, but they are most often promoted on the basis of their ability to do change work.

Pattern 2: Middle managers shift back and forth between operational and change work more than either frontline managers or senior leaders do.

Pattern 3: Senior leaders spend more time doing change work than operational work, and they are almost always valued more on their ability to do change work than operational work.

Pattern 4: Change work is considered more important to an organization than operational work because it is the basis of creating value for the future.

Pattern 5: Leaders who perform change work effectively are considered more valuable to an organization than those who perform operational work effectively.

Pattern 6: Younger managers, Gen-Xers or millennials as they are called, born since 1980, demonstrate more natural agility as a general rule. They have been socialized and acculturated in a rapidly changing environment. In many cases, members of this demographic have known nothing but external change and continuous adaptation. The agility gap between many younger managers and their older counterparts can be a serious impediment to organizational change when younger managers seem innately familiar and comfortable with change, while older baby boomers see it as foreign and threatening. Furthermore, younger managers tend to be more indifferent to authority and hierarchy, whereas baby boomer managers tend to be more deferential to both.

What does this have to do with physical agility? First, it takes more physical agility to do change work than operational work. Second, doing change work in addition to operational work, and going back and forth between the two, can be physically taxing.[25] Physical agility is part of the ability to move adroitly between the realms. It's never easy, and the emotional and psychological demands of change work take a heavier toll than do those of operational work. Just ask yourself whether you sometimes feel like a grief counselor or a triage nurse. If you do, you're probably doing change work. Being physically conditioned to do it will pay important dividends over the long term. I believe that the whole notion of the so-called corporate athlete has evolved in part from the increasing demands placed on leaders to do change work. There are ample grounds to argue that the new physical requirement for agility is more demanding. The environment is more intense and demands more flexibility and stamina. A colleague of mine, for example, worked with a senior executive team at a major teaching hospital in the United States to conduct a massive project to improve bed economics and discharge times. After several months of work, members of the executive team started taking three times the number of normal sick days. They had hit the wall and had to make some adjustments to keep their efforts sustainable.

The increasing demands of change work should prompt you to consider the fundamental elements that contribute to physical performance. Consider, for instance, the following elements, and then think about ways that you can improve each one and increase your own physical agility:

- Diet
- Exercise
- Rest
- Pacing and spacing, renewal cycles
- Work-life balance

In the process, it's vital to respect the principle of renewal because you can't break that principle; you can only break yourself against it. As one leader notes, "We all have a well from which we draw to meet our responsibilities and there are times when that well runs dry and needs refreshment."[26]

A Final Word on Personal Agility

Work patterns are changing. Leaders are spending more time performing change work than ever before. They're also shifting back and forth between operational and change work more frequently. The problem is that you don't have the luxury of saying, "I want to be a manager who does exclusively operational work," or "I want to be a leader who does exclusively change work." You have to do both.

Leaders at all levels, whether they are formally designated as managers or not, are responsible for creating value today and tomorrow. Due to the hypercompetitive business environment, more change work is now being required, which puts a premium on those who can do it and a blemish on those who can't. Indeed, with competitive advantage always under siege, the source of sustained competitive advantage shifts to the nimble and resilient leader who stays in a constant state of readiness to take on the next adaptive challenge. These are the leaders who are most in demand—those with agility who are willing to tackle the challenges of change work.

ASSESSING ORGANIZATIONAL AGILITY

Now that we've addressed the three basic categories of individual agility, let's turn to organizational agility. Like individuals, organizations also vary in their ability to respond quickly and effectively to an adaptive challenge. Leaders can increase organizational agility, so it's not by chance that an organization becomes highly adaptable. It's a matter of conditioning. Without conditioning, most organizations become complacent, sluggish, and highly resistant to change. They become soft, slow, and clumsy when they cease to be aware of competitive reality. Several obstacles tend to reduce the agility of organizations.[27] For example, Anne Mulcahy, the CEO of Xerox, points out, "If you're not nimble, there's no advantage to size. It's like a rock."[28] Think about your organization and what might be getting in the way of becoming more agile. Ask yourself the following questions:

- Does size or age get in the way by creating deeply entrenched or encrusted ways of working?
- Is your organization possibly too stable? Do you cling to false beliefs about what the organization is even though circumstances have changed?
- Has the organization experienced unbroken success that has created intractable complacency?

- Has the organization experienced too many repeated failures and false starts that have created fear, fatigue, and unrelieved pessimism? Does the organization bear the impress of accumulated traumas?
- Do people in your organization understand the concept of competitive advantage?
- Are people in your organization aware of what's going on inside and outside your industry? Is the organization insulated or opened up to the outside world?
- Do people in your organization understand your strategy? Is it clear and actionable?
- Do people in your organization trust the leaders? Are these leaders credible?
- Does the organizational culture energize employees or put them to sleep? Do the prevailing cultural norms foster risk taking, innovation, and dissent, or do they encourage conformity and compliance?
- Are people in the organization challenged in their jobs? Are they expected to grow, develop, and take on stretch assignments?
- Do organizational values, structure, and processes support continuous learning?
- Are there entrenched organizational systems that are difficult to change or overcome in order to implement change?
- Are people properly recognized and rewarded for confronting and overcoming challenges?

CREATING ORGANIZATIONAL AGILITY

Organizational agility means that the organization possesses both the will and capacity to respond to adaptive challenge. It means that leaders can deploy willing and capable people as well as the resources necessary to respond to change at the moment of need.[29] You can create or increase the agility of your organization using best practices that have been developed. Most of them are based on two key principles to keep in mind: agility is best cultivated through actual experience, and people seem to learn more when they step outside their own environment.

For example, Great Ormond Street Hospital for Children, Britain's largest children's hospital, has redesigned its patient hand off techniques by imitating the choreographed pit stops of Italy's Formula One Ferrari racing team.[30] This approach has led to a reduction in mishaps that result from poor coordination, such as transferring a patient from the intensive care unit to surgery before the ventilator is ready. In this example, the hospital meets both criteria: the approach is based on experience, and the members of the organization learn from an environment different from their own.

To experience something is better than to observe something. To observe something is better than to hear something.

What follows is a list of best practices for increasing organizational agility. The list is a compilation of tested ideas that have come from other leaders and organizations. I encourage you to read through the list and identify only two or three things that you can do right now to bring your organization's agility to the next level. The most important part is to sustain your efforts, so don't take on too much and don't make it too complicated. If you do, it will never last in spite of your best intentions.

Creating agility is very much like maintaining a personal exercise regimen. Most people don't keep it up because the regimen is too demanding and they lack the personal commitment to stay with it. The whole key is sustainability, which dictates simple measures that you can maintain. What you're after is building agility over time so that it becomes a cultural trait infused throughout the entire organization. The other reason leaders shy away from conditioning for agility is that it deliberately disturbs the organizational system and requires keeping it perpetually disturbed at least at some minimum level. Maintaining creative discomfort is painful and requires more leadership energy to do it. But it works. General Electric, for example, does this through its performance management practices. The ongoing process of measuring an individual's performance and comparing that performance against peers no doubt creates anxiety. Bill Conaty, GE's executive vice president of human resources, explains, "We want to create angst in the system."[31]

Ways to Create Agility

- Be approachable in your relationships with people in your organization. Show them that you are curious about and interested in their ideas.
- Organize events or contests to challenge employees to provide innovative solutions to existing needs or opportunities.
- Deliberately hire people from varied backgrounds and experiences to add new thinking and a challenging element to the organization.
- Create more opportunities for involvement and collaborative work to foster the sharing of ideas across departmental lines.
- Reduce hierarchy in both structure and culture to create more boundaryless behavior and open communication.
- Train employees in critical and analytical thinking skills.
- Allow employees time to work on discretionary tasks of their own choosing.[32]
- Create expectations, standards, and tools for fact-based analysis of current performance.
- Teach people to think in terms of cycles or the run of competitive advantage in which there is an end point.
- Assign a person or function to constantly monitor the outside environment, trends, and external factors and report to the rest of the organization.
- Hold team, department, and company meetings to share hard numbers and facts about the competitive reality.
- Hold simple brainstorming sessions throughout the organization.
- Assemble groups that are highly diverse, in terms of workforce demographics as well as from all reaches of the organization. Ensure that you represent every category of diversity in order to stimulate new thinking and seed the organization with new ideas.
- Assemble a cross section of the entire organization for a conference to explore the past, the current state, and what the future might look like.[33]
- Expose employees to new industries through conferences and other cross-industry forums to bring in thinking from beyond the confines of the industry.

- Teach employees general business acumen, including how the business, organization, and industry work.
- Organize regular forums for speakers to address relevant topics in the industry.
- Formally communicate trends in the industry through a newsletter, corporate videos, or other means of delivery.
- Organize regular speaker forums.
- Set progressively higher goals to stretch people gradually.
- Keep the organization challenged by constantly tinkering with things through small project teams.[34]
- Communicate change as far in advance as possible.
- Reward risk-taking and entrepreneurial behavior.
- Train employees in decision making under pressure.
- Assign employees to specific projects or job assignments to stress-test them for conditions of ambiguity and uncertainty.
- Give employees the opportunity to work in frontline positions to understand the emotional side of a particular job or role.
- Share more information with the shop floor employees.
- Train employees in business simulations to mirror competitive situations.
- Take on small change initiatives to build up to larger ones step by step.
- Give people assignments to monitor the external environment.
- Decide which attachments, connections, anchors, or familiar aspects of people's jobs you will preserve in the change process. Communicate this up front.
- Create a culture of reality by demanding candor and an honest assessment of the facts.
- Increase the dialogue and free flow of ideas in your organization.
- Create a culture where ideas compete on their merits regardless of the position or authority of those who propose them.
- Accelerate developmental opportunities for employees by giving them stretch assignments early.
- Train people in time management skills.
- Support measures that encourage work-life balance.
- Support physical wellness with policies, events, sponsorships, speeches, and reward programs.

- Pace and space change initiatives in order to conserve energy and capacity.[35]
- De-layer the organization to make it less bureaucratic.
- Increase ways to solicit employee feedback.
- Audit the decision-making process. Make it faster and simpler where possible.
- Conduct employee surveys to assess strategic alignment and engagement levels.
- Benchmark the best practices of competitors to raise awareness and understanding of competitive realities.
- Interview customers to get an intimate view of the customer experience from beginning to end.
- Communicate historical examples of how the organization had to change in response to adaptive challenges.
- Create formal feedback channels for employees and hold managers accountable to gather it.
- Create human resource systems and processes that develop and support leading change as a key competency

Summary

Key Points

- Agility is the ability to respond quickly and effectively to an adaptive challenge. It's a state or condition of initial change readiness. It's the state of preparation and the latent or stored energy of the organization. Agility is both natural and conditioned, individual and organizational. There are three dimensions to agility: intellectual, emotional, and physical.
- Intellectual agility is based on understanding the nature of competitive advantage, which consists of two basic paths: low cost and high value. Understanding competitive advantage in the context of rapid change creates a planned abandonment mentality.
- Competitive advantage is a perishable commodity with a shelf life and expiration date.
- Planned abandonment is a mentality that assumes and anticipates the continuous loss of competitive advantage.

- Emotional agility is based on understanding and accepting the dual nature of leadership, which refers to the paradoxical role to simultaneously preserve and disturb the status quo by performing both operational and change work.
- Operational work is performed to execute the current strategy using current culture, systems, processes, structures, and tools in order to create value today.
- Change work is performed to prepare an organization to execute future strategy by changing or reconfiguring aspects of current culture, systems, processes, structures, or tools in order to meet an adaptive challenge and create value tomorrow.
- The psychology of work changes in the move from operational to change work. People need to be prepared and carefully guided through change work because it is unfamiliar and poses a variety of risks.
- Physical agility helps a leader succeed in the midst of changing work patterns. For example, leaders switch more frequently between operational and change work, and change work is normally performed in addition to operational work responsibilities.
- There are a variety of ways to increase the level of organizational agility. For best results, leaders should narrow their focus to two or three things that they will do to increase organizational agility.

PART THREE

PREPARE

As an organization moves from evaluation to preparation, the second EPIC stage, it makes the transition from a relatively flat line on the power curve to a gradually sloping upward line. The gradual incline represents the additional work—change work—that a leader must now ask the organization to perform. It requires more energy to perform this work, which includes analyzing alternatives for change, testing them, selecting a course of action, and planning for implementation. All of that has to be performed on top of the operational work of running the organization, so it requires a new exchange of energy for discretionary effort. In the figure shown here, the arrow indicates the preparation stage.

THE GRADUAL INCLINE OF PREPARATION.

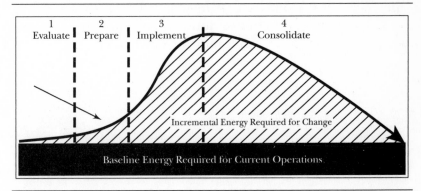

The transition from evaluation to preparation also marks a psychological shift. It's the point at which the leader deliberately disturbs the organization. Although usually not severe, this initial disturbance begins to destabilize the organization from its patterns of operational continuity. As you can see from the power curve in the figure, preparation doesn't involve the steep grade that implementation does, but it does mark the end of stability or equilibrium and the beginning of a transition period that won't end until change is firmly rooted in the organization during consolidation. Although it's not as demanding and taxing as implementation, it rattles and shakes the organization out of its orbit of inertia.

Your organization may be a stodgy, bureaucratic company with a culture of entitlement, a nimble and responsive organization with a culture of continuous improvement, or something in between. In any case, you've decided that there's a gap between current reality and where the organization needs to be.

Most large-scale change initiatives succeed because of leaders who patiently and meticulously prepare their organizations in advance. They front-end load the work during the preparation stage to gain maximum momentum to meet the steep grade of the implementation stage that follows. Most arduous change initiatives require that energy be laid in store for the implementation stage, so the preinvestment during preparation is substantial. According to the EPIC methodology, no fewer than four of the seven primary energy sources must be activated during preparation: urgency, credibility, coalition, and vision. This doesn't imply that their influence will die out later. Rather, it will be long lasting, but it's vital that they are activated during preparation so that there's adequate energy to carry over into implementation.

CHAPTER FOUR

PREPARE WITH URGENCY

The disposition of a fleet, while proceeding on a
voyage, will in some measure depend on particular
circumstances; as the difficulty of the navigation; the
necessity of dispatch, according to the urgency or
importance of the expedition: or the expectation of an
enemy in the passage.
WILLIAM FALCONER, SCOTTISH POET

PREPARE WITH URGENCY.

EPIC Stage	1 Evaluate	2 Prepare	3 Implement	4 Consolidate
The Leader's Role	**Equilibrium step** Supply energy for the ongoing evaluation of competitive reality, internal performance, and change alternatives.	**Ignition step** Replenish energy to supply a gradual increase in work performed and stress absorbed during preparation.	**Refueling step** Replenish energy to supply a significant increase in work performed and stress absorbed during implementation.	**Refueling step** Replenish energy to supply a gradual decrease in work performed and stress absorbed during consolidation.
Energy Sources	**1. Agility**	1. Agility **2. Urgency** **3. Credibility** **4. Coalition** **5. Vision**	1. Agility 2. Urgency 3. Credibility 4. Coalition **5. Vision** **6. Early Results**	1. Agility 2. Urgency 3. Credibility 4. Coalition 5. Vision 6. Early Results **7. Sustained Results**

What can urgency do? Consider the case of the Liberty ships during World War II. By 1940, all of continental Europe had come under Nazi control, and there was an urgent need for the United States to provide a massive sealift of food and war supplies to aid Allied forces. There was just one problem: the American merchant marine fleet was undersized and woefully unprepared to respond. Without delay, President Roosevelt announced an emergency ship building program to assemble a standardized cargo vessel that became known as the "Liberty ship." At 441 feet long and weighing thirty-five hundred tons, the Liberty ship could carry more than nine thousand tons of cargo. It had enough space, for example, to carry three thousand jeeps in a single haul. By early 1941, nine shipyards were built around the country, and the vessels started rolling off the production lines. The average production time for a Liberty ship in 1942 was 108 days.[1]

But the demand kept increasing. The German Reichsmarine was attempting to strangle Britain with a blockade of shipping routes to America. Britain was now consuming more supplies each month than it was receiving.[2] The German U-boats were also wreaking havoc on all Allied vessels. For example, in the spring of 1942, 680,000 tons of Allied ships were sunk. Roosevelt and the Maritime Commission responded by constructing another nine shipyards along the Atlantic and Pacific coasts. In all, eighteen shipyards employed 1.5 million workers to cut, weld, rivet, paint, and deliver what in the end would be 2,710 Liberty ships, constructed with 592,000 man-hours each.

By the end of 1943, the average production time had been cut by more than half. Instead of 108 days, it now took fewer than 40 days to construct a vessel. In fact, at Kaiser's yard in Richmond, California, workers set a record, assembling the USS *Robert E. Peary* in only four days. In the end, the American merchant marine delivered an astonishing six thousand tons of cargo every hour through the duration of the war, clearly playing a pivotal role in the Allied victory. That's what urgency can do.

URGENCY AS AN ENERGY SOURCE

Urgency ignites or catalyzes the change process. During the first EPIC stage of evaluation, an organization is in an operating mode and a state of relative equilibrium. Because the evaluation stage requires a comparatively small amount of additional work and stress absorption, it's often imperceptible that anything other than running the organization day to day is going on. With the exception of those who are evaluating the external environment and internal performance, the organization often doesn't detect additional demands. Everything seems normal and undisturbed. Once the organization decides to pursue change, however, there's a new requirement for work and energy to fuel that work.

As the table at the start of the chapter indicates, four of the seven primary energy sources come into play during preparation: urgency, credibility, coalition, and vision. Each must be activated in the proper sequence in order to fuel the preparation stage and build up energy for the taxing implementation stage that follows.

The initial task of urgency is to help move the organization from thinking to doing. What formally signals the transition from evaluation to preparation is a decision to pursue change. That transition is usually more gradual than abrupt because the organization takes on additional work slowly as it prepares for implementation. Urgency becomes the essential first energy source during preparation because it has the power to move an organization from an intellectual state of analysis to an emotional state of action. The other energy sources in the first two stages—agility, credibility, coalition, and vision—can't accomplish this. Without urgency, people may believe that change isn't necessary. Only urgency provides the all-important thrust that moves people from seeing the need to feeling the need. Without a felt need born of urgency, people seldom do anything about it.

DEFINING URGENCY

Urgency is a state or condition requiring immediate action or attention. It's the raw emotion that motivates people to move away from something because of risk, fear, or pain or to move toward something due to potential reward. It's a state of dissatisfaction in which there is motivation at some level to change the way things are today.

Urgency springs from both fact and emotion to create a felt need. As a source of motivation that calls forth the discretionary effort of people, it

---

Urgency: A state or condition requiring immediate action.

---

can be positive or negative in nature. There can be a sense of urgency to move toward something desirable or away from something undesirable. An example of positive urgency is Microsoft, which observed the remarkable success of Apple's iPod music player and its 75 percent market share in the portable music player business. Microsoft felt positive urgency to create a competitive product, the Zune music player, in order to compete with Apple in this lucrative market. An example of negative urgency is Wal-Mart, which sold all of its stores in Korea after struggling for several years to establish profitable operations in a country and culture where its value proposition fell flat with consumers.

The higher the level of dissatisfaction is, the greater are the urgency and motivation to change.[3] When the pain of certainty associated with the status quo becomes higher than the pain of uncertainty associated with change, people tend to act.

INITIATING CHANGE ON THE BACK OF A CRISIS

Like agility, there is both natural and conditioned urgency.[4] This means that with any condition that might prompt change, there will be a level of urgency naturally associated with that condition. Sometimes the level of natural urgency is high. Referring to his predecessor, the current CEO of IBM, Samuel Palmisano, explained, "When Lou Gerstner came here in 1993, there was clearly a burning platform. In fact, the whole place was in flames. There was even talk of breaking up the company."[5] Gerstner went on to achieve one of the most significant corporate transformations in history. No doubt the high level of inherent urgency within IBM worked in his favor. It was an energy source that he drew on liberally from the beginning of the change process.

Initiating change is clearly easier on the back of a crisis because it generates massive amounts of energy to fuel the discretionary efforts of people. It lightens the burden of the leader by reducing the need to sell change. When survival is at stake, people understand quickly. They run the risk-reward calculation in their heads, and it tells them that the impending loss is greater than the risk of change. That's when change appears as a road to deliverance—a road that represents less danger than staying the course. This can be a welcome and powerful source of energy.

Another benefit of urgency in crisis is that it can impose a deadline. An organization facing business failure can't go on indefinitely. The leader must fix the problem quickly or the business will fail. I worked with a manufacturing firm that was bleeding cash at the rate of $2 million a day. The company's poor performance made it unable to borrow more money against its assets, so the leaders had to stop the hemorrhaging or the company would face liquidation in a bankruptcy court. In the end, the company couldn't stop the bleeding, and the company was forced into bankruptcy. Not seeing any viable alternatives, the bankruptcy judge ruled in favor of shuttering the production facilities and liquidating the remaining assets. This may seem like an extreme example. It's not. Once an organization enters into crisis (that is, any threat to viability as a going concern), the clock immediately starts ticking toward demise. Crisis generates high levels of urgency, but it also imposes a deadline.

INITIATING CHANGE WITHOUT A CRISIS

Now consider the opposite situation. In 1996, Jack Welch launched Six Sigma, a statistics-based quality improvement program, as a major corporate initiative at General Electric. The backdrop is that in 1995, GE had produced record earnings and profits. Revenues had climbed from $60 to $70 billion, and net earnings had increased from $2.8 billion to $3.9 billion during the same period.[6] When Welch announced the initiative, he explained, "You could see the interest level in the audience plummet and eyes glaze over."[7] I talked to several individuals who worked at GE when Six Sigma was announced. When I asked them what the organization's level of urgency was to embrace the initiative, they looked at me in bewilderment. "How could we have any sense of urgency about it?" they replied. "We didn't even know what the word meant." You get the point. If there's no crisis, you have to sell change. But you're limited because you can't sell survival very well in flush times. You've got to come up with a rationale, and it has to be compelling or no one will be buying.

Regardless of the rationale for change, if there's no crisis, there will be less urgency. People are much more reluctant to part ways with the status quo when there's no clear and present danger. The reason is simple: everyone does a private risk-reward calculation, and if there's no visible risk to keeping the status quo and no certain reward for leaving it, people will vote to keep it every time. Remember that urgency is an energy source because it's a form of motivation. But unless people have a compelling reason or a felt need for change, they won't have any natural urgency to pursue it. The difficulty is that urgency is rarely on the leader's side if he or she tries to make a move ahead of the market. Often such a leap of faith is the best strategy, but it underscores the loneliness of truly visionary leaders who seek new platforms for growth before others do.

THREE CATEGORIES OF ADAPTIVE CHALLENGE

There is a different level of natural or inherent urgency associated with every change.[8] It depends on the strength and direction of the incentives connected to the change. At any given time, every organization possesses some level of dissatisfaction to change or satisfaction to keep things the way they are. If we look closer at what causes the variation, we can make some interesting observations. First, urgency is based on the combined perception of what's going on inside and outside the organization. Second, if a company is doing well internally, there's less natural urgency, as we observed in the GE example. Third, the level of urgency often depends on whether there is an adaptive challenge, what it looks like, and how close or far away it is. Let's take a closer look at the third pattern and discuss the three categories of adaptive challenge:

• *Opportunity.* When there is no clear adaptive challenge, change can only be based on opportunity, like the Six Sigma example at GE. It is a difficult category of adaptive challenge to deal with because nothing is prompting change, nothing is shaking the organization from its state of comfort, and nothing is provoking it to sharpen its focus except the leaders themselves. For example, a medical device company with industry-leading profits announced that it would decentralize from three large divisions into eleven operating units in an effort to foster innovation and entrepreneurship, speed up product development, and decrease overall time to market. In this case, internal performance was good and there was no visible external adaptive challenge, so change could be based only on perceived opportunity. There was little immediate pressure inside or outside the company to pursue change because the adaptive challenge was neither visible nor felt.

• *Threat.* To understand this category of adaptive challenge, let's bring it a little closer. A computer software company has decided to acquire an IT consulting firm in order to offer bundled solutions of software and consulting services to the marketplace. The company has had average profits for the past three years. On the outside, competitors are embracing a solutions business model by bundling software with services, so the firm is concerned about being left behind. In this case, the organization is pursuing change based on a threat. A threat is more than an opportunity because the adaptive challenge is visible and may be exerting some degree of competitive pressure on the organization, but not intense pressure.

• *Crisis.* In a crisis, the adaptive challenge is at the door, or it might even be leaving footprints on your back. For example, a major producer of home furnishings is losing market share to manufacturers in China: it has experienced declining sales growth for the past three years. After much deliberation, corporate leadership has decided to outsource all manufacturing to China and focus its efforts on core competencies such as new product design, managing and building its brand, and expanding its services. In this example, the adaptive challenge is both clear and present and the competitive threat immediate and intense based on the proximity of the adaptive challenge.

As you consider change, or find yourself in the midst of it, a helpful diagnostic is to assess the nature and distance of the adaptive challenge that you're addressing. Ask yourself what it looks like and how close or far away it is. Using a scale from 1 to 10, where 1 means "no urgency" and 10 means "the highest possible urgency," rate the level of urgency for the change initiative that you're currently working on. Then check to see if your assessment corresponds with the categories of opportunity, threat, and crisis. An opportunity usually equates to an urgency rating of 0 to 3; a threat, 3 to 6; and a crisis, 6 to 10. Figure 4.1 illustrates this pattern. The three bars show the relative differences in urgency that are normally associated with the three categories of adaptive challenge.

As you make your assessment, consider that if you have a track record of success, that fact alone will sometimes limit your ability to spot adaptive challenges that lie ahead and thus make an objective assessment. Past success has the ability to blind minds, dull senses, and lull us into complacency. A final point is that given the velocity with which external change moves, sometimes it's hard to tell the difference among the three. What looks like an opportunity could really be a threat, and even that threat could develop into a crisis rapidly. Andy Grove, the former chairman of Intel, once observed with language borrowed from the poet Carl Sandburg, "Most strategic inflection points, instead of coming in with a bang, approach on little cat feet."[9]

What did you determine? A standard rule of thumb is that if you rated the natural level of urgency somewhere between 0 and 6,

FIGURE 4.1.   THREE CATEGORIES OF ADAPTIVE CHALLENGE.

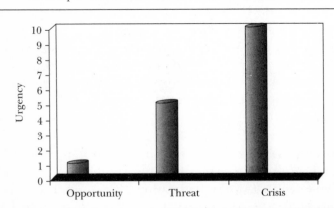

ask yourself why. If urgency is low, complacency is high. Answer these probing questions to get to the root cause:

- Are your people falsely secure in their belief that the organization is competitive and performing well?
- Are your people denying that certain competitive threats aren't real, let alone serious?
- Is your organization tired, discouraged, or disaffected from previous false starts? Is it suffering from a state of fatigue that has induced a survival mentality and has made people apathetic toward change?
- Are your people making unrealistic assumptions about market conditions? Are they betting that things will improve?
- Are past organizational success and a proud heritage preventing you from seeing the reality of the organization's vulnerabilities?
- Are you tracking trends closely enough so that people are aware of new market developments?
- Are there leaders who are protecting the status quo to benefit themselves and at the same time putting the organization at risk?
- Do members of the organization understand the basic and underlying economics of the business so that they are able to properly diagnose the need for change?

Once you identify the most important sources of complacency, you have the opportunity to try to increase urgency through deliberate means.

Increasing Urgency: Appeal to Reason and Emotion

One of the biggest mistakes that people make in leading change is to rush into a change effort that has low natural urgency without making efforts to create more. If urgency isn't an unalterable given, what can you do about it? How can you create or increase urgency when you don't have enough? How can you enroll people in the effort by convincing them of a need? Clearly external sources of urgency are the most powerful, but if there aren't visible external sources of urgency that are getting people's attention, the job of creating urgency falls to you as leader. First, there are several possible ways to increase urgency: "No single intervention alone is sufficient to diffuse dissatisfaction properly."[10] What's important to understand is the principle behind the best practices: appeal to reason and emotion. Both are important. People need information and logic, but they also need to witness something compelling or feel something viscerally before they really get motivated.

C. K. Prahalad, a professor at the University of Michigan's business school and a leading strategy guru, was hired by Philips Electronics in 1991 to do a weeklong brainstorming session with senior leaders. On the first day of the session, he started by sharing something he said he had read in the *Financial Times* that morning: Philips was heading into bankruptcy, the article speculated, and bankers wanted to know what the management game plan was going to be. He said, "Forget what we are supposed to talk about. There is a major crisis. You had better figure out what you are going to do about it." He broke the stunned executives into two groups, and they returned several hours later with ideas for radical restructuring involving up to fifty thousand layoffs. Then Prahalad admitted that he made the article up.[11] I'm not advocating his methods in this case, but the example illustrates the power of new facts and elevated emotion to spur people to action. In almost every case in which a leader is able to increase urgency, there is new information presented or a new emotional condition created.

Sometimes the rationale for change is clear and compelling but not enough to get people's attention. For instance, a steel supplier to Caterpillar, the well-known maker of heavy equipment, was in danger of losing its supplier relationship because the surface quality of its steel was so poor. Management responded by taking a team of hourly workers to the Caterpillar plant to see firsthand why good surface steel is critical to make parts for a backhoe or earth mover. The hourly workers were given the opportunity to talk to their hourly worker counterparts at Caterpillar. Although brief and limited, the time the workers had together proved to be a significant emotional experience that created a deep inner commitment to improve quality and meet the customer's standards. Surface quality immediately improved after the visit.

A variation on that theme is an approach taken by Ravi Kant at Tata Motors in India. To get up close and personal with adaptive challenge in his business, he put his people face-to-face with competitive threats: "We exposed our people to products of competitors by tearing those products apart and analyzing the good and bad and comparing them with our own, thereby making people see why customers buy someone else's products rather than ours."[12]

The power of personal interaction can't be overstated. To begin the turnaround at IBM, CEO Louis Gerstner spent thousands of hours making personal appearances to his employees around the world. When asked why, he responded, "To shake them out of their depressed stupor, remind them of who they were."[13] Another successful change leader, Corrado Passera, CEO of Banca Intesa, also uses this approach: "It's a long process, but you have to put your face in front of the people if you want them to follow you."[14]

Here are some simple suggestions to increase urgency on both sides of the equation:

Appeal to Reason	*Appeal to Emotion*
Share new and relevant information about a problem or opportunity. Some people need to be drowned in data. Give them as much as they need.	Use a vivid story or anecdote. Use a vision of what the future state will look like. Make a customer visit so you are up close and personal.
Assign people to study a problem or opportunity and come to their own conclusions.	Get a customer to give you candid feedback about what is working and what isn't working.
Assign those closest to the problem to explain the need for change. Explain the long-term consequences of not pursuing change.	Make personal emotional connections with people. Get face-to-face.

THE POWER OF URGENCY: NECESSARY BUT NOT SUFFICIENT

The strongest forms of urgency are based on fear, loss, and pain. But even that is often not enough to motivate change. The specter of dire consequences may not arouse people enough to get them to change.

Consider the following clinical example. You've had a serious heart attack. Fortunately, you're pulling through, but you had to undergo coronary bypass surgery. You're now recovering, and your doctor has warned you that unless you make certain changes in your diet and exercise, your heart disease will continue to threaten your life. Would you be willing to make the necessary lifestyle changes? According to Edward Miller, dean of the Medical School at Johns Hopkins University, the answer is most likely not. He reports that "ninety percent of patients who've had coronary bypass surgery don't sustain changes in the unhealthy lifestyles that have worsened their severe heart disease and greatly threatened their lives."[15]

We can't deny the enormous power that urgency can supply. It's a vital energy source, but we have to keep in mind that although it's necessary, it's never sufficient. In the change process, urgency has an important role to play to fuel a gradual increase in work as the organization leaves the state of relative equilibrium. And even after the preparation stage, urgency can have an important cumulative impact on change during subsequent stages. But it is only one of seven critical energy sources.

There remain some instances of change for which urgency is low (a rating of 0 to 3), and you can't find ways to increase it. Even when urgency is high, organizations behave the same way individuals do. It's not uncommon to see an organization faced with a serious crisis or threat, or even extinction, respond with complacency and indifference.

Urgency has another limitation as well: it tends to act more like a spark than a sustained source of motivation to change. Although urgency may have the ability to catalyze change, it doesn't provide the skill, discipline, and stamina that are required to get all the way up and down the power curve. When urgency is based on a particular need or pain point, it tends to have a short shelf life.

URGENCY AS A PERMANENT STATE OF MIND

Most of the time, urgency is the consequence of immediate circumstance. It's a temporary condition caused by an opportunity, threat, or crisis that exists today. But what if there is no such condition? Can you still have urgency when there is no opportunity, threat, or crisis on the horizon, when there's no visible danger or potential reward? The answer is yes. Urgency can become a cultural condition that isn't based on an immediate situation. It can become a permanent state of mind or a cultural trait that defines the way the organization sees the world. As leaders and their organizations become more accustomed to change, they become socialized to believe that the next adaptive challenge is always just around the corner, regardless of prevailing business conditions or how well the company may be doing. As Jack Welch has noted, "Great leaders are constantly looking around the corner, anticipating and smelling out issues."[16] Two leaders in the auto industry exemplify this pattern.

The first is Katsuaki Watanabe, the CEO of Toyota Motor Company. Despite Toyota's recent ascendancy to become the world's largest carmaker and despite the fact that it has overtaken General Motors to become the world's largest carmaker, Watanabe carries with him a constant sense of urgency. He's concerned about Toyota's competitive position, slipping quality, engineering practices, and efficiency of plants. A perpetual dissatisfaction with the status quo is such a part of his mind-set that he engenders a "severe dose of institutional paranoia" throughout the organization.[17] This is a man who when he arrived at Toyota was concerned about the amount of rice being wasted at company cafeterias due to pre-served portions, and as a result implemented changes to allow employees to serve themselves.

Some of his counterparts aren't any different. Take Carlos Ghosn, for example, the CEO of both Nissan and Renault: "Mr. Ghosn functions as if collapse lurks around the next corner. He is fueled by a sense of crisis and urgency, mixed with impatience and passion, as he runs, simultaneously, two of the largest car companies in the world. At Nissan he preaches vigilance and the risk of getting complacent; at Renault, where he took the chief executive title in April of last year, he imbues the ranks with a sense of being in danger as they try to remake a profitable but mediocre company into a great one."[18]

ASSESSING URGENCY

To assess the level of natural urgency in the change initiatives that you're involved with, ask yourself the following questions:

- Is there a felt need today as a result of stress, fear, risk, pain, or loss? Explain.
- On a scale from 1 to 10, rate the level of urgency associated with the change initiative that you're working on. Is the adaptive challenge you confront an opportunity, risk, or crisis? Explain your rating.
- Do you need to increase the level of urgency associated with your change initiative?
- If so, what can you do to increase the urgency associated with the change initiative?
- What can you do to appeal to reason? What can you do to appeal to emotion? How will you do this?

Summary

Key Points

- Urgency is a state or condition requiring immediate action. It's the raw emotion that motivates people to move away from something because of risk, fear, or pain or to move toward something due to potential reward. As the first energy source in the preparation stage, it plays the role of igniting or catalyzing the change process.
- There are two kinds of urgency: natural and conditioned. The level of natural urgency associated with a change depends on the nature of an adaptive challenge, how close or far away it is, and how much competitive pressure it is exerting on an organization.
- An opportunity represents an adaptive challenge that is either invisible or off in the distance. It typically represents the lowest natural level of urgency.

- A threat represents an adaptive challenge that is visible and exerting some degree of competitive pressure on the organization. It typically represents a medium level of natural urgency.
- A crisis represents an adaptive challenge that is clear, present, and exerting significant pressure on the competitive position of an organization. It typically represents the highest level of natural urgency.
- If you assess the natural level of urgency associated with a particular change to be between 0 and 6 on a scale of 1 to 10, you should consider ways to increase urgency through deliberate means.
- Increasing urgency is best accomplished through appeals to reason and emotion based on an accurate portrayal of circumstances.
- The strongest forms of urgency are based on fear, loss, and pain. But while urgency is necessary, it is never sufficient because it lacks other requirements to bring about successful change such as leadership, strategy, vision, and resources. It tends to act more as a spark than a sustained source of motivation.
- A permanent sense of urgency can become a mind-set, or cultural trait, that defines a leader's fundamental approach to managing an organization. Increasingly, this trait is valuable to guard against the risk of complacency.

CHAPTER FIVE

PREPARE WITH CREDIBILITY

There is no edict in the world that will make people take risks.
JACK WELCH

PREPARE WITH CREDIBILITY.

EPIC Stage	1 Evaluate	2 Prepare	3 Implement	4 Consolidate
The Leader's Role	**Equilibrium step** Supply energy for the ongoing evaluation of competitive reality, internal performance, and change alternatives.	**Ignition step** Replenish energy to supply a gradual increase in work performed and stress absorbed during preparation.	**Refueling step** Replenish energy to supply a significant increase in work performed and stress absorbed during implementation.	**Refueling step** Replenish energy to supply a gradual decrease in work performed and stress absorbed during consolidation.
Energy Sources	**1. Agility**	1. Agility **2. Urgency** **3. Credibility** **4. Coalition** **5. Vision**	1. Agility 2. Urgency 3. Credibility 4. Coalition 5. Vision **6. Early Results**	1. Agility 2. Urgency 3. Credibility 4. Coalition 5. Vision 6. Early Results **7. Sustained Results**

I once worked with a large organization that was struggling financially and badly in need of major change. At the end of my first week with the client, I had the opportunity to attend the company's big tent meeting during which the CEO unveiled a plan for massive restructuring. I took a chair in the large conference room along with several hundred employees. I sat and mingled with members of the executive team until the CEO made his appearance. Smartly dressed, this articulate man approached the podium, raised himself to his full height, and began a dazzling presentation.

With the aid of multimedia, he explained the company's long-term aspirations. We watched three-dimensional animations of new systems and equipment that would soon come online. We followed his laser pointer as it bounced over pro forma business plans full of ginned-up assumptions concerning future growth. In well-milled prose, the CEO explained how the company would outwit its rivals, both domestic and global, to become the market leader. The carefully choreographed event was a rich sensory experience, polished, full of substance, and incredibly well executed. After the meeting, the CEO left immediately to catch a plane, so I lingered for more conversation to get a sense of employee reaction. I was surprised at what I both saw and heard.

The employees were unmoved and uninspired. Many of them just sat in their chairs for a few minutes in what appeared to be a stupor. After talking to several of them, I learned that almost without exception, the CEO's presentation came across as hollow and gratuitous. It had been a brilliant performance of oratory and chartsmanship, but it had elicited no visceral response. The advocacy skills, verbal artistry, and evangelical fervor didn't matter. To the employees, it was noise. They simply set his words at the curb for pick up. "Why?" I asked. "Because he's not credible," came the response. "Staged and scripted ceremonial nonsense," voiced another. "He doesn't pass the smell test," commented a third. The employees were unwilling to sign on for change and give their discretionary efforts to the cause. Only after the CEO's unmourned departure did the organization begin to respond seriously to calls for change.

CREDIBILITY AS AN ENERGY SOURCE

Peter Drucker explained that "the manager is the dynamic, life-giving element in every business."[1] This isn't just a high-minded statement. It's also correct in an operational sense when you consider how credibility works in conjunction with the other six primary energy sources to move change along the power curve.

Credibility means you deserve to be trusted. It's the hard currency of change leadership and the basis of your legitimacy to lead. When you're credible, you meet the qualifications that people place on trust, so they grant you what Mark Moore, professor of Criminal Justice Policy and Management at Harvard's Kennedy School of Government, calls an "authorizing environment" in which to lead.[2] Credibility is your legitimacy or permission to lead. In times of organizational change, it gives you greater capacity to ask for and gain discretionary effort. Credibility is so vital a leadership attribute that lasting and meaningful change doesn't happen without it. Because organizational change is dependent on a leader's ability to supply, replenish, and manage organizational energy, it must precede other energy sources in order to put them in motion. Credibility is the actuator, the mechanism that catalyzes the other energy sources. It's that life-giving element, wellspring, or original source from which all real change leaders draw their ability to motivate, organize, direct, and lead.[3] Authority, power, and position are just contrivances that we use to manage the complexity of an organization. They work on a short-term basis and out of fear of loss. Sustainable performance-based change requires credibility.

In Chapter Four, I identified urgency as the first energy source that is based on the productive dissatisfaction people have with the status quo. I noted that undesirable circumstances often evoke the discretionary efforts of people. Remember, however, that urgency alone is unproductive. Unless there is a credible leader to channel that urgency, it normally turns to indifference or despair. As the second energy source in the change process, credibility is also unique in its origin: it's the only energy source that derives its power from within the leader. All of the others trace their origins to something outside the leader:

- Agility is based on an organization's condition.
- Urgency is based on undesirable circumstances.
- Coalition is based on common interests.
- Vision is based on a compelling picture of the future.
- Early results are based on visible and tangible outcomes.
- Sustained results are based on visible and tangible outcomes over time.

But credibility draws its power from characteristics that reside in the person. It's the energy source that harnesses, directs, and compounds the others. In the example that opens this chapter, employees had urgency to change, but because the CEO was not credible, the urgency resulted in despondency. No one believed that the CEO could lead them to a better place, so the change process never got off the ground.

According to the EPIC methodology, credibility is the third energy source and the second one needed in the preparation stage. Its function is to provide renewed energy for the additional work and stress that the organization must perform and absorb in preparation for change.

One question commonly arises at this point about vision: Why isn't it the first or second energy source? The answer is that a clear and compelling vision takes time to develop. What moves you out of evaluation is a decision that change is necessary. In the early stages of preparation, you evaluate the options for change, test them, and finally decide on a course of action. All the while, the vision is incubating. Rare is it that you will have a crystalline vision of change until well into the preparation stage, and it's not uncommon to find that the vision is still developing during the implementation stage.

Let the vision incubate.

Bob Lane, the CEO of John Deere & Company, vividly illustrated this principle when he embarked on an operational and cultural transformation of the 164-year-old maker of farming and construction equipment. In 2000, when he launched the effort, he explained the concept of an evolving vision this way: "I held up a great big meat bone in front of the group and told them that while our strategic direction and performance imperative was clear, we would put more meat on the program's bones over time. The details came after we were already sharing with everybody how the business was going to be organized."[4]

Given that a vision for change is usually raggedy as you move through the process of discovery, or what some people call "ideation," you have no choice but to rely on urgency and credibility as energy sources. Vision will certainly play a critical role, but it needs time to come into focus.

It's also true that of the seven primary sources of energy, credibility is the one that requires the most advanced preparation. It is without question the most potent and enduring energy source. Along with agility, credibility is the only other energy source that can be stored and used at a future date. Credible leaders must build up reserves of credibility over time and then draw on that inventory in times of change. They can use the credibility they've garnered as a residual stock of goodwill to enlist discretionary effort.

Finally, credibility is the most delicate energy source. It can vanish in an instant if a leader behaves in a way that violates trust. Leaders can't anoint themselves with credibility any more than they can decree trust in their organizations.[5] There are no simple formulas to follow or tonics to administer to become a credible leader. You have to earn it. As Marcus Buckingham and Curt Coffman explain, "You are always on stage. Your misplaced time and attention is not a neutral act."[6] In other words, it damages credibility and thus reduces your ability to generate energy. As a leader, you should expect to be placed under the lamp of those you lead as they assess your credibility again and again.

GOING AT RISK

The best way to understand credibility as an energy source is to understand personal risk. Every time you ask people to embrace change, you're asking them to go at risk. So another way to define credibility is the extent to which members of an organization will go at risk to support change.

There's more to it. When it comes to major change, the request to go at risk becomes more personal than

Credibility: The degree to which people will go at risk with you.

institutional. Not only are you asking someone to go at risk, you're specifically asking that person to go at risk with *you*. You're asking others to cast their lot with you and rely on you for a positive outcome. You're asking them to hang their fortunes largely on your abilities as a leader.

To understand why people are willing to go at risk with their leaders, I asked more than three hundred managers, "In your career, think of someone you were willing to go at risk with. Why were you willing to go at risk with that particular person? Be specific." Despite the fact that the managers I interviewed came not only from business but also from higher education, health care, government, and the nonprofit sector, the results fell into the same general four categories. I call these the "four gauges" of credibility.

THE FOUR GAUGES OF CREDIBILITY

The four gauges of credibility represent the primary areas in which people consciously or subconsciously evaluate their leaders before making a decision to go at risk with them. Figure 5.1 illustrates the four gauges: character, competence, commitment, and concern. The most effective change leaders combine strengths in all four areas.

FIGURE 5.1. THE FOUR GAUGES OF CREDIBILITY.

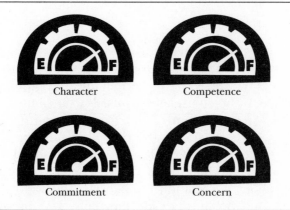

Character

Competence

Commitment

Concern

Two gauges, character and concern, are general characteristics or attributes; the other two, competence and commitment, are traits that must be specifically directed to a proposed change. Maximum leverage comes from the balance, stability, and power of having high levels of all four, and a seriously low reading of one or more gauges will usually limit anyone's effectiveness. In fact, a glaringly low level on one gauge can become a fatal flaw that prevents you from leading change at all. Nevertheless, you can't expect a perfect reading on all four gauges. As a violin teacher once said to her student, "You don't get everything in one violin." So it is with leaders. No one leader possesses every attribute, but there are threshold requirements associated with each gauge that you must achieve to realistically expect others to go at risk with you.

I asked an unusually effective leader how he was able to combine high levels on all four gauges. He responded, "To become strong on all four gauges is the quest of a lifetime. Leadership is very hard work. I've managed to have some success as a leader, but I've also made plenty of mistakes and had my share of failures. Those experiences have been my tutorials. From it all I've learned that to become effective on all four gauges of credibility, you have to focus on each one and commit yourself to making steady progress. It requires a deep and ongoing commitment to personal development. It also requires a lot of courage to continually seek feedback, accept it as a gift, and then do something to make yourself better."

GAUGE 1: CHARACTER

The anchor gauge of character was cited first by six of ten managers whom I interviewed as the basis for making a decision to go at risk with someone. Why does character hold the apex position? Here's what I learned. Character relates primarily to attributes of honesty and fairness. We can certainly argue from a moralistic standpoint that being a leader is simply the right thing to do. But there's more to it. Professor James O'Toole, a noted leadership scholar, writes, "Leaders fail when they have an inappropriate attitude and philosophy about the relationship between themselves and their followers."[7] But why and how do they fail? How does character increase the chance of success? How does its absence increase the chance of failure? Why does high character in a leader provide more energy to a change effort than low character?

The reason is simple. Beyond moral and philosophical arguments, leaders of low character create more risk of pain or loss for those who are being led. Low-character leaders routinely place their own interests above other people and principle. Those who are led by them understand this. If trust is erringly granted, leaders run the constant risk of neglect, betrayal, and loss in many forms.[8]

Leaders without character, as defined by honesty and fairness, quickly break the trust equation. As a result, people recoil and withdraw their discretionary efforts. Because a leader's behavior poses a constant risk to followers, leaders are subject to constant scrutiny. Instinctively, people listen: Does the leader make professions of honesty and fairness? Then they observe, scanning for intent and concentricity: Does the leader's behavioral patterns show evidence of honesty and fairness? Are words consistent with public pronouncements? Does he or she walk the talk?

If there is credibility, trust is imparted, and the leader can more easily call on the discretionary efforts of people. Some leaders try to justify questionable behavior on grounds of legality. Will people lose trust if leaders do something illegal or felonious? Certainly. But to abide by a legal instead of a moral standard is unwise for any leader. People overwhelmingly judge leaders by a moral standard first. They understand that law grows out of morality and that what's legal is usually weak, riddled, and permissive compared to what's moral. As Mark Hurd, the CEO of Hewlett-Packard, explains, "Whether legal or not, we have a higher standard than legal."[9] People look for both because they understand that what may be legal may not be moral. Leaders who unfairly enrich themselves with company perquisites may be acting perfectly legally, but their actions may be a body blow to their credibility.

Sometimes in an attempt to speed up the production of trust, a leader will change his or her vocabulary yet carry on with the same behavior. Not only does this not work, but it erodes self-awareness if the leader continues the charade. Others play along in public but privately withhold their discretionary efforts. The leader is left to go it alone, deprived of the efforts and the honest counsel of others.

When describing leaders of character, the managers I interviewed responded with comments such as the following:

"He didn't try to take credit for other people's work."

"She maintained her point of view even when it wasn't popular."

"He gave candid feedback."

"The guy doesn't trade favors."

"She's fair, firm, and consistent."

"She has always done what she said she would do."

"She actually left the company because she refused to be beholden to the CEO's personal agenda."

"He was always good for his word."

"She told you the truth even when it wasn't what you wanted to hear."

"He didn't play games or make deals with people."

"She wanted to advance her own career, but she didn't do it at the expense of what was in the best interests of the organization."

"This person would bridle his self-interest for the good of the company."

Every leader has different skills, but character isn't a skill. It's not based on endowments of personality or the charismatic arts. Character isn't costume jewelry that you put on to suit the occasion. It has to do with substance, not style; motive, not message; and intent, not technique. Yet I still see leaders clamoring for the latest leadership fad or fashion, tool or technique instead of giving more serious attention to character building.

Character is about deeply held values that are exceedingly difficult to conceal from the people you work with every day. Sooner or later, character or its absence comes out. You can't help but reveal yourself in what you say and do. Character is not about pedagogical tricks. It's not the manipulation of symbols or atmospherics. Nor is it executive presence, kinesthetic energy, and how you use your body. Leaders with character don't necessarily possess a puckish sense of humor or Churchillian eloquence. That's all secondary. Those things are condiments and relish.

As I deconstruct large-scale organizational change initiatives, I'm usually analyzing bet-the-company decisions in which senior leaders put all of their reputational assets on the line. These high-stakes situations tend to disclose character or its absence more quickly than when leaders are performing operational work. You can see when people respond to a call to action and when they don't. Major change helps the scales fall from our eyes as we strive to understand leadership better. When an organization is in the middle of a steep crawl to effect change, when taut nerves are starting to fray, when morale is cratering, and when results have not yet arrived, these are the golden moments to observe. When these circumstances combine, change leadership is most clearly revealed.

The central question is always, "What keeps people going?" One unassailable answer is character. If you don't have it at that moment, it's too late. It can't be manufactured. There are no short cuts to possess it, and nothing can compensate for its absence. It flows from a person's fundamental ethos. Columnist Peggy Noonan cautions, "You can hire pragmatic, and you can buy courage and decency, but you can't rent a strong moral sense."[10] Leaders who have little compunction to say or do things that compromise character don't comprehend the leverage they throw away at that moment. Leaders should nudge, cajole, harangue, and challenge. But when they breach character, they trade away the stock-in-trade of change leadership.

Finally, don't confuse character with loyalty. When people consistently advantage each other, it may have the appearance of character, but even criminals are good at trading favors. Witness the scandalous meltdown of Enron, WorldCom, and Tyco as a result of secret, or off-balance-sheet, activities. To temporarily suspend one's code of conduct is to suspend one's change leadership ability. In financial terms, we can say that people grant trust against the collateral of character. In manufacturing terms, we can say that without character, leaders can't build hedge inventories of trust for times of change.

GAUGE 2: COMPETENCE

The second gauge of credibility is competence, which relates to skill and experience. In a traditional sense, competence means that a person is qualified to do his or her job. In the case of change, it goes a step further. It means that others believe that this person's capability is both relevant and sufficient to reduce the risk of failure in navigating change and making the difficult decisions that have to be made along the way. People want to go at risk with leaders who know what they're doing technically, organizationally, and strategically based on the requirements of change. The risk management principle of competence is based on the idea that past performance is a good predictor of future performance and that a leader's ability to make certain types of good decisions in the past will translate into good decisions during the change process.

For example, if your organization is installing a new enterprise system and you've already directed three successful implementations, you'll score high on competence. If your company has just acquired another organization and you have personal experience with merger integration, people will feel confident that you have enough knowledge and experience to make the right decision in a given situation. To trust you is in part to place faith in your competence. But if you're a brilliant software engineer and you've just been asked to lead the newly restructured sales function, your competence will be held in question.

GAUGE 3: COMMITMENT

If competence is about skill and experience, commitment is about desire, decision, and enthusiasm. But commitment in this case must be narrowly focused on the specific change being considered. When you ask people to go at risk with you to embrace change, the fact that you might have a deep, emotional commitment to the organization or a strong personal commitment and drive to succeed are helpful but too broad and abstract. Your colleagues want to know if you are committed to accomplishing the specific change at hand.

Change forces a personal decision. Unless you can bring an end to your own vacillation and replace it with resolution, unless you can terminate doubt and controversy, unless you can cross over from resistance and neutrality as they relate to change, your attempts to secure the commitment and discretionary efforts of others will be feeble. Any chance that you have of succeeding must be preceded by a clear, personal decision to undertake change. When you make that decision, your personal commitment becomes a source of energy. It gives others the assurance that they aren't alone, that you will join their efforts with yours, and that you're excited at the prospect and rewards of change. The eighteenth-century evangelist and founder of Methodism, John Wesley, said, "I set myself on fire and people come to see me burn." With a personal commitment to change, you're in a position to light other fires. Change work is passion work. People want to look in your eyes and see your steely resolve. It releases energy and emboldens them to venture into the unknown.

With nearly every change, people respond to the invitation to pursue it according to the normal bell-shaped adoption curve first advanced by Everett Rogers, a celebrated communications professor and researcher. At the far left of the curve are the early adopters who embrace change right away. At the far right are the laggards and grim-faced mourners of the status quo who either resist it all the way or eventually get on board after a long personal struggle. In the middle are the majority, who decide to support change at different times during the implementation stage.

But you don't have the luxury to wait and see. Because of your role as leader, you're under obligation to wrestle early with any proposal for change, reconcile your concerns, get your questions answered, and declare your position. I'm not implying that you should exercise blind faith. Far from it. You need to make a studied effort to understand change and its implications. But you have to decide. Otherwise your ability to provide energy to the effort will be lost in your postponement. Sometimes procrastination is a good business principle, but this isn't one of those times. You have a personal responsibility to contribute, and this requires the voluntary act of committing to change.

This is especially important when you don't have the opportunity to participate in formulating change in the first place, which is the case for most people most of the time. During an average career, the majority of change initiatives that a leader

will be asked to lead will be ones that
he or she doesn't personally have a
hand in designing or deciding. They
will be change initiatives that are
inherited from higher levels of the
organization but that the leader is

Leaders inherit most of the change they are asked to lead from higher levels in the organization.

responsible to implement. This can be tricky given the mixture of incentives and risks that normally accompany change. The important point is that a personal commitment to the change at hand is important to increase credibility and release the discretionary efforts of people.

GAUGE 4: CONCERN

Demonstrating personal concern is not a concept that is frequently mentioned in the literature of change, yet it emerged as vitally important in my interviews and analysis. When managers perform small acts of personal concern that benefit or advantage others but at the same time conspicuously fail to advance themselves, they release enormous energy into a change effort. Acts that demonstrate personal concern for another can cement trust and boost the credibility to lead in an unmistakable way.

On one occasion, the CEO of a large software organization gave his executive parking pass to an administrative assistant whom he didn't know. The woman had undergone knee surgery and had to use crutches for several weeks. His gesture was communicated quietly and reverently throughout the campus. That small act of concern was electrifying. People were clearly moved by it at a deep emotional level. Speaking of the CEO, one employee commented, "I'll go to the wall for him." That one move set off a dramatic chain reaction that prompted other employees to perform similar acts of concern for their fellow employees. In this case, a small act of concern greatly enlarged the CEO's credibility. Why did this happen?

Apart from being loyal to the organization, people want to know that you care about them personally. They want to know that as an individual, you matter in the grand scheme of things. Acts of concern reveal this. They provide evidence that you won't arbitrarily disregard or disadvantage them during times of change. By contrast, I have observed instances where others have the sense that a leader is living large while employees are bearing the heaviest burdens of change. When this happens, there is no sense of shared sacrifice, so credibility is injured.

I also note that it's more difficult for leaders of unbridled ambition and narcissistic temperament to show genuine and consistent concern for their colleagues simply because it's not a core value for them. When there's intense pressure to lead major organizational change, this can become a serious liability.

Acts of concern: deliberate acts that subordinate personal interest for the greater good and create enormous amounts of energy to call forth discretionary effort.

Finally, many leaders have long been taught that those who occupy a leadership position should maintain professional distance from their colleagues. This principle seems more suitable for and rooted in the stable environment of the past in which leaders didn't have to earn their living by asking employees to trade security for the risks of the unknown and then try to lead them safely there. In the global age, it's critical to use direct and personal interaction as a way to foster thick trust through both private and public acts of concern.

THE FOUR REALITIES

The sin of many well-intentioned leaders is to create unrealistic expectations when confronting change. In an effort to be empathetic, they can easily slip into a pattern of overpromising in an attempt to remove anxiety and assuage fear. It doesn't work. Don't promise success and the absence of emotional bloodshed; you can rarely promise anything. Under conditions of extreme stress and uncertain outcomes, you should rely on a simple declaration to do all you can. You should be confident and show it, but you can't guarantee what you can't control. People know this without being told. Anytime a leader asks people to go at risk in the pursuit of change, there are four realities that people intuitively understand about that request:

Reality 1: You don't have all of the facts.
Reality 2: You can't remove all risk.

Reality 3: You can't promise zero loss.

Reality 4: You can't eliminate the pain.

People don't have to formally analyze anything; they know instinctively that leaving the status quo moves them into a state of transition. They know that many factors are at

Avoid the temptation to overpromise in an attempt to reduce uncertainty.

work and that no leader can control the outcome. All you have to offer to replace the uncertainty is your credibility. Nevertheless, there is a temptation to project certainty and overpromise.

REPLACING THE SECURITY OF THE STATUS QUO

Think about your own career. Think of someone you were willing to go at risk with. Why did you do it? What was it about that person that made you willing to leave the status quo with him or her? This is the question others will ask you as leader. Think about the question in an intimately personal way because your people will ask it with you in mind. The answer to this question is largely the way credibility is measured. In other words, the extent to which others are willing to go at risk with you represents your credibility score.

Keep in mind too that the bigger and more complex the organization and the more people you are trying to lead, the more your credibility becomes reputational and the more you have to cultivate trust at a distance. You have to ask people who don't know you and may never work with you directly to go at risk with you. Particularly with a distributed workforce or a virtual organization, people have to calculate their decision to go at risk from very little information, most of which comes indirectly.

The true essence of leadership comes to the surface when we ask people to go at risk. They usually don't do it because of the title we hold, the position we occupy, or the formal authority we possess. When people make the decision, they usually strip those things out of their calculations and focus on what is a better indication: your personal credibility. Think about it from the other person's perspective. What else is there? What else can you offer? Your credibility is it. It becomes proxy for what people are giving up. Thus, among the seven primary energy sources, credibility has another unique role: it acts as a replacement for the comforts, security, and attachments of the status quo. It can reduce fear in spite of uncertainty. Urgency doesn't necessarily reduce fear, and vision comes later, so a lot rests on credibility. During change, people think about the fear of loss before the prospect of gain.

In times of change, the leader becomes the repository of people's fears.

Given a choice, most employees don't trade away security, but this is exactly what you're asking them to do every time you undertake change. Once you move an organization into transition, security shrinks. Credibility can reduce the resistance, but it can't fully remove the potential for loss. Trust doesn't restore normalcy. Nothing can overcome the fact that people can become arbitrarily disadvantaged as a result of major change. Even the best leaders can't guarantee that once change is set in motion, everyone will share equally in the rewards. But credibility can lessen the problem.

If you're credible, people will have some measure of confidence that the range of negative and arbitrary things that could happen to them when it's all over will be less than otherwise. This simple perception makes employees more willing to go at risk. They replace their security with faith in leadership. The leader becomes the focal point of stability during a period of destabilization. In times of great commotion, a general affection for the organization in the abstract is far less comforting. People want to trust you, and they will if they've earned good returns on trusting you in the past.

In times of change, credibility does not restore normalcy or the potential for loss, but it can reduce uncertainty and the threat of arbitrary disadvantage.

Figure 5.2 illustrates that going at risk means asking people to transfer their attachments from the status quo to you. They can't transfer their attachments to anything else because the future state doesn't yet exist. You're going into a state of transition.

FIGURE 5.2. TRANSFER OF ATTACHMENTS.

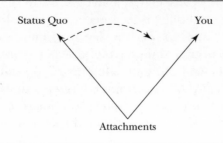

You're asking for their trust, so you can see why they need to ask you for credibility in return.

When you ask people to go at risk, you're asking them to leave the normal state and give up or release their attachments to it.[11] Every member of an organization is attached or tied to their organization in the following ways:

- Emotional
- Social
- Political
- Technical
- Financial
- Professional
- Physical

To commit to change means that people willingly offer to transfer their attachments from the status quo to something else. At least in the near term, that something else is you—and the general goodwill of the organization in a more general sense. The rest is uncertainty. And even when people don't voluntarily want to support change, that change will most likely estrange them from the status quo anyway. Somewhere during the change process, whether people have willingly supported change or not, they will be looking to leadership for security and a place to connect—temporarily at least—their attachments.

Assessing and Building Your Own Credibility

Credibility is best revealed under pressure. When it's being tested, you find out if it's really there. If it's not under attack and called into play, it might be dormant, or it might not be there at all. What counts is the way you are known and perceived. It doesn't matter what you think about yourself. What matters is how others see you. They are the judges who decide if you have credibility and how much you have. In the case of change, people will make conservative estimates of your credibility because they are trying to manage risk and avoid personal loss.

You should personally assess your own credibility. The best way to do this is to think about it through the eyes of those you lead. In the assessment in Exhibit 5.1, there are four questions—one for each of the four gauges of credibility. Notice the way they are written. Each begins, "I am known..." The questions are worded this way because the perceptions of others count rather than your own. In this exhibit, I have operationalized credibility by breaking it down into four measurable components using a five-point Likert scale. Read each of the four questions, and then rate yourself according to the four gauges of credibility on a scale of 1 to 5 by circling the correct number: 1 means "strongly disagree," 2 means "disagree," 3 means "neutral" (neither agree nor disagree), 4 means "agree," and 5 means "strongly agree."

As a general rule, if you gave yourself a score of 3 or lower on any one of the four gauges, you have some work to do. A score of 3 isn't poor; it's just neutral. It means that for whatever reason, you haven't shown yourself to be on the positive side of that attribute. So the good part is that it may not be a liability for you. The bad news is that it's probably not an asset either. Your minimum goal, and the basic requirement for effective change leadership, is to increase the levels of all four gauges until they are positive attributes. There should be at least some visible evidence that you possess them.

One last question is vital to the entire analysis: When do you have enough credibility? The answer must be relative and not absolute. Within the context of the EPIC methodology, the goal is to move forward along the power curve. To do this, you have

EXHIBIT 5.1.   CREDIBILITY SELF-ASSESSMENT.

	Strongly Disagree	Disagree	Neutral	Agree	Strongly Agree
Character gauge: I am known as a person of high character and can use this asset to influence others to support change.	1	2	3	4	5
Competence gauge: I am known for my professional or technical expertise and can use this asset to influence others to support change.	1	2	3	4	5
Commitment gauge: I am known for my commitment to this particular change initiative, and I can use this asset to influence others to support change.	1	2	3	4	5
Concern gauge: I am known for my ability to show concern and therefore motivate others, and I can use this asset to influence others to support change.	1	2	3	4	5

to replenish each energy source in sequence in order to continue to fuel the discretionary efforts of the people involved in the change process. If you view the process in stages and according to energy sources, it's clear that your immediate goal is to move successfully through preparation. The next energy source in the preparation stage is a coalition, so the logic of the methodology is that the required amount of credibility is the amount required to assemble a coalition. You need enough credibility to be able to influence and persuade key opinion leaders to support change. If you can assemble a strong and influential coalition, you have enough credibility. The coalition will then take on the role of providing energy for the next stretch of the journey. If you don't have enough credibility to build a coalition, you shouldn't proceed to the next step because the change process will falter and you will not make it very far into implementation before the effort is overcome with inertia and resistance. To help increase your credibility, do the following exercises:

- Based on the self-assessment you just completed, identify your strongest and weakest gauges of credibility.
- Evaluate and list specific ways that you can increase your weakest gauges.
- Based on the specific needs of the change initiative, determine if you have enough credibility to build a coalition. Explain.
- If there are gaps in your ability to provide enough credibility to assemble a coalition, determine how you will fill those gaps and supplement your need.

If you can build a sufficiently strong coalition, you're ready to move to the next step. If you can't, you've got to find a way to increase your own credibility first or borrow from the credibility of others.

SPONSORSHIP

There are times when you may not personally possess enough credibility to assemble a coalition and yet there isn't time to increase it. Your only other option is to borrow credibility from somewhere else. In other words, when you need shade, look for a big tree. That tree could be a person, a group, an idea, or an organization. I call this concept *sponsorship*. To sponsor is to promote, support, or endorse the ideas or actions of another. To gain a sponsor is to borrow the persuasive and reputational assets, such as name, brand, prestige, popularity, power, and influence, of another source and attach it to the change effort.

Here's an example of the simplest form of nominal sponsorship. You call your coworker and say, "I need the report by the end of the day." Your colleague responds, "Well, unfortunately, I'm not going to be able to get it done by the end of the day." Then you say, "The boss says he absolutely needs it by the close of business." Your colleague says, "I think I can find a way to get it by the end of the day."

There are several forms of sponsorship. These are the five most common:

- *Nominal sponsorship:* Borrowing another person's credibility through his or her name
- *Institutional sponsorship:* Borrowing the credibility of another organization
- *Concept sponsorship:* Borrowing the credibility of a concept or idea
- *Brand sponsorship:* Borrowing the credibility of a brand
- *Data sponsorship:* Borrowing the credibility of third-party data

In my review of large-scale change initiatives, nearly all of them use forms of sponsorship in one way or another as a way to supplement credibility:[12]

- One young hospital administrator recruited the more tenured and respected chief financial officer to provide critical support for his initiative to redesign the pharmacy supply chain in the face of strong opposition from several leaders.
- A bankruptcy judge wouldn't approve a company's plan for reorganization under Chapter 11. Finally the company CEO, on his own initiative, called in a well-known bankruptcy adviser who had served as a court-appointed trustee to several other bankruptcy cases. When the expert put his independent stamp of approval on the plans, the judge changed his decision.
- A board of directors at a large shipping company was about to reject an expensive plan to redesign the organization's logistical software system until the vice president of operations

mentioned that the system would be based on the concept of lean manufacturing and the Toyota production system.

The goal is to continue in the preparation stage and make the transition to the next energy source, a coalition. As you move through the change process, constantly assess your ability to provide enough credibility to the effort, through both your own credibility and sponsorship. You should periodically check to see if the credibility you can produce is equal to the magnitude of the change. If for some reason you're attempting to lead more change than you can reasonably handle from a credibility standpoint, rethink your plans. A noted change expert has said, "Don't engage in any more change than you can properly sponsor."[13] Otherwise you may end up inducing stress and disruption that can't be adequately managed or directed to a positive outcome. You'll likely veer off the power curve into a failure pattern.

Title, Position, and Authority

One of the most important principles about leading change is that title, position, and formal authority often don't count for much because organizational change is dependent on a willing offering of discretionary effort. I learned this lesson in a profound and painful way several years ago when I was promoted to the position of plant manager over a manufacturing facility. Under my charge were twenty-three hundred hourly workers and four hundred managers. Soon after my promotion, our company entered into contract negotiations with the union representing the hourly workforce. The negotiations for a new collective bargaining agreement began to stall and eventually reached impasse. At that point, the president of the local union issued a call to his membership to "work safe," which in union-speak meant to slow things down. He wasn't calling for a work stoppage, just enough of a reduction in throughput to exert some indirect negotiating leverage at the bargaining table. Ultimately productivity trailed off to 50 percent of normal for six weeks. Despite my title, position, and formal authority, I had less power at that particular time than the local union president did. His ability to motivate and direct the discretionary efforts of the workforce was much greater than mine.

Summary

Key Points

- Credibility is the most potent and enduring of the seven energy sources in its ability to elicit a willing offering of discretionary effort from others. It's also the only energy source that originates from within the leader.
- Credibility is the second of the seven energy sources in the EPIC methodology and the first of four energy sources that must be activated during the preparation stage. It can be defined as the quality of deserving to be trusted or the extent to which people will go at risk with a leader.
- The four gauges of credibility are character, competence, concern, and commitment. A leader achieves maximum leverage to lead change through the balance, stability, and power of all four. A weakness in one or more gauges will seriously limit a leader's capacity to lead change.
- A leader with character behaves according to principles of honesty and fairness and subordinates his or her own personal interests when they conflict with these principles.
- A leader with competence is one who possesses skill and experience that are relevant and sufficient to reduce the risk of failure in leading a particular change initiative.
- A leader with commitment is one who has made a clear personal decision to support change and demonstrates a sustained willingness to contribute his or her personal efforts to accomplish the change.
- A leader with concern is one who demonstrates a genuine interest in others through acts of personal concern that are not calculated to advance his or her own interests.
- In times of change, people understand instinctively that a leader doesn't have all of the facts, can't remove all risk, can't promise zero

loss, and can't eliminate the pain. Therefore, leaders should avoid the temptation to guarantee success or overpromise a positive outcome.

- Because change severs people from their personal attachments to an organization, credibility becomes a proxy, or replacement, for the comforts and security of the status quo. Attachments are defined as the social, emotional, political, cultural, financial, physical, and professional ties that connect an individual to an organization and create a particular human experience for that individual.
- Credibility doesn't restore normalcy or the potential for loss, but it can reduce uncertainty and the threat of arbitrary disadvantage.
- Sponsorship is the process of borrowing credibility from the reputational assets of outside sources. Acquiring sponsors is vital when a leader doesn't personally possess enough credibility.
- A leader has enough credibility when he or she is able to assemble the needed coalition to move change forward to the point of implementation.

CHAPTER SIX

PREPARE WITH A COALITION

An organization is a coalition of coalitions.
ROBERT E. QUINN, *Deep Change* (1996)

PREPARE WITH A COALITION

EPIC	1	2	3	4
Stage	**Evaluate**	**Prepare**	**Implement**	**Consolidate**
The Leader's Role	**Equilibrium step** Supply energy for the ongoing evaluation of competitive reality, internal performance, and change alternatives.	**Ignition step** Replenish energy to supply a gradual increase in work performed and stress absorbed during preparation.	**Refueling step** Replenish energy to supply a significant increase in work performed and stress absorbed during implementation.	**Refueling step** Replenish energy to supply a gradual decrease in work performed and stress absorbed during consolidation.
Energy Sources	**1. Agility**	1. Agility **2. Urgency** **3. Credibility** **4. Coalition** **5. Vision**	1. Agility 2. Urgency 3. Credibility 4. Coalition 5. Vision **6. Early Results**	1. Agility 2. Urgency 3. Credibility 4. Coalition 5. Vision 6. Early Results **7. Sustained Results**

Identifying a need for change and crafting a solution certainly can come from the executive suite, the shop floor, or somewhere in between. But implementing change is a different story. You can't hide change and try to implement it as a covert action. As Alan Mulally, the CEO of Ford, puts it, "You can't manage a secret."[1] Although change may begin in some small corner of the organization, it must become known, understood, and supported by those affected by it, or it can't become a reality. In almost every case, change must be handed off for implementation. Unless there is broad-based action by many people, change won't take place.

Change usually affects far more people than those who identify it as a need. For example, when Carlos Ghosn arrived in Tokyo in 1999 to turn around Nissan Motors, he commissioned nine teams of ten members each and a few subteams to study the company's problems and recommend a change agenda. At the time, Nissan had lost money in six of the previous seven years and was saddled with $22 billion in debt. The teams studied everything from product planning to power trains to purchasing. After three months, they reported their findings and recommendations, all rolled together in what became known as the "Nissan Revival Plan."[2] But creating that plan was still only preparation. Nissan would then have to engage its 140,000 employees around the world to begin the implementation stage because the change was a huge enterprise and required the participation of every single employee in some way.

How do you go from a couple of hundred people who are involved with change in the preparation stage to thousands of people in the implementation stage? How do you scale an influence strategy? Do you just give the directive and march forward? Sometimes you have no choice, particularly if you're in a state of crisis. But it substantially increases the risk of failure. Ideally the most effective approach is to enlist the help of a coalition in order to build support for change and scale it across the organization. A coalition is a mechanism to diffuse both understanding and commitment. It's the second of the four sources of energy that must be activated during preparation.

In terms of sequence, a coalition necessarily follows credibility, because without credibility in place, there is no means by which to bring a coalition together. The credibility of the first leader, or group of leaders, who supports change becomes the catalyzing force, and based on that credibility, it has the ability to recruit others to the effort.

Even if you are a credible leader, you can't lead change by yourself. Even leaders with astounding capacity and force of will can't pull it off. Nor can you prepare every person who will eventually participate in the implementation.[3] You need a coalition through which you can replenish energy. Without a coalition, success will largely be based on contingency and luck.

A COALITION AS AN ENERGY SOURCE

A coalition is an alliance of people, inside or outside an organization, that supports change. The first and most obvious benefit of a coalition is that it can perform much of the additional work that you give the organization during the preparation stage. But a coalition does more than perform work: it also creates energy to help motivate the rest of the organization. There are four attributes that turn an effective coalition into an indispensable energy source: assets, effort, influence, and intelligence.

ASSETS

An effective coalition possesses several key assets that it uses to perform work, and all are critical in drawing out the discretionary efforts of people. They are in fact the same assets that a credible leader has, albeit extended from a single individual to a group. Certainly people must judge not only the leader of a change effort but also the coalition of individuals who sign up to support it. If people perceive that the collective assets of the coalition are strong and that they represent the capacity to see change through and persuade others to support it, they will be much more likely to join the coalition themselves. An effective coalition normally possesses strong assets in the following categories:

- Authority
- Reputation
- Influence

- Knowledge
- Skills and expertise
- Experience
- Relationships

Effort

If a coalition is a group of individuals who support a proposed change, by definition, this means they are willing to apply their own discretionary efforts rather than withhold the assets they have. There are two ways to do this: formally, or publicly, support change or informally, and sometimes privately, support change. Being willing to use the assets doesn't mean that the coalition will apply its assets unsparingly. There are always limits, conditions, and restrictions. For example, during a major systems implementation, a programmer once called to tell me that he knew exactly who was supporting and opposing the effort and why, based on certain technology issues that I had no idea about, let alone understood. He then told me what we needed to do to win the support of the hard-line resisters by making certain changes in the functionality of the system.

Influence

An effective coalition is able to use its assets to diffuse its influence and win the support of others to support change. Because of the personal yet scalable way a coalition performs its work, no other energy source can rival its impact. The energy that a coalition is able to generate is based on power embedded in its assets. In other words, in the context of complex social situations that no other energy source can handle, a coalition spreads influence like a virus. This viral approach allows it to increase support exponentially within an organization to achieve the maximum possible impact. As W. Chan Kim and Renée Mauborgne state, "In any organization, once the beliefs and energies of a critical mass of people are engaged, conversion to a new idea will spread like an epidemic."[4] Without a coalition, however, it's almost impossible to reach this point.

INTELLIGENCE

An effective coalition is able to gather critical intelligence through-out the course of the change process and feed it back to leadership, allowing leaders to make adjustments and avoid making costly mistakes. The game of football provides a good illustration of this capability.

In critical offensive situations, the team with the ball often breaks the huddle and fans into formation as if to proceed with the next play. Rather than take the snap and execute the play, the quarterback will call a time-out and then jog to the sideline to consult with the coaches. Why? The offense is trying to gather as much intelligence as it can before execution. By taking the field, it forces the opponent to line up and thus reveal its defensive scheme. In a like manner, an effective coalition, through its relationships and collective corporate dialogue, can identify resistance before implementation begins.

The status quo always has defenders. But without a coalition, you're severely handicapped in knowing exactly where those defenders are, who they are, and what they're defending. The risk you run in not assembling an effective coalition is that you will see only visible and active resistance, while the invisible and passive resistance will go undetected. As a leader, you are limited to your own line-of-sight visibility of resistance. Beyond that, you have to rely on others to be your eyes and ears. Based on the way a coalition spreads influence and gathers information in the context of a web of relationships and social interaction, it can gain access to resistance that is both passive and invisible when that resistance is partially or totally hidden from your view. The leader has an impaired view, while the coalition usually has 360-degree vision.

Figure 6.1 illustrates this difference. The leader (bottom left-hand corner) has an unobstructed view of visible and active resistance but a blocked view of the resistance that is invisible and passive because he or she is removed from relationships, interactions, and information outside his or her immediate circle. Members of the coalition (lower right-hand corner), however, are usually aware of the more invisible and passive resistance that surrounds a change initiative because they are involved

FIGURE 6.1. A LEADER'S OBSTRUCTED VIEW.

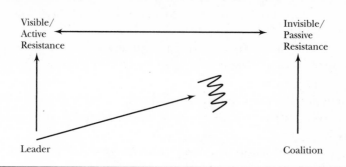

in relationships, participate in interactions, and have access to information throughout the organization.

For example, a consumer products company had decided to outsource its entire IT function. It sent out a request-for-proposal to potential outsourcing partners. Once it selected the right partner, it would move forward with the change plan. In the process of evaluating potential partners, several members of the coalition discovered that an influential vice president was silently opposed to the change and that she was going to try to block the change once the company selected an IT partner. The coalition members recommended that this executive be appointed a member of the official team who was evaluating the vendors. The executive was brought onto the team, and her opposition quickly turned to support once she was given an important role to play. Without the coalition, the company would have encountered costly and disruptive resistance downstream.

BENEFITS OF A COALITION

I have discussed the four attributes of an effective coalition. Now I'll get even more specific about what a coalition can do to replenish energy, avoid obstacles along the way, and increase the chances of a successful outcome. Consider that a coalition can:

- Spot conflicting priorities.
- Surface concerns and assumptions.

- Flesh out the available options for change.
- Scrutinize the implementation plan as it relates to adequate scheduling, resources, role assignments, coordination, and accountability.
- Identify who has the power to kill change.
- Identify potential pitfalls or misguided approaches that might cause change to fail.
- Identify shortages in resources up front.
- Understand who cares about the change, what they care about, and why.
- Help define roles and responsibilities during the change process and after transition.
- Identify the change alternatives that are possible to test or pilot and how to do it.
- Identify and overcome operational obstacles that could jeopardize the change if they are not addressed.
- Help others make the emotional and psychological transition that must accompany change before it takes place.
- Provide vital emotional support to the effort when the change process becomes difficult and people are tempted to quit the change.
- Implement change faster through more efficient coordination and more effective dialogue.
- Commit fewer errors in execution due to better communication.
- Perform less damage control with employees who were surprised by change.
- Perform less remedial training for unanticipated requirements.
- Neutralize those who will resist or threaten the change effort.
- Map the flow of informal influence traffic in your organization to understand who talks to and influences whom.

THE DILEMMA OF PARTICIPATION

A coalition can make a significant contribution during preparation. It can vet a proposed change, debug it, challenge it, improve it, and essentially make it ready for prime time. But an equally important role is to prepare the organizational soil for planting the change. In other words, the coalition is uniquely qualified to prepare the other members of the organization who have not yet been involved in the change process. A coalition is essential to perform this role because organizations often face *the dilemma of participation*.

A well-known principle of successful change is that participation builds commitment. Without participation, people tend to resist what they don't help create because they're not emotionally invested in the process. Theoretically, leaders should involve as many members of the organization in the process of formulating change as possible in order to build commitment as deep and wide in the organization as they can. As researchers Richard Pascale and Jerry Sternin describe it, "The key is to involve the members of the community you want to change in the process of discovery, making them the evangelists of their own conversion experience."[5] Yet employees often find themselves at the far end of the whip. There is no perfect architecture that allows everyone to participate they way they want to.

The bigger and more complex the change is, the less practical it is to have large numbers of people participate in the process of deciding what and how to change. Through the first two EPIC stages of evaluation and preparation, the fewest number of people are involved in the process. From a practical standpoint, most members of the organization don't and can't be expected to participate in these early stages; they are busy doing operational work and running the system. They are excluded as an organizational necessity.[6] Eventually, when the change process moves to the implementation stage, the rest of the employee population will get involved. In most cases, they are the ones who will do the actual implementation. In fact, there's no way to accomplish large-scale change without the rest of the organization making a multitude of decisions during tactical implementation. No organization has the time or money to weigh the opinions of thousands.

It's impossible for everyone in the organization to decide what to change and how to do it. It's also impossible for leadership alone to implement change. This is the dilemma of participation.

Figure 6.2 shows the dilemma of participation. The rectangle represents the total population of an organization over time. A diagonal line running from the lower left corner of the rectangle

FIGURE 6.2. THE DILEMMA OF PARTICIPATION.

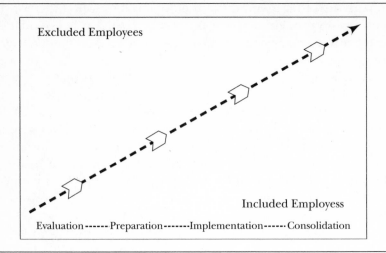

to the upper right corner represents the typical pattern of participation during the change process. The area of the rectangle above the dotted line indicates the proportion of the total employee population excluded from the change process, and the portion below the line represents those who are included. When the change pro-

The dilemma of participation: it's impossible for everyone in the organization to decide what to change and how to do it. It's also impossible for leadership alone to implement change.

cess begins, most members of the organization are excluded from the process, primarily during the stages of evaluation and preparation. As the change process advances, more people become involved. Depending on the scope of change, the process may expand to include a much larger proportion of the organization's employees. More narrow change initiatives may not enlist the participation of more people as they move into implementation and consolidation, but enterprise-wide efforts can expand to include every member of an organization as they progress through all four EPIC stages.

A coalition can help overcome the dilemma of participation by creating needed support for change based on factors other than participation. As in the example of Carlos Ghosn and Nissan, in most large-scale change initiatives, you won't have the luxury of involving most members of the organization, so you'll have to resort to other means. A coalition can help you work around this inherent limitation.

WHY LEADERS NEGLECT COALITIONS

Despite all of the benefits of coalitions, leaders neglect them. In fact, Harvard Business School professor and noted change expert Rosabeth Moss Kanter argues that "coalition-building is probably the most ignored step in the change process, yet a change without a coalition usually turns into an unfunded mandate."[7] Why does this happen?

The answer is that there are natural incentives to avoid building a coalition. Every manager I interviewed confessed to having done this at least once. Many had made a habit of proceeding with change without so much as a backward glance to see if anyone was with them. Are any of the following reasons familiar to you?

- *A bias for action.* "We've been taught to execute and are socialized with this mind-set. The idea that we need to slow down to build a coalition seems a terrible waste of time. If success is about speed and first-mover advantage, how can I possibly wait for you to get on board? People have a choice: get on board or get out of the way."
- *My thoughts are your thoughts.* "You've got the information I've got, so it's obvious what we need to do. The change imperative is self-evident. Once I arrived at the conclusion to move ahead, so did you. So let's go."
- *Pressure to perform.* "We're in trouble. Our competitive position is under siege. Let's just march, and I'll explain it later."
- *You wouldn't understand.* "I'm too tired and too busy, and if I tell you exactly what we're doing and why, you'll just resist it more. It's better to keep you at least partially in the dark. Just trust me, and things will work out on the other side."
- *It's really my job.* "According to our roles and responsibilities and the division of labor, I'm the leader here. It's my job to be the visionary and chart the course. It's your job to implement

the plan. I'm the strategic guy; you're the tactical guy. If I do my
job and you do yours, it will work.''

- *I'm consumed with the technical requirements.* ''It's my top priority.
  It's all I think about. I'm so focused on getting the details right
  that I forgot about the human dimensions of change. I've been
  pouring over the specs, the budget, the schedule, and the
  technology, and I just forgot about the impact it would have on
  people.''

- *It's about me.* ''This change initiative is my baby, and I'm not
  going to let anyone get in the way. Plus, I don't buy the concept
  of moving fast to move slow. That's just the oversold rhetoric of
  soft-side consultants. The best thing to do is march forward and
  let people work it out. There are casualties in any large change
  endeavor anyway.''

- *I'm a dynamic leader.* ''People want to follow me even if they
  don't fully understand where we're going and what's going to
  change.''

HANDLING INHERITED CHANGE

There's another scenario to discuss. In Chapter Five, I noted the
importance of personal commitment to change as one of the four
gauges of credibility. And I also noted that there are two kinds of
change: those that you help formulate yourself and those that you
inherit.

When it comes to building a coalition, an inherited change presents
a unique challenge. It should come
as no surprise that the first member of your coalition must be you.
But if the change is inherited, it
introduces an additional step into
the coalition-building process. Never
assume that you automatically support change and have an immediate commitment to help make it happen. In some cases, you will
support it right away. In other cases, you'll have serious reserva-
tions. In still other cases, you might be opposed to it. What should
you do?

> *Inherited change: change that
> you did not design, develop, or
> decide on but that you are in
> some way responsible to
> implement.*

I've already mentioned the danger of trying to implement change without a coalition. That will almost guarantee failure. Another poor option is to go out and immediately start building a coalition. That won't work because every coalition has to begin with one member. If you aren't personally committed to the change, you still don't have your first member. Obviously you won't be effective in recruiting others to the coalition if you oppose the change effort or harbor serious misgivings about moving forward. Your efforts will seem disingenuous. Others will see that you're playing the part and giving the party line, and it will work against you. Those you lead will expect you to take issue with things that you question. If you don't, your failure of nerve will count as a breach of your own character.

As a leader, you get paid to think, add value to ideas and potential courses of action, challenge and contest points of view, and create better solutions. By virtue of your role, others need and expect you to do this to increase the chance of a successful outcome. But there's another reason: you're also the delegate and custodian of your people. It's your job to represent them, advocate for them, and stand as a buffer between them and senior leadership. People expect it even more during times of change. When the stakes are higher and the tension is thicker, people would rather have their leaders be in front and represent their views rather than doing it themselves.. This is especially true if the culture of the organization is not tolerant of dissent, open debate, and direct challenges to the status quo. A lot of organizations like to claim that they invite candor, but these professed norms of participation seem to disappear when an organization is under intense pressure.

TAKING PERSONAL OWNERSHIP

If you've inherited the change imperative, your first responsibility is to recruit yourself. You must take personal ownership for the change and become the first member of your own coalition. Don't rush out to start implementing change because you're loyal, a high performer, or a good soldier. In the long run, it won't benefit you or the organization. But once you're on board, that commitment will provide the following benefits:

- You'll have more credibility as a leader because you've gone through the process of building personal commitment. You've increased your ability to solicit the discretionary efforts of others.
- The change initiative will have a higher chance of success because you have tested and challenged the proposed change based on your own concerns, questions, and objections.

It's not easy to reconcile yourself with a proposed change that you question. It's even more difficult to align yourself with one that you oppose. But you've got to confront the issues and work through the process because the moment of truth will come when you try to implement the change. In the privacy of personal conversations, your colleagues will ask you, "What do you think about this change?" To a large extent, success or failure will depend on your answer to that question.

To take personal ownership for an inherited change, anticipate that you will often pass through four emotional stages before you can embrace change:

1. Resistance or rejection
2. Denial
3. Acceptance
4. Commitment

To help move through the process of taking personal ownership for inherited change, think about the following questions:

- Did you help design or develop the change initiative, or did you inherit the change initiative from higher levels of the organization?
- What is the level of personal ownership you currently feel for the change on a scale from 1 to 10, with 1 being the lowest and 10 being the highest?
- How do you explain your rating?
- What concerns do you have about the change? As you assess your concerns, review the what, where, when, who, and how aspects of the change. How will you resolve your concerns?

- Who are the right people to discuss your questions and concerns with?
- How can you test assumptions or aspects of the change that might concern you?
- Do you clearly understand your personal role in implementing the change? If not, how can you resolve any questions about it?

Passing through the emotional stages isn't automatic. People get stuck and stay stuck if they don't do something to move themselves along. Here are suggestions:

- Assume positive intent on the part of others.
- Ask questions so you thoroughly understand the case for change.
- Express your concerns.
- Challenge assumptions.
- Focus on the "how." The organization is most likely relying on you to figure out how change should be implemented. Often it's the discovery of the "how" that finally persuades you that it can be done and that it's the right thing to do.
- Offer alternative approaches if appropriate.
- Sleep on it.

Ultimately you must make a clear and conscious decision to support change. Recognize that it's your job to help your colleagues pass through these stages as well.

How to Build a Coalition

The best way to build a coalition is to use a formal process and systematic approach using some kind of tool. The tool must be detailed enough to be meaningful yet simple enough that you will actually use it. The tool that I've included here has been developed through field-testing with several change initiatives. It aims to strike the proper balance between simplicity and complexity and tempt you to actually use it.

Following is a case study and then an explanation of how to build a coalition using a tool called the coalition grid. Read the case and then walk through the process using the tool.

Exhibit 6.1. Coalition Grid.

1. Stakeholder	2. Interests	3. Potential Impact	4. Potential Support	5. Assets	6. Role	7. Strategy
Chief nursing officer (CNO).	Having a full and motivated nursing staff.	New scheduling plan could positively or negatively affect nurse attrition.	CNO does not currently support the plan.	CNO has formal position and authority over all nurses. She is also a knowledgeable, respected leader.	CNO must play the central role in leading any kind of change. The initiative won't succeed without her support.	Recruit. We must address CNO's concerns until we have an alternative she can support.

Coalition Case Study

You are the vice president of human resources for a large and successful hospital. After many years of growth, however, your hospital is experiencing a nursing shortage. Compounding the problem is that nurses are leaving the hospital in greater numbers than before. The attrition rate among nurses, for example, increased from an average of 8 to 20 percent last year. Consequently, there are eighty nurse vacancies, which is causing the hospital to staff its nursing shortage with more expensive contracted and per diem nurses.

Together with the CEO and CNO (chief nursing officer), you have studied the issue carefully. All three of you have reached the same conclusion: a big part of the problem is the scheduling plan that covers the thirteen hundred nurses. The current plan richly rewards the more experienced nurses who have been with the hospital five or more years and who work in the critical care units. The schedule, however, is less and less attractive to newer nurses who are scheduled for weekends and holidays. Many of the young and talented nurses are leaving because they can find more accommodating schedules elsewhere.

In spite of acknowledging the flaws in the current scheduling, the CNO is strongly opposed to a new plan. She thinks she'll lose her most experienced and most successful nurses and set the hospital back even further. The CEO wants a new scheduling plan to attract more nurses and retain the current force. He's asked you to design and implement it. As you finished your last discussion with the CEO, his parting words were: "Make sure you come up with something that everyone can support."

Now review the coalition grid in Exhibit 6.1. Filling out the grid is a matter of identifying all possible stakeholders who may be connected to the change in some way and then answering the questions listed below for each one. Answer the questions for each stakeholder and fill in your responses row by row on the grid. The chief nursing officer is listed on the first row to show you an example of how to complete the grid.

Coalition Grid Questions

1. *Stakeholder:* Identify the stakeholder. A stakeholder is any individual or group with an interest in the outcome of a proposed change.
2. *Interests:* What does the stakeholder care about? Why?
3. *Potential impact:* How will the change likely affect the stakeholder?
4. *Potential support:* What is the likelihood that the stakeholder will support the change?
5. *Assets:* What assets does the stakeholder have? Identify any tangible or intangible resource or quality that a stakeholder possesses that could be used to support or help implement change, such as authority, influence, experience, knowledge, expertise, reputation, technical resources, or money.
6. *Role:* What role, formal or informal, could the stakeholder play in a coalition?
7. *Strategy:* What is your strategy for the stakeholder? There are three main options:

   - Recruit to the coalition.
   - Address concerns or resistance but do not recruit to coalition.
   - No action required.

By identifying all stakeholders and answering the questions for each of them, you will be able to systematically identify which stakeholders should be members of the coalition and why. The exercise will also help you think through your response to stakeholders whom you determine should not be members of the coalition. In the end, the goal is to identify and address all stakeholders in a systematic way. The completed coalition grid is never perfect, but it can be enormously helpful. Not using a tool or systematic process usually results in a poor and incomplete analysis.

BENEFITS OF A SYSTEMATIC PROCESS

There are several benefits to completing a coalition grid and several risks for not doing so:

- It will reveal surprising gaps that you don't otherwise see.
- The bigger and more complex a change is, the more detailed and comprehensive you should be in completing a coalition grid.
- If you're dealing with a relatively simple change, perhaps with two or three stakeholders, you may be tempted to just think through the coalition informally. But there is still a risk that you will miss something. It's always better to force yourself to go through the discipline of completing a coalition grid.
- The coalition grid can help you track progress during the coalition-building process.
- If you don't keep a coalition grid, you may think you are ready to move to the implementation stage before you really have a coalition in place. The coalition grid will help you avoid relying on faulty assumptions about who supports the change.

Let's summarize your progress at this point. You have started the process of building a coalition. In the real world, you then take the completed coalition grid and implement the strategy that you've defined in column 7 for each stakeholder group. It's important to complete the strategy for each stakeholder regardless of whether you have identified the stakeholder as a coalition member.

Depending on the situation, you may want some coalition members to support the change effort formally or informally. Big and complex change projects require that you commission a formal team to guide the implementation and carefully weigh the advantages and disadvantages of formal versus informal participation based on the assets that a coalition member possesses.

Summary

Key Points

- A coalition is a group of people who supports change and is willing to use its assets, formally or informally, to help change succeed.
- A coalition possesses the same assets as an individual leader and represents the extension of credibility from the individual to the group.

- A coalition's assets are authority, reputation, influence, knowledge, skills and expertise, experience, and relationships.
- A coalition is incredibly effective and efficient in spreading influence and gathering information in the context of complex social situations.
- A coalition usually has an unobstructed view of invisible or passive resistance to change that exists in an organization, whereas the leader sees mostly the resistance that is visible and active.
- The dilemma of participation means that although it's important to involve people in the change process to win their support, it's often organizationally impossible to involve everyone in the initial stages of formulating change. This dilemma illustrates the vital role of a coalition because a coalition can win the support of others through influence and relationships when the option for direct participation is not available.
- Leaders neglect coalition building for many reasons, including having a bias for action, assuming that other people think the way they do, believing that people will resist more if they know more, and being preoccupied with the technical side of change.
- Moving to the implementation stage of change without a strong coalition in place usually leads to failure.
- A leader who inherits change from higher levels in the organization must take personal ownership for the change before attempting to build a coalition of support.
- The most effective way to build a coalition is to use a formal process and tool to guide the effort. The bigger and more complex the change is, the more this becomes necessary.

CHAPTER SEVEN

PREPARE WITH VISION

History marches to the drum of a clear idea.
W. H. AUDEN

PREPARE WITH VISION.

EPIC Stage	1 Evaluate	2 Prepare	3 Implement	4 Consolidate
The Leader's Role	**Equilibrium Step** Supply energy for the ongoing evaluation of competitive reality, internal performance, and change alternatives.	**Ignition Step** Replenish energy to supply a gradual increase in work performed and stress absorbed during preparation.	**Refueling Step** Replenish energy to supply a significant increase in work performed and stress absorbed during implementation.	**Refueling Step** Replenish energy to supply a gradual decrease in work performed and stress absorbed during consolidation.
Energy Sources	**1. Agility**	1. Agility **2. Urgency** **3. Credibility** **4. Coalition** **5. Vision**	1. Agility 2. Urgency 3. Credibility 4. Coalition 5. Vision **6. Early Results**	1. Agility 2. Urgency 3. Credibility 4. Coalition 5. Vision 6. Early Results **7. Sustained Results**

Is a vision essential for organizational change? If change requires new levels of performance rather than simply passive compliance, the answer is yes. The leader is commissioned to give others sight, allowing them to behold greater vistas. Through the emotion of that experience comes the energy. What vision provides is a lasting stimulus for people to perform work and absorb stress. If urgency is about selling a need, vision is about selling an ambition. It opens a window through which to view the future. Without some kind of portrait of what that future might look like, it's almost impossible to summon and redirect institutional will and capacity.

To understand vision as an energy source, you need only look at organizations that have a poor one or none at all. What you see are institutions that are either stalled or not progressing well. You see a tangled mess with people going in different directions. A good vision gives an organization both direction and the inspiration to pursue it. The German philosopher Goethe said, "The important thing in life is to have a great aim and possess the aptitude and the perseverance to attain it." But what I find is that the aptitude and perseverance are not independent of the aim. Instead, the very act of having the aim in large measure provides the aptitude and perseverance needed to achieve it. Vision does this because it taps deeply seated emotions. It stirs people, kindles their passion, and propels them forward.

As the final source of energy during the preparation stage of the power curve, a compelling vision can provide enormous energy for change before the effort moves into implementation. As Peter Senge observes, "Truly creative people use the gap between vision and current reality to generate energy for change."[1] Of course, it's not the gap but the unsatisfied aspiration to close the gap that motivates. In fact, in a global survey of communications and human resource practitioners, respondents cited "communicating a clear vision of the future" as the most important action of a senior leader.[2]

VISION AND ITS TWO SIBLINGS

Vision has two siblings: mission on the left and strategy on the right. The three elements tend to blend into each other in most organizational plans and communications. That's fine. There's no reason to be a purist about keeping them separate as long as you answer the questions they raise and can use vision as a critical energy source. In fact, a vision usually needs to include aspects of mission and strategy in order to do its job. Let me briefly review the conceptual distinction among mission, vision, and strategy.

MISSION

Strictly speaking, a mission answers the question, "Why?": "Why are we here, and why do we exist?" For example, Google's mission is "to organize the world's information and make it universally accessible and useful." Northwestern Memorial Hospital's mission is "to improve the health of the communities we serve by delivering a broad range of services with sensitivity to the individual needs of our patients and their families." Disney's mission is "to make people happy." Mary Kay Cosmetics' mission is "to give unlimited opportunity to women." And the United Nations' mission is, in part, "to save succeeding generations from the scourge of war, which twice in our lifetime has brought untold sorrow to mankind."

Some organizations don't have statements that set out the fundamental purpose of the enterprise. It may be unwritten, assumed, or self-evident. For example, I can find no written mission statement for NASCAR. But does it really need one? From the standpoint of leading change with vision, including elements of mission may be powerful in providing the backdrop of larger purpose.

In some organizations, the mission possesses a certain magnetism and deep sense of purpose that literally brings people in the door. For example, Teach for America, a nonprofit organization based in New York City, has motivated seventeen thousand high-performing college graduates to forgo more lucrative options in order to teach disadvantaged children in inner-city schools. The mission, "To enlist our nation's most promising future leaders in the movement to eliminate educational inequality," is a good example of providing powerful impetus that moves people from working for money to dying for a cause. Contained within that mission statement are critical elements of vision and strategy that give a sense of where the organization is going and how it's going to get there: by recruiting the best and brightest college graduates and deploying them in urban centers of most need throughout the country.

VISION

A vision answers the questions, "What?" and "Where?": "What do we want to become or achieve?" and "Where do we want to go?" By painting a picture of the future in broad and bold strokes, a vision defines a new identity and destination that is essential to pump motivation and direction into the veins of an organization's members. Visions aren't necessarily discrete from either missions or strategies, but they tend to provide a narrower definition of what you plan to be and where you plan to go, whereas missions generally don't do that. Missions tend to lose power due to breadth and abstraction. For example, Microsoft's mission is to "to enable people and businesses throughout the world to realize their full potential." How difficult would it be to lead change under this banner? It doesn't tell anyone what or where. It's trite, abstract, and of little use to the change leader.

At a minimum, a good vision has something to say about what and where. When Jack Welch demanded that every division at GE become number one or number two in its market, that constituted an operational vision removed from abstraction and blue-sky aspiration. It defined what and where in terms of market position, performance, and profitability. That dictum is now legendary, precisely because it demonstrated the ability to pull energies out of an organizational system.

Think for a minute about the simplicity and power of the vision to be number one or number two. It's not fancy or bathed in the lather of marketing copy. It's not sparkling with imagery or gleaming with the description of some utopian future state. It's actually a bare-bones directive with no evocative language. So why did it work? Why did this call to action create such an overwhelming response? There are several reasons, but one is that it contained unmistakable intent about answering the questions what and where. It gathered its strength in doing those two things. It became resonant, high, and daring. It caused people to quiver and quake with both fear and excitement. In the annals of organizational vision, this epigrammatic example helps us understand as much as anything else what a vision is as it occupies space between mission and strategy.

STRATEGY

Strategy answers the question, "How?" specifically, "How do we choose to achieve the vision and fulfill the mission?" The purpose of strategy is to maximize the accomplishment of the vision. Referring back to Welch's "number one or number two" vision, it clearly doesn't say anything about how, which is often the case. That had to come later. I've analyzed many visions that did the same thing. It's not necessarily incumbent on the change leader to know the "how" in order to harness the energy of vision.

Each of the three elements answers a different question:

Mission	Why does the organization exist?
Vision	Who or what does the organization seek to become?
Strategy	How will the organization fulfill its mission and achieve its vision?

"THE VISION THING"

If an organization is fighting for survival, it has a vision. Survival is the vision. People can't lift their eyes to higher goals if their organization's very survival is at stake. Self-preservation tends to black out and temporarily suspend all other ambitions. There's a crucial distinction and motivational basis between survival and a vision. It goes back to Abraham Maslow's hierarchy of needs. When lower-level needs are unmet or at risk, those needs consume all of our time and attention. But if an organization isn't fighting for survival, it needs a vision if it wants to progress from where it is.

The requirement of a vision is an organizational necessity on several levels. Don't be fooled by Louis Gerstner's famed statement: "The last thing IBM needs right now is a vision." IBM already had a vision. What it lacked was the ability to execute the vision, which is something entirely different. Clearly it's impossible to execute a vision that doesn't exist.

Why do we tend to deride "the vision thing"? Is it our way of making light of a poor vision? Does it provide a bit of consolation when we can't win hearts and minds? Unfortunately, it gives the impression that vision is a third sock in the organizational gym bag. Be careful not to indict the role of vision just because a particular vision is ineffective. Most visions create little or no energy, but we shouldn't denounce the role vision can play. What we need to do is look closer at what makes a vision moving and powerful.

THE KITE STRINGS OF VISION

In the cases of large-scale change that I studied, I carefully analyzed the role and power of vision. In several instances, the change vision was impoverished and rang hollow because it lacked proper leadership support. In other instances, the vision was transcendent and captivating. What I observed is that visions with power are like kites held up by strings.

I was once flying a kite with my daughter, when she asked me to let go of the strings to let the kite fly higher. I told her that the strings actually hold the kite up, and that if I let go, the kite would fall to the ground. Looking up at the kite and seeing the tension on the strings, she couldn't understand this, so I let go to demonstrate this counterintuitive relationship. The kite plummeted to the earth. So it is with visions. They fly and maintain their altitude when they are attached to strings of credible leadership and sound strategy.

To understand the kite string of credible leadership, consider the sequence of energy sources on the power curve. The credibility of the leader comes first because the leader must infuse a vision with power and bring it to life. Good visions are to a large degree an extension of a leader's personal credibility.

One of the cases I analyzed involved a professional services organization that tried to restructure its IT function. The organization had seven fairly autonomous IT departments that resulted from several acquisitions over the years. At the top was a chief information officer who presided over a consortium of seven IT directors—one director attached to each of the seven consulting practices in the firm. Given the lack of standardization, redundancy in systems, high costs, and overall inefficiency, it became clear to leadership that the organization should centralize the IT departments into a single shared service department. The new model made sense to everyone. It would reduce costs and increase efficiency. The vision was logical, easy to communicate, and strategically superior to the old approach.

The CEO explained the change and announced that the CIO would be charged with leading the initiative. There was no visible backlash to the announcement, but there was a deep undercurrent of skepticism among the seven IT directors who reported to the CIO. It hadn't been widely known because of the decentralized structure of IT, but the CIO was not seen as highly credible among his direct reports. As a result, the directors mounted stiff but hidden resistance. They engaged in subtle sabotage by stretching out deadlines and delaying the schedule for consolidating systems. Eventually the delays created problems that started affecting clients. After an entire year of implementation, the organization reversed course and went back to stovepiped IT departments for each consulting practice. The vision was sound, but there was no kite string of credible leadership to hold it up and give people the assurance that there would be commitment and capacity to implement the vision.

The second kite string of vision is sound strategy. Many leaders don't understand this. To a large extent, a vision is only as good as the strategy. If a vision simply resembles the competition, don't expect people to get very motivated about it. There isn't much luster and vitality in a me-too strategy. In the cases that I observed, the leaders who didn't take vision seriously were often those who didn't understand its connection to strategy.

Leaders in this category tend to view vision as a gimmick. I observed a pattern in which some leaders open the phrase book every couple of years to put new clothes on old clichés and trot them out for a new showing. The problem is that clichés, generalities, and amorphous aspirations struggle to provide a lasting stimulus. They're usually apologies for visions that don't provide purpose or direction. They are direct reflections of leaders who haven't thought hard enough about their organizations and what they want those organizations to become or accomplish in the future. Or they reflect disingenuous leaders who believe employees can feed on a diet of superficial corporate-speak. Clearly the substance of a vision is more important than style. In the course of my research, I learned that one of the most revealing questions to ask of any leader—a question that tends to reveal the leader without addressing him or her directly—is simply, "What is your vision?" Vision reveals the person's understanding of leadership, strategy, and execution and all of the interconnecting linkages.

Michael Porter, a leading strategy expert, makes the point that "there's a striking relationship between really good strategies and really strong leaders."[3] The corollary is that there's also a striking relationship between really good strategies and really good visions. Good visions can't be drawn out of thin air. They need the grist of good strategy, which is based on understanding who and what you are in the competitive landscape and what you have the ability to become. Visions gain clarity and force when they are founded in good strategy. You can expect that people will think hard about the vision to test its assumptions and question its realism. A good vision has to counterbalance inspiration with feasibility. That feasibility comes of sound strategy, which is the second kite string. Jim Collins underscores this point when he explains that "Bad BHAGs (big, hairy, audacious goals) are set with bravado; good BHAGs are set with understanding."[4]

THE THREE ROLES OF VISION

A vision has three related roles—education, motivation, and coordination—each of which helps replenish energy and direct the discretionary efforts of people. There's a natural sequence to the three roles: an effective vision first educates, then motivates, and finally coordinates. People need to progress through cognitive understanding before they become emotionally motivated to support change and coordinate as an organization behind it.[5] Figure 7.1 illustrates this progression.

A VISION EDUCATES

Getting to first base as a change leader means having people understand your vision of change. Unfortunately, this can be

FIGURE 7.1. THE ROLE OF VISION.

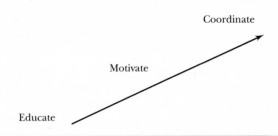

Coordinate

Motivate

Educate

difficult. Several studies show that a striking percentage of employees don't understand their organization's direction. In one study, an amazing 95 percent of employees were either unaware of or did not understand their organization's strategic vision.[6] Think about how difficult it would be to win support for change when the members of an organization don't understand the direction of the organization in the first place.

One prominent example of an executive who had difficulty creating a shared understanding of vision was the former CEO of Hewlett-Packard (HP), Carly Fiorina: "A survey asked 94,000 HP employees to grade the management in 15 categories and, while HP got high marks in seven segments, the workers gave below-average grades in three: The troops said they don't yet understand the adaptive strategy and feel stretched thin in their new roles."[7] Battle-fatigued employees who don't understand the goal won't achieve the goal.

What makes this all the more clear is the speed with which the new CEO, Mark Hurd, has been able to educate, motivate, and coordinate HP since he arrived in 2005. He has articulated an exceptionally simple vision of growth, operational excellence, and cost discipline that has resonated and circulated with amazing velocity and impact. Why? Because everybody gets it, and they get it immediately. It wasn't without pain, however. He laid off more than fifteen thousand people soon after arriving. But the employees still signed up for his vision, in part, simply because there was understanding.[8] People need to understand change at some basic level before they support it. They need to understand the rationale for change; how it fits with overall strategy; why, how, and when it will take place; and what part they will play in the process.

In one case of change that I studied, a software company decided to redesign the sales compensation plan for the entire sales force. Knowing that the mere mention of tampering with a sales compensation plan strikes terror in the hearts of salespeople and usually leads to an immediate loss in sales productivity, executive management decided to announce the change at the annual sales meetings where there would be enough time to explain and discuss the details of the new plan.

The new plan called for a series of revenue gates for which salespeople would earn graduated commissions to replace the flat commission structure of the old plan. There was a

People don't embrace change ahead of their understanding and motivation.

series of other changes designed to create richer rewards for higher performance and fewer rewards for lower performance. The initial unveiling of the system met with a mixed reception, and in fact no more than half of the salespeople were actually happy about it when it was finally implemented. Ten percent of the sales force left the organization as a result of the new plan. And it wasn't until several months later that a majority of the sales team felt comfortable with the plan and supported it. Regardless of the overall success of the change, the case illustrates that a vision must educate if it hopes to motivate and coordinate.

To understand better the first step of educating, let's go back to the principle of exchange that I discussed in Chapter Two. I explained that a change leader must maintain an ongoing exchange of energy for the discretionary efforts of people. Not only do people exchange effort for the energy supplied by leadership, but they also examine any proposal for change based on its perceived future benefits. In the short term, change almost always requires sacrifice. People don't tend to offer a willing sacrifice unless it's exchanged for a perceived benefit of some kind now or in the future. They know that change usually means delayed gratification and planned deprivation. They know you want them to make sacrifices now for potential benefits later.

As one CEO explains, "Each person in the organization has to find a credible reason for making an effort and supporting the project. I call this the 'return on sacrifice.' If you fail to get the right mix of sacrifices and benefits, the process will either start with various components moving in different directions or it will not get under way at all."[9] Vision is the first piece of information needed to help an individual calculate the ultimate return on sacrifice. With a poor or absent vision, the potential benefits of change are difficult to figure.

A VISION MOTIVATES

An interesting aspect of human nature is that people want to be motivated and readily accept sources of motivation. For example, the question that newly minted M.B.A.s most frequently ask potential employers is, "What the organization's vision?" They want something to get excited about. To motivate is the primary emotional function of a vision and the source of its greatest power. It does this in two ways: it gives people the motivation to go forward to receive future benefits and the security to leave the present based on assurances of fair treatment. Vision provides the crucial performance motive beyond the survival instinct. It does this by showing people an attractive place to go and a reason to go there. The emotional side of vision communicates why a change is attractive based on future potential benefits. Simply knowing the grand intention of an enterprise—the big vision—often motivates people toward it. Without vision, organizations tend to suffer from emotional and cognitive deficits that are reflected in lower productivity and poor execution.

Visions can also motivate by providing security. Under conditions of change, vision compensates for the chill winds of uncertainty. By giving employees something to hold on to, along with the credibility of leadership, it further replaces the comforts of the status quo. A vision provides much-needed continuity when an organization has been deliberately disturbed. Crisis can make survival the vision, at least for a time, but survival doesn't generally provide sustainable energy to an organization's long-term change efforts, especially if people have alternatives. In time of war, for example, there is no option but to fight. But in time of peace, it takes a vision to persuade people that things need to be different.

In one case I studied, a large retail organization decided to divest one of its store chains, which it had acquired only five years earlier. The chain had never integrated well into the larger retail portfolio. When the employees heard that they were being placed on the auction block, they welcomed the news in spite of an uncertain future. Of course, context had everything to do with motivating the employees to embrace the vision. The vision itself was nothing more than the news that the chain would be sold. But the fact that this simple message could galvanize an employee population so dramatically testifies to the power of vision to motivate.

A VISION COORDINATES

Vision coordinates efforts among people because they share common understanding and motivation. It removes fault lines and splices territories. As Stanford professor James Phills states, "Performance depends not just on effort or motivation but on the coordination of efforts. Individual behavior has to be in the service of organizational goals, not just personal goals."[10] An organization that isn't coordinated is hobbled when it attempts to execute anything.

Under the leadership of Charles Quigley, the Center for Civic Education, based in Los Angeles, has become the world's most influential nonprofit organization dedicated to civic education and democratic process. The organization's simple yet clear and compelling vision is to teach young people the principles and practices of democracy. That vision has attracted and coordinated thousands of scholars and educators around the world to voluntarily create standard curriculum materials and programs to offer to schools on every continent. The center has now educated more than 30 million students in seventy countries. In the United States alone, twenty-two thousand schools have participated in its programs.

Without a coordinating vision, the center would have little impact because it relies on the mass collaboration of volunteers to move its work forward. The nonprofit sector in particular

FIGURE 7.2.   THE RECIPROCAL RELATIONSHIP OF HEAD, HEART, AND HANDS.

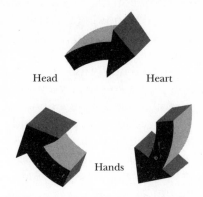

Head   Heart

Hands

Educate—Cognitive role: create understanding.
Motivate—Emotional and psychological role: create a bond.
Coordinate—Organizational role: create shared purpose.

illustrates the power of a coordinating vision because it must rely on the vision to do much of the work. Without a coordinating vision to infuse the organization with direction and attract volunteers from around the world, the organization would simply disappear.

The progression from understanding to motivation is not a simple linear process. It involves reciprocal influence of head, heart, and hands (Figure 7.2). But generally people move through the cognitive steps before the emotional ones.

THE ECONOMICS OF A GOOD VISION

We tend to emphasize the emotional role of vision, and for good reason. Our emotional response to vision is what we remember. Not only do we understand that vision can exert tremendous power, but most of us at one time or another have felt it. More than anything else, it was something we responded to emotionally. But I want to come back to the educational role of a vision because there's more to it.

If a vision successfully creates understanding, it has performed work—very important work. It does this by gently and almost imperceptibly imposing order on the organization. Knowledge has economic value, but shared knowledge created through vision has even more economic value because it makes a direct contribution to increase the efficiency of the production process. A vision that cascades consistently and uniformly through an organization turns that organization into a cognitive community in which the members share a common understanding about direction and are able to implement that direction more efficiently. While a vision may seem like only a lofty appeal to emotion, it's as necessary as a map is to a wandering traveler.

Consider the tactical reality of how vision is communicated and implemented within an organization. A leader communicates a vision from

Vision can lower the unit costs of performing certain kinds of work.

the top. Depending on how clear and actionable it is, people at various levels will apply the vision to their own work. A good vision will help coordinate the tactical and operational work that people perform every day, whereas a poor vision won't inform those efforts, leaving them potentially scattered and unconnected. A good vision enables an organization to perform work based on knowledge economies of scale. The vision becomes a force multiplier by mass-producing certain inputs for the organization.

Vision can lower the unit costs of:

- Communicating
- Collaborating and problem solving
- Decision making
- Implementing

When vision performs these types of work, it also indirectly performs some other highly valuable kinds of work, such as:

- Attracting and retaining employees
- Attracting and retaining customers
- Creating market demand

The economic value of vision comes in reducing the time and cost of asking questions, analyzing issues, and making decisions.

It allows people in many cases to direct themselves. It organizes assumptions, values, words, actions, and resources. It influences strategy, systems, and structure.

A clear and compelling vision answers thousands of questions, guides employees in thousands of small decisions, and eliminates the ambiguity that might otherwise create the need for thousands of conversations. Through implication, it is the mass production of answers. It increases an organization's capacity to perform work by creating more efficient and effective coordinated action. It increases the efficiency of organizational metabolism. In other words, it reduces the energy required in the sum of its processes to convert inputs into outputs.

Going back to the GE example, think of what the unit production cost was for making a tactical operating decision. Even the last employee hired could at least attempt to do the basic analysis with an eye toward the vision, asking: "Does this get us closer to being number one or number two in our market?" One former manager at GE told me that with the aid of the vision, many decisions were self-evident.

Now think about the opposite. Without the clear vision of becoming number one or number two, what kind of calculus do people go through? It's unclear, but one thing we do know is that it would cost a lot more time and money to make a decision because people don't know where the organization is going. You'll get as many different answers as the number of people you ask. It can't be otherwise. If you think about an organization as one person, that one person armed with a clear vision can make clear decisions and act on them. Without it, thinking is cluttered, and there is no basis to make decisions. A vision unclutters thinking, which unclutters decision making, which unclutters execution.

Another practical consequence of poor vision is that it puts a heavier operational burden on leaders at every level. Because employees can't make decisions and execute them based on their coordination with the vision, the leader assumes an unnecessary babysitting role. By necessity, the leader has to repeatedly provide general guidance and direction because the vision isn't there to perform that work.

Does a vision answer every question about strategy and resource allocation? Of course not. A vision leaves out most of the detail, so there are many more questions. And leaders have to stay involved in the details.[11] But a good vision can provide the broad coordination that allows an organization to move quickly through basic issues of direction and priority in order to spend time and energy on strategic and tactical implementation. Clearly good vision directs people to direct themselves.

SPLINTER, PEEL, AND FRAY

Creating an effective vision is one of the most difficult leadership challenges. A good vision comes from a delicate balance of reality and possibility. As one executive put it, the vision "must be at one level, a dream but also achievable. Too much of a dream and people will not believe in it. Too much emphasis on survival and they will not accept the sacrifices."[12] A vision is an image, rendering, or articulation of what an organization aims to be and where it aims to go. It represents a reality that doesn't exist but could be achieved. That's all straightforward. But vision doesn't appear on its own or communicate by itself.[13] This is the leader's work, and it's harder than it may appear.[14]

In several failed cases of change, I observed that the vision was not durable. It couldn't make the organizational journey. As it traveled, it would become badly mauled and often unrecognizable by the time it moved from one end of the organization to the other. In order to have any opportunity of doing its job—to educate, motivate, and coordinate—a vision must hold together. It has to be able to take a hit, endure damage in handling, and yet remain intact. Only visions that survive the communications journey are able to create widespread understanding, motivation, and organizational coordination. The two greatest threats to a vision are that it will be changed or lost.

The average vision takes a pounding as it moves through an organization. Think about some of the obstacles that it must encounter and overcome:

- *Interpretive filters.* Words are highly open to interpretation. They mean different things to different people depending on many factors.

- *Cultural bias.* Especially in organizations that extend across many cultural and national boundaries, cultural bias can often affect the way a vision of change is interpreted and communicated.
- *Competing assumptions.* People hold differing assumptions and beliefs about almost every aspect of an organization. Unless the assumptions are made explicit, people often draw different conclusions about information based on differing assumptions.
- *Informal networks.* When groups of people come together informally, they do so based on having something in common. They exert tremendous influence in the way vision is communicated and interpreted.
- *Communication handoffs.* The bigger and more complex the organization is, the more communication handoffs there are across business units, functional areas, and organizational layers.[15] There are also more indirect and impersonal communication channels in use, such as e-mail, teleconferencing, video, and print.
- *Chain of command.* The editorial filter of the chain of command can be clumsy or predatory with vision. Often leaders simply won't pass the vision down or explain and interpret because it requires additional effort. What's worse is when leaders in the chain don't like the vision and deliberately try to undermine it by distorting it or withholding it to maintain personal power. This is a common form of self-preservation when change becomes a personal threat to a leader.

It's daunting to see the full scope of the communications challenge that a vision must square up to. Unfortunately, there's no way around it. If a vision breaks down or gets lost, it can't do its job, and organizational illiteracy develops. Rather than creating a cognitive community, the vision splinters, peels, and frays into different messages. When leaders persist in communicating visions that are not understood, they run the risk of engaging in a grand illusion, which is to proceed as if people understand.

At a large multinational construction company, there was a deep cultural divide between management and the construction workers. Although the company wasn't unionized, the fault line was unmistakable, and it produced some hostility that resulted in constant miscommunication. Anyone in management was labeled a "cell phone," and anyone doing the actual construction was labeled a "tool belt." The cell phones and tool belts liked to keep to their own group and avoided interaction if at all possible. These are the kinds of obstacles a vision has to face.

THE CONCEPT OF HIGH FIDELITY

In my research, I discovered that some change visions travel well, stay together, and perform all three functions: educate, motivate, and coordinate. They possessed certain attributes that allowed them to resist distortion errors and thereby maintain consistent meaning. In spite of the obstacles, some visions emerged intact. They survived the ravages of the organization without being materially changed or hopelessly lost. I call these survivors high-fidelity visions, after the stereophonic term, because I observed that they could be reproduced with accuracy and maintained fidelity or faithfulness to the original version as they traveled.

I asked the next logical question: What properties combine to create a high-fidelity vision? From my analysis of successful change cases, I identified three elements that high-fidelity visions nearly always have in common:

1. Clarity
2. Relevance
3. Memory

Visions with clarity allow leaders to create, manage, and control the message.[16] Relevance explains the connection to strategy, mission, and values of the organization. Memory creates a lasting impression of the vision in mind of the person receiving it.[17] When a vision contains all three elements, it becomes capable of generating significant energy to a change effort. The combination of these three elements can produce the high-fidelity effect illustrated in the Venn diagram in Figure 7.3.

CLARITY

In a scene from the movie *Philadelphia*, Denzel Washington, who plays a lawyer, turns to his client, played by Tom Hanks, and says:

FIGURE 7.3.   THE THREE ATTRIBUTES OF A HIGH-FIDELITY VISION.

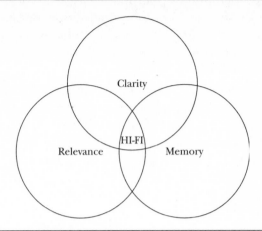

"Tell me like I'm a third grader." When it comes to vision, this is good counsel. It's not a new imperative for leaders to craft clear visions, but it remains the single biggest obstacle and point of failure to high fidelity. If a critical message is not clear to begin with, it only becomes less clear as it moves through an organization. An unclear vision typically splinters as it passes through organizational layers and moves laterally through departments. Instead of speaking with one voice, the organization speaks with many. In the end, there will be little chance of coordination because the vision can't be reproduced with accuracy as it gets passed around. If a vision is opaque from the beginning, it's in trouble. It's not like a rough stone that has its corners knocked off and rough edges smoothed as it rolls down a streambed. You have to design clarity into a vision from the beginning. As Marcus Buckingham has stated, "Effective leaders don't have to be passionate or charming or brilliant. What they must be is clear—clarity is the essence of great leadership."[18] Without clarity, there's no dispersion and pooling of knowledge, so an organization is in the dark.

Being clear seems easy when we're on the receiving end. But clarity is deceiving: it seldom reflects the work that goes into its creation. Clarity is usually the result of a painstaking process to refine and purify something that was rough and impure at the start. As the French philosopher Blaise Pascal famously remarked, "The present letter is a very long one, simply because I had no leisure to make it shorter."[19] Clarity has its price. Not surprisingly, there are several reasons that we fail to achieve clarity:

- *Lack of clear intent.* If you don't have clear intent about what you want the organization to be or where you want the organization to go, your vision will reflect that unrefined intent. Language is a reflection of thought. Unclear vision is symptomatic of unfinished or poor thinking. Yet clarity isn't in any way the opposite of grandness. When President Kennedy held up a thunderous vision to go to the moon, that vision was grandiose yet exceedingly clear.

- *Competition.* Your vision has to compete with many other messages. It's more difficult than ever before to gain mind share with so many messages vying for attention. This makes it harder to create a vision that can rise above the noise and clamor of other competing messages in the digital age. Organizational communication has become a zero-sum game. Members of organizations have to choose what to listen and pay attention to. When Alfred Sloan was running GM in the 1940s, he sent out memos to his people that didn't have to compete with others' message. He could take as much mind share as he wanted. Today only the high-fidelity messages get through.

- *Misunderstanding.* The best organizations have learned to simplify their visions. The assumption is that strategy, and therefore vision, is conceptually simple. An inability to communicate a vision in simple and clear terms that the front line can't immediately grasp reflects a fundamental misunderstanding of the concepts of competitive advantage. By its very nature, strategy implies clear choices and simple concepts. Thus, a high-fidelity message of strategy is not dumbed down but simply highly refined.

In explaining his own approach, Procter & Gamble's CEO, A. G. Lafley, states, "It's *Sesame Street* language—I admit that. A lot of what we have done is made things simple because the difficulty is making sure everybody knows what the goal is and how to get there."[20] It seems that leaders of the biggest organizations soon learn the importance of clarity. They are tutored early by their failures to understand that clarity is the only way to have any chance of moving an enormous enterprise forward. Carlos Ghosn, the CEO of Renault and Nissan, who doesn't speak Japanese, acknowledged this lesson from his experience at Nissan: "Once the men and women of Nissan were given a clear vision, a clear strategy, clear priorities, and a framework for action, they did change."[21]

- *Ego.* Jack Welch explains that clarity might imply that a leader isn't very sophisticated and thus tempt him or her to complicate a message to make it appear more intelligent. I've witnessed several CEOs try to regale their employees with complexity in an effort to impress. Keep in mind Welch's statement: "One of the hardest things for a manager is to reach a threshold of self-confidence where being simple is comfortable."[22]

RELEVANCE

When it comes to change, how many times have you heard people wonder, "Why are we doing this?" People rarely get on board if they don't know why. If your vision doesn't show how change is relevant, others will see it as disconnected: done in isolation, unrelated to everything else, and worst of all, arbitrary. Relevance comes out of context to show how change is tied to current reality. When people don't see the relevance of proposed change, they see change as pure pain.

Change seen as irrelevant is considered pure pain.

I've seen many instances where the need for change wasn't clearly communicated. In times of crisis, the need for change often communicates itself because of overwhelming evidence of poor performance and the prospect of catastrophic loss. But even in crisis, people often misinterpret or don't see a clear cause-and-effect relationship that says, "We need to change, and this is why."

I interviewed a restaurant manager of a large and well-known national chain who had been brought in to take over a particular location that had been losing sales for six consecutive months. I asked her what her number one priority was in turning the operation around. She responded, "That was obvious from day one. The restaurant has not been kept clean. A key part of our brand is to provide an immaculately clean environment for our customers." I then asked her how the employees were responding to her change vision. With a disappointed look, she informed me that at first, the team had reacted with surprise. They believed the property was clean enough. They didn't understand the deep connection between clean and the brand's promise to its customers. The new manager had to explain the high standard of cleanliness and its relevance to restaurant sales based on the brand's value commitment to the market. Once they learned the central importance of the standard, they could implement it. Figure 7.4 illustrates the importance that relevance played in this particular change vision.

MEMORY

George Wright, the marketing manager of Blendtec, a small company that makes industrial blenders, had a tiny ad budget. One day after watching the blenders undergo motor testing by chewing up pieces of wood,

> *Assume that your vision will be communicated with the sole aid of memory and by word of mouth.*

he wondered if the blenders could blend other hard materials like marbles. He tried it, and the blender reduced a bowlful of marbles to a pile of glass dust. He did it again and this time recorded the experience on video. He posted it on YouTube, and to his amazement, his video proved to have viral marketing qualities. More than 11 million people viewed the "Will It Blend?" series of videos. They were amazingly memorable: as a result, revenues soared.[23] The second attribute of high fidelity is memory.

FIGURE 7.4.   SEEING THE RELEVANCE OF CHANGE.

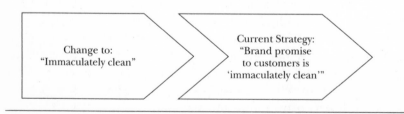

High-fidelity vision resists distortion in large part because people remember it. Most large-scale change initiatives are communicated through multiple communication channels and repeated numerous times. With large-scale change, it's good practice to train managers with a communications tool kit to help them move a vision message throughout an organization. Most managers need the help of talking points and process for soliciting and reporting feedback about the vision of change. But that's still the exception. Most of the time, vision has to be relayed, explained, interpreted, and translated informally for the sake of efficiency and speed. We tend to reserve the use of formal communications processes for major initiatives that affect the entire enterprise. Most change is local, affecting a function, department, process, team, structure, or some other part of the organization instead of the whole thing, so we communicate change with the sole aid of what we remember. We expect others to pass it on the same way. The key observation is this: change communications is still primarily an oral tradition that relies on word of mouth.

Because vision relies heavily on memory, visions that capture memory are much more likely to achieve high fidelity.

Incorporating qualities of memory into a vision is extremely difficult because we remember things that are different rather than things that are common. Most organizational changes aren't original or exciting in any particular way. There simply is no algorithm for stickiness.[24] But if we can isolate one attribute of memory, it is the ability to create a visual image.

Creating an image is the most effective way to create memory.

As James O'Toole points out, when Ronald Reagan explained in his budget message that a trillion dollars was enough money to reach to the Empire State building, he captured memory and found support to reduce federal spending.[25] An image grabs mind share faster and better than any other communications attribute. The element of memory can cut through the clutter. As Sanaz Ahari, a lead program manager at Microsoft, points out, "Create something cool, and people will distribute your brand for you."[26] Of course the challenge is figuring out what's cool. Chances are greater that if you can inject vision with an attractive image, people are usually more than happy to distribute that vision rapidly and accurately.

More than 150 years ago, Ralph Waldo Emerson said, "If a man can...make a better mouse-trap, ... the world will make a beaten path to his door." Unfortunately, this isn't remotely true today. Unless you can break through the airwaves to capture attention, you will have no chance of explaining the features and benefits of the new mousetrap; your new invention will remain unknown. The context of organizational communications is unlike any previous age. A generation ago, Herbert Simon, a Nobel Prize winner in economic science, prophetically alerted us to the concept of attention economics. "What information consumes is rather obvious," he said. "It consumes the attention of its recipients. Hence a wealth of information creates a poverty of attention and a need to allocate that attention efficiently among the overabundance of information sources that might consume it."[27] So what's the consequence?

The spamming of the human mind in the global age is forcing everyone to organize and filter information more aggressively. With an increased volume of messages seeking an audience, the discarded pile of messages continues to grow as a percentage of the total. This phenomenon is both a cognitive and an emotional necessity. A person can absorb and process only so much. We are easily the most filtering generation of communicators in the history of the world.

The obvious risk of increased filtering is that important messages will be filtered out. From a probability standpoint, every message has a lesser chance of being heard and understood. Second, with the increasing number of messages being sent, it becomes more difficult for the listener to determine which ones are worth listening to. All messages are not created equal, but how can you tell when so many claim the same level of relevance and importance?

How to Build a High-Fidelity Message

The three elements of high fidelity—clarity, relevance, and memory—might be easy to understand, but they are hard to create and combine. There are in fact high barriers to entry when it comes to putting such a vision together. What follows are several best practices that I observed in the most successful cases of change.

USE A DESIGN TEMPLATE

Design vision messages according to the way the human brain wants them. This means giving the punch line, or summarizing idea, first and supporting information second.[28] The template in Exhibit 7.1 illustrates the questions and information sequence that you should normally answer to craft a high-fidelity vision.

COLLABORATE IN THE CREATION

Vision isn't the first energy source because it takes time to develop. It starts out fuzzy and has to incubate. But it doesn't do this by itself, and rarely can a leader do it in isolation. Don't bring a

EXHIBIT 7.1. VISION TEMPLATE.

1. Give the main message first. Answer the question, "What?"	
2. Give support to answer the question, "Why?"	
3. Give support to answer the question, "How?"	
4. Explain the personal impact: costs and benefits.	
5. Does the impact change based on the stakeholder? Are there variations of the message that you need to develop for different audiences or stakeholders?	

carved-in-stone vision of change to your organization and present it from on high. Bring a draft vision, and let people have at it. Let them challenge and disagree. Let them shoot holes in it and make it better. The best visions are generally the product of a collaborative process in which senior leaders invite the participation of other employees, sometimes far down into the organization.[29] Why? Because the ability to reach employees with a motivating and enabling vision means that you connect with them by first meeting them where they are and then lifting their eyes to something higher. Teaching other members of the organization the elements of high fidelity and then visioning together to create a compelling image of the future works far better than trying to do it yourself.

SEEK DIRECT FEEDBACK

In large organizations especially, don't be afraid to try out draft visions on randomly selected members of the organization and then gather their feedback about what works and what doesn't. Put some bait on the water, so to speak, and see if anyone snaps at it. They will tell you if a story, image, metaphor, or concept works or not and why. They will tell you if something isn't clear. They will tell you if the change that you're contemplating makes sense and fits with current strategy or whether it seems disconnected. A recent task force concluded the following in its study of American higher education, "There is no greater factor in a president's success than the ability to elicit and inspire the thinking of others in a shared vision of the institution."[30]

BETA TEST THE SPOKEN VERSION

It might sound like worn advice to advise you to communicate the vision, but too many miss the point here. A vision isn't done with a written document. That's only the beginning. Now comes the beta testing. Your vision may be clear on paper but unclear to others. You have to track how the vision is interpreted and translated. You have to audit the process whereby the spoken version is developed. Much of the final refining of the vision will come in the dialogue of testing and discussing it.

CREATE A COMMUNICATIONS PLAN

If you are undertaking large-scale change, you have an even bigger communications challenge: creating a formal communications plan. Otherwise you won't be able to get the message out effectively and collect the valuable feedback that you need.[31] For large-scale change, communications must become nothing less than a strategic business system. A communications plan should address the following elements:

- Multiple audiences and their specific needs
- Different communication channels
- Communication tools and training
- Timing
- Sequence
- Feedback loops

Summary

Key Points

- The three elements of mission, vision, and strategy are related organizational elements, but each answers a different question. Mission answers the question, "Why do we exist?" Vision answer the question, "What do we want to become or achieve?" Strategy answers the question, "How do we achieve the vision and fulfill the mission?"
- Elements of mission and strategy are often not only helpful but also necessary to create a compelling vision.
- A good vision is attached to the kite strings of a credible leader as an extension of his or her credibility and strategy, which provides a way to understand how the vision is possible to achieve.
- Vision replenishes energy for change by performing three different but related roles in an organization. First, a vision educates to provide cognitive understanding of change. Second, a vision motivates by providing the allure of future benefits and the security of fair treatment when one leaves the status quo behind. Third, a vision coordinates people within an organization based on shared understanding and purpose to pursue new organizational goals.

- When vision performs its three functions, it performs work and creates economic value. Based on knowledge economies of scale, vision can reduce the unit costs of communicating, solving problems, making decisions, and implementing those decisions based on the understanding and self-direction it creates.
- The two greatest threats to a vision of change are that it will become changed or that it will become lost. Change visions often fail because they aren't durable messages that can survive the damage in handling that normally occurs when a vision takes its journey through the organizational gauntlet, which is beset with a variety of communication obstacles.
- A high-fidelity vision represents a durable message that can be reproduced with accuracy by resisting transmission errors. The three attributes of high fidelity are clarity, relevance, and memory.
- Clarity is the most important attribute of vision. It conveys unmistakable intent concerning the aims and rationale for change. It also allows a leader to control and manage the meaning of a message so that it won't splinter into multiple messages.
- Relevance shows how change is tied to context and current strategy. Specifically, change should link to the strategy, mission, or values of the organization. When change is seen as irrelevant, it is considered pure pain.
- The attribute of memory allows vision to create a lasting impression. The most important quality of memory is the ability to create a visual image. Leaders must assume that change visions will be communicated with the sole aid of memory and by word of mouth.
- To build a high-fidelity vision, a leader should use a design template, collaborate in the creation, seek direct feedback, beta test the spoken version, and create a communications plan.

PART FOUR

IMPLEMENT

Once you have completed the preparation stage of change, you will have generated significant amounts of energy from the first five energy sources: agility, urgency, credibility, coalition, and vision. You will need this as you move into the stage of implementation and begin to climb the steep slope of the power curve.

The energy that you have tapped from the first five sources provides the momentum to carry you into the implementation stage and the stored energy to carry you through until you can replenish it again with early results. You have, so to speak, a running start, which is exactly what you need. If you try to move into implementation from a standing, or homeostatic, position, with little preparation and energy, the effort will likely fail for lack of energy. Most successful cases of change enter the implementation stage with anticipation and a head full of steam from the combined power of the first five energy sources.

Implementation is the stage in which the organization performs the most work and absorbs the most stress. It is therefore the stage that requires the most energy to fuel that exertion. In the power curve figure shown here, the arrow indicates the steep slope of the power curve, representing the significant increase in energy requirements that normally accompanies the implementation stage.

IMPLEMENTATION STAGE.

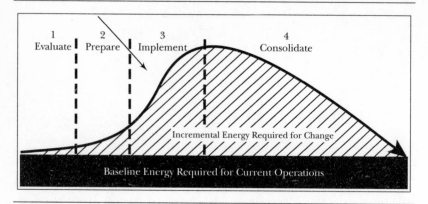

Even large reserves of energy can soon be depleted during implementation when the process is strenuous. If change calls for significant additional change work to perform and stress to absorb, it takes away massive amounts of energy. The other important fact is that implementation can take a long time. Organizational transformations usually take years, whereas more localized changes may take only days or months.

Regardless of how long it takes to implement change, keep in mind that the first five energy sources you bring to implementation will act as a booster rocket that will fuel only the first phase of implementation. Your immediate concern will be to switch engines in order to replenish energy from the next critical energy source for the next stage of the journey. The next energy source is early results. When a change effort starts to produce early results, it crosses over to the realm of evidence, which is the natural expectation of all human beings who embark on change. When this happens, the weariness and fatigue are swallowed up in the positive effects of actual progress.

Chapter Eight

Implement with Early Results

Running a transformation effort without serious attention to short-term wins is extremely risky.
John Kotter, *Leading Change* (1996)

Implement with Early Results.

EPIC Stage	1 Evaluate	2 Prepare	3 Implement	4 Consolidate
The Leader's Role	**Equilibrium Step** Supply energy for the ongoing evaluation of competitive reality, internal performance, and change alternatives.	**Ignition Step** Replenish energy to supply a gradual increase in work performed and stress absorbed during preparation.	**Refueling Step** Replenish energy to supply a significant increase in work performed and stress absorbed during implementation.	**Refueling Step** Replenish energy to supply a gradual decrease in work performed and stress absorbed during consolidation.
Energy Sources	**1. Agility**	1. Agility **2. Urgency** **3. Credibility** **4. Coalition** **5. Vision**	1. Agility 2. Urgency 3. Credibility 4. Coalition 5. Vision **6. Early Results**	1. Agility 2. Urgency 3. Credibility 4. Coalition 5. Vision 6. Early Results **7. Sustained Results**

When she was appointed president of Texas Southmost College in 1986, Juliet Garcia became the first Hispanic woman to lead an institution of higher learning in the United States.[1] Together with faculty, staff, students, and the community in the border town of Brownsville, Texas, Garcia created a bold vision to advance the institution beyond its role as a small community college. In her mind's eye, she saw a flourishing university deeply committed to academic excellence and community engagement. The vision was inspiring, but now loomed the ominous task of making it a reality.

In her first year as president, she and her team made several landmark policy changes to put the college on the path toward growth and an expanded role. Theoretically it was an important early win. The problem was that almost nobody knew about the policies or understood their implications. They were essentially invisible to students and the rest of the community and supplied little, if any, energy to the broader change effort.

That same year, Garcia helped persuade the community to raise a public bond to fund a campus expansion. When the bulldozers arrived on campus and started digging dirt, everything changed. The reality of heavy equipment carving away the past and erecting the future communicated change with absolute clarity. Energy spiked in support of Garcia's vision, giving her renewed energy to move forward.

The next year Dr. Garcia's team set its sights on creating a scholarship endowment program to provide more incentive and opportunity to many disadvantaged young people. To do it, the college would need to raise a million dollars. In other college settings, this may not be an ambitious goal, but in this, the largest city of the Rio Grande valley, where the average per capital income is $9,762, 36 percent of residents live below the poverty line, and only 52 percent have earned a high school diploma, it seemed insurmountable.

Garcia realized that she would have to be willing to win in inches and feet. She needed participation from every corner of the community because economic resources were scarce. Instead of glitzy fund-raisers with big donors, the college sponsored car washes and bake sales. Through a community-wide campaign,

Garcia enlisted every segment of society. It was a grassroots effort for nickels, dimes, and quarters, with the goal that "everyone would own the victory." For instance, at one local elementary school, students skipped lunch for three days so they could donate their lunch money to the scholarship campaign.

Each time there was an event and communication of progress toward the goal, that event and that progress would fuel momentum to keep the effort alive. The milestones along the way signaled progress and motivated people to continue their efforts. In the end, Texas Southmost College raised the million dollars. Indeed, the achievement of the endowed scholarship fund became an early win in the context of the institution's grand vision. In 1991, the college achieved university status and became part of the University of Texas system as the University of Texas at Brownsville. As a case study in large-scale organizational change, Garcia's approach illuminates the critical importance of the sixth energy source—early results—and the leadership process necessary to unleash its power.

Almost without exception, large-scale change is accomplished through the energy created by early results. Early results, also known as small wins or quick hits, become the immediate goal once you enter the implementation stage. The role and power of early results was introduced into organizational theory by social psychologist Karl Weick in 1984. He defined a small win as a "concrete, complete, implemented outcome."[2] Since then, leaders in every field have validated the importance of this concept. Not only do early results generate energy when they arrive, they also generate energy before they arrive. Early results offer these twin benefits:

- Giving people confidence that a vision is achievable by breaking it down into smaller pieces, which makes a daunting goal seem possible.
- Giving people a vision within a vision. Setting goals for early results gives people visibility to those results before they happen. That visibility alone is a source of power before the actual results show up.

THUNDER DON'T WATER THE CROPS

At some point in every change effort, energy must be replenished with real results. The effort must enter the realm of tangible evidence in order to continue the exchange of energy for discretionary effort. Witnessing movement toward vision becomes a test of obviousness. During the preparation stage, people get a sense of forward motion. But during implementation, they ultimately need the hard evidence of actual results as compensation for their continued efforts. Sometimes results don't come for a long time, as in the case of large and complex change. In these instances, you have no choice but to rely on reserves of stored energy created during the stages of evaluation and preparation to bridge the span to early results.

A common failure pattern occurs when the implementation stage is long and grueling. If the combination of energy reserves provided by agility, urgency, credibility, coalition, and vision is not sufficient to maintain the generation and exchange of energy for effort until early results appear, the change process will suffer a nontechnical leadership failure. I classify it as a leadership failure because it is squarely the job of leadership to build up reserves of energy to supply the journey up the steep slope of the power curve. Thus, the longer you think it will take for results to appear in a given change effort, the more front-end-loaded your preparation should be in order to fuel this stage of the journey.

I repeatedly observe leaders, boards, and even venture capitalists who don't pay attention to this kind of assessment as it relates to investment decisions. Whether an organization is a start-up or an underperforming business that requires a turnaround, it's as important as financial due diligence to forecast the length of time needed to achieve early results—and often the early results are not financial—and then compare that forecast with an analysis of energy reserves that the organization can draw on until those results appear. As a rule of thumb, I advise investors to add 50 percent to their assumptions as to when results will come and then carefully discern whether they have sufficient stored organizational energy to last that length of time. This qualitative assessment is as important as projecting the break-even point based on the cash burn rate. Many people do these kinds of calculations subconsciously, based on gut and instinct, but I'm convinced of the need for analytical rigor in the formal process.

I witnessed one venture capital (VC) firm provide a $15 million second round of funding to a technology company that after eighteen months was still having trouble commercializing its product. The VC firm placed this bet based on its confidence in the technology, the market opportunity, and the president of the company. What they treated lightly was how much energy, or "juice," was still available to keep everyone going. Unfortunately, they didn't see the warning signs in the CEO's waning credibility, the teetering vision, the growing disillusionment, and the cracks in the coalition. All they needed to do was conduct interviews two layers down in the organization to discover these warning signs. Instead, because they were impressed with the president of the company, they didn't spend much time with the employees other than the leadership team. The start-up collapsed after four months because it couldn't reverse the flight of talent. Unfortunately, the VC firm missed the most important piece in analysis of their intangible assets. You place the bet on these assets every bit as much as you do on the technology itself.

When a leader makes the transition from preparation to implementation, he or she is now leading the change campaign based on stored energy until results appear. Successful cases of change show that people can stay productive and hopeful for a very long time. They can keep trudging with little or no evidence of progress if the prior five energy sources have something left to give. But these energy sources don't last forever. At some point, they must be replenished. The first five energy sources can be strong and enduring, but they can't match the motivating power of actual results. They are, after all, based on things other than real evidence of change, such as people, reputation, ideas, and emotion. These things can provide energy until early results can refresh the effort, but the question always is, Will it be enough?

THE SPAN OF UNCERTAINTY

People can go with their heads down for only so long. At some point, they need to see results during implementation and at intervals thereafter. Early results are meant to generate large amounts of energy at exactly the same time the organization is exerting itself the most. In almost any organization, there will be those who get on board right away to support change. But there's a large contingent who won't get on board until they see results. As Jim Collins found in his own research, "When people begin to see tangible results, that's when the bulk of people line up to throw their shoulders against the wheel and push."[3] This is the skeptical, but not necessarily the resistant, cohort. Often this cohort supports change wholeheartedly once he or she is persuaded that it can be done. This group is simply more risk averse from the beginning. It adheres to the old saying, "Thunder don't water the crops," so they wait for rain. As a leader, you want to take a conservative approach and have the expectation that fewer people are with you at the start and that it is your job to win over skeptics and resisters through actual results. Second, you want to bridge to early results as soon as possible.

As the sixth source of energy in the EPIC methodology, early results provide vital emotional lift to a change effort. They may be small, but they're real. They're not gimmicks even though many times their most important function is symbolic. If early results are pursued with real intent, they signal that intent. They are way stations on the road to the ultimate destination. But to achieve early results, you have to know how to set the right goals, based in part on the spans of uncertainty of the people in the organization. A span of uncertainty is the length of time a person or group will continue to give discretionary effort without seeing actual evidence of progress.

Of course, the first five sources of energy will affect this span, as will the individual attributes and makeup of each individual. As a leader, it's important to learn how to read the vital signs of your people so you can

Span of uncertainty: the length of time an individual is willing to give discretionary effort without seeing actual results.

adjust the pressure and tempo of the change effort if necessary. People can only perform so much change work and absorb so much stress. You must ensure that the change effort doesn't dip into a failure pattern because you are losing the discretionary efforts of people. Moreover, when you begin the implementation stage, there are often many people who are deeply ambivalent to change and take a wait-and-see approach before they contribute any discretionary effort. So another objective is to enlist those who are sitting on the fence. It all comes back to early results.

Setting Goals for Early Results

The immediate aim of the implementation stage is to replenish energy with early results as soon as possible. Some change efforts have more opportunities for early results than others. But a determining factor in achieving early results is knowing what early results will matter like the bulldozer.

One of the best-known examples of early results comes from New York City under the leadership of Rudy Giuliani. When he was elected mayor in 1994, he knew full well that his vision of change would take several years to accomplish, but he also knew that he had to replenish energy to keep the change process fresh and alive. When he took office, he faced massive, even overwhelming, challenges, but he understood the power of early results. Instead of focusing on his long-term goals to reduce crime, he carefully identified specific short-term goals that, if achieved, would produce early results and the rejuvenating energy that goes with it. He carefully selected goals based on battles that he knew he could win, battles for which the victory would generate even more energy:

- Eliminating squeegee men (unsolicited window washers who wash your windows and then ask for money while you are stopped at a red light) from traffic intersections
- Getting taxi drivers to wear collared shirts
- Cracking down on turnstile jumpers in the subway
- Shutting down pornographic emporiums
- Removing graffiti from subways cars

He did this throughout his administration as a way to maintain the exchange of energy for discretionary effort until he was able to conquer the larger and more intimidating goal of making New York safer.[4] During his two terms in office, from 1994 to 2001, crime fell by an astonishing 65 percent. Homicides in particular fell 70 percent. The results in crime reduction were dramatic and unmistakable. Eventually the FBI named New York City the safest big city in America.[5]

The same principle of early results applies to other settings. Another example is Mike Ullman, the CEO of JC Penney with its 150,000 employees.[6] In attempting to relax a 104-year-old formal, elitist, and rigid corporate culture, Ullman gained initial energy from the following quick hits:

- Asking employees to address each other by their first names
- Selling the company's art collection
- Reinstituting business casual attire and allowing jeans on Friday
- Giving all employees access to all parts of headquarters, including the executive elevators and suite

Finally, at a software company I studied, the CEO knew his engineers needed more than a year to bring a new product to market. But he had a problem. Based on his interviews with them, he determined that their span of uncertainty was less than a year. After all, these were top flight software developers who received calls from headhunters every week, trying to lure them away with new offers. How could he keep them on board? What would create excitement and maximum energy?

For this boutique firm, the normal pattern of commercial progress for a new software product was to secure a customer who would first pilot the software, purchase the software, deploy the software, and have it work. Normally it didn't matter who the first customer would be, but in this case it became clear that what would make an enormous difference to the engineers would be to secure a name brand customer. Not only would that customer be highly referenceable to other prospects, but the name brand customer would provide significantly more energy to his software developers simply by virtue of the brand recognition. It would give them a much bigger sense of success and faith in the future.

The president and vice president of business development put a laser focus on this goal. Four months later, they committed one of the big-four accounting firms to beta test the new software. The energy associated with landing this high-profile client retained the engineers and accelerated the product development process.

Setting the Right Goals

Setting the right goals for early results is half the battle. The key is to understand what criteria have the biggest and most lasting impact. From the cases I studied, five criteria came to the surface as most important. It's not possible for every goal to include all five, but to the extent that you can, look for goals that meet as many of these:

1. *Truly achievable.* Is it something you can accomplish in the short term?
2. *Outwardly visible.* Is it something that will be obvious, that people will notice?
3. *Easy to measure.* Is it something that you can easily measure and track?
4. *Easy to communicate.* Is it something that you and others can communicate far and wide in the organization?
5. *Symbolically important.* Is it something that sends an important signal about the overall change and course that you are pursuing?

At the same time, be careful that you don't set goals for early results in a vacuum. There are other factors that you need to consider when setting goals for early results. It's important to identify potential conflicts that might arise between the new goals and the old way of doing things. It's also important that you are prepared to follow through with the communication and reinforcement that is necessary once you meet your goals. Here are five guidelines that should govern this process:

- Ensure that your financial and nonfinancial incentives do not work against the goals you set.[7]
- Communicate early results formally and repeatedly.
- Draw attention to and celebrate the early results.
- Recognize and reward employees for accomplishment.
- Express sincere appreciation face-to-face.

Now, based on the five criteria and five guidelines, carefully analyze what early results would give you the biggest bang for the

EXHIBIT 8.1. SETTING THREE GOALS FOR EARLY RESULTS.

Goals for Early Results	Criteria
1.	
2.	
3.	

buck. What will really get people's attention, instill confidence, and clearly signal that you are committed to your long-range change objectives and that you have the ability to achieve them? Start with at least three because it's a manageable number yet significant enough to replenish energy. Using Exhibit 8.1, identify your three goals for early results and indicate which criteria they meet.

MORE COMPLEXITY, LESS CONTROL

Once a major change initiative moves into full-scale implementation, two fundamental changes take place: things get more complicated, and the change leader loses a degree of control.

During implementation, the organization exerts itself at its highest levels. It performs more work and absorbs more stress than at any other time during the change process. The shift from preparation to implementation introduces a whole new set of variables into the organization based on the new activity and resource allocations that are part of making change happen. In other words, things get more rather than less complicated. There are now more moving parts that can interact in all sorts of unpredictable ways, potentially leading to unpredictable and unintended consequences.[8] One of the unavoidable realities of change leadership is that you must first introduce more complexity into the system before you have the opportunity to change it and make it better.

A major change initiative, for example, usually houses hundreds and even thousands of smaller changes within it. One organization that I studied shut down several offices around the country in an effort to reduce its fixed costs and allow more employees to work from home. The new organizational design would be simpler and more efficient, but getting there was quite complicated, because hundreds of tasks had to be scheduled and carefully executed. The change required a dedicated project manager who spent all of his time managing the process using an intricate Gantt chart to manage a critical path of tasks and their contingencies, involving everything from real estate leases to uninterruptible power supplies to new letterhead. Once they accomplished change, however, the new reality was far more simplified.

> *Implementation introduces complexity, which increases the chance of failure.*

Implementation introduces complexity, which increases the chance of failure. But that's not all. What compounds the challenge is that the instant you launch the implementation stage of change, you also lose a measure of control. For change leaders who understand this principle, the temporary trade-off is planned for and expected. For those who don't, it's an unwelcome surprise. Implementation usually means the following:

- More variables and moving parts
- More people involved
- More dependencies
- More assumptions about relationships, cause and effect, performance, and implications
- More opportunity for outside interpretation
- More influence by more participants
- More uncertainty and risk of unintended, unplanned, and undesirable consequences
- More chance of change taking its own path
- More loss of direct knowledge, control, and decision making
- More loss of ability to provide direct observation, guidance, and adjustment

Certainly no leader would purposely choose these conditions without the promise of change.

MANAGING RESISTANCE

Is it any wonder that resistance can surface from anywhere at any time? Once you start implementation, the race is on to achieve early results before you deplete your reserves of stored energy. The problem is that things become a lot less predictable. In my research, I observed a fairly consistent pattern in which change leaders are ambushed by resistance they didn't see or anticipate. On the technical side of change, we normally rely on standard tools such as a schedule, a budget, a formally commissioned team, key measurements, and so forth to gauge how things are going. These tools help monitor progress along the way. We can usually detect a hard-side problem in its early stages, before it becomes a major problem—for example:

- If we are falling behind, our schedule will tell us.
- If we are starting to spend too much, our budget will tell us.
- If technology is not quite doing the job, negative indicators will tell us.

This isn't always true. Sometimes we don't catch technical problems early enough, but we do have tools and instruments to help us predict problems before they happen or identify them when they're small. The bigger challenge is predicting problems on the human side. Leaders often don't understand the principle that governs resistance. Several leaders told me that resistance was just plain unpredictable. Some said that it was arbitrary and that it's pointless to try and prepare for it because you don't know where it will come from or how strong it will be.

The general pattern, then, is that leaders respond to resistance after it has become a problem and threatens the success of change. This is a defensive position that gives the leader very little latitude to maneuver. What if you could spot or predict problems before they happen? What I found is that it's possible to gain a measure of predictive power in dealing with resistance. The key is to understand what the organization and its members care deeply about. One of the most valuable questions that a change leader can ask of the organization and specific individuals is this: "What does the organization, or this individual, cherish?" The answer to that question will normally lead you to those things that the organization will stoutly defend. Peter Senge observes that

> resistance to change is neither capricious nor mysterious. It almost always arises from threats to traditional norms and ways of doing things. Often these norms are woven into the fabric of established power relationships. The norm is entrenched because the distribution of authority and control is entrenched. Rather than pushing harder to overcome resistance to change, artful leaders discern the source of the resistance. They focus directly on the implicit norms and power relationships within which the norms are embedded.[9]

Senge's point of view is helpful as we look at the organization as a whole. It's critical to understand that the prevailing norms of an organization shape dominant behavioral patterns within the culture. It's also important to uncover the distribution of power, both formal and informal, in order to see the patterns of influence that really matter.

But when it comes to assessing individuals, you have to look at impact. This, I believe, is the principle that governs resistance. In case after case, I observe that resistance to change is not proportional to change. It's proportional to the expected personal impact of change.[10] Furthermore, there is often a natural tension between what is in the best interests of the organization and what individual members of the organization want for themselves.

Resistance to change is not proportional to change. It's proportional to the expected personal impact of change.

Resistance to change is not proportional to change. It's proportional to the expected personal impact of change.

Based on this principle, it's possible for relatively small organizational changes to spark enormous resistance if those changes threaten people with enough loss or pain. In several cases, I observed that small changes created a chain reaction that led to the unexpected failure of an entire initiative.

A Mouse of Change, a Lion of Resistance

When major initiatives fail unexpectedly, leaders usually find themselves sifting through the wreckage, looking for clues that might explain what happened. The irony is that with many such cases, the effort begins with good leadership, a solid plan, and ample resources and seems destined to succeed. And yet despite having all of the essential elements presumably in place, it fails.

A closer look reveals a striking pattern in which failure is traceable to small and seemingly insignificant changes within the larger initiative that provoked enormous resistance. I term these small changes *mice* because of their ability to sire lionlike resistance. Let's look at two examples: one of unexpected failure, the other of early failure.

At a midsized luxury goods company, an IT project team was working feverishly to configure a new enterprise computer system to meet a deadline two months away. The team had fallen behind as a result of late requests for new features and functionality and was now working long hours to get back on schedule.

Gradually the company's revenues started dropping off as the economy turned down and consumers backed away from big-ticket purchases. As the company plunged into negative cash flow, leaders attacked the cost side of the business. As part of the effort, they decided to suspend daily overtime pay to IT personnel. On paper, they would save several thousand dollars a month, which was considered a small yet important part of the cost reduction effort. This change became the mouse. The manager of the project tendered his resignation the next week. Two programmers followed him out the door, and the company had to end the project after completing three-quarters of the work.

In this case, senior leadership was obsessing about its liquidity problem and made a foolish exchange: trading some incremental cash flow for a failed major initiative. In the end, the project became a sunk cost three hundred times the savings of the rescinded overtime pay. And the project became an unexpected failure.

Now let's take an example of early failure. At a large manufacturing company, executive management decided to launch a major change initiative to improve its bulging inventory problem. The implementation plan included applying lean manufacturing and automatic replenishment signals to speed up cycle times. The initiative also called for organizational restructuring. All of the functional silos relating to activities from order entry through billing and shipping—everything except manufacturing itself—were to be brought together in a new process-based department to be called "order fulfillment." It was a well-conceived plan that promised a step change improvement.

Midway through the implementation, executive management concluded that it would help the effort if the director of production planning (let's call him Vernon), a respected leader in the organization, relocated to the billing and invoicing wing of the building. They insisted that having Vernon there would break down interdepartmental barriers and foster a new level of cooperation. The initiative had been embroiled in controversy, but the chief operating officer had worked hard to build a coalition to see it through, enlisting Vernon along the way. But Vernon steadfastly resisted the request. When upper management would not relent, his resistance turned into a withdrawal of support for the initiative. Eventually Vernon's negative influence persuaded others to withdraw support for the change. After a few weeks, the coalition supporting the change fractured. Senior management had to back away from the initiative.

POTENTIAL RESISTANCE

In these two examples, the mice were not big changes in magnitude, scope, or duration, but each created a train of consequences that eventually brought down a major initiative. In each case, a mouse led to lionlike resistance—not out of its own size or strength but out of its ability to disrupt. The danger of mice lies in the enormous potential resistance they carry. In fact, a closer examination of mice provides further insight concerning resistance.

Major change initiatives consist of many smaller change elements. In order to implement major change successfully, you have to break down the initiative and assess the potential resistance embedded within the individual elements based on expected personal impact and expected organizational gain.

Resistance is widely regarded as arbitrary because it can come unexpectedly and is often disproportionate to a change. What I find instead is that resistance behaves with remarkable consistency when viewed with these two concepts in mind.

The amount of potential resistance associated with individual change elements results from the interaction of two factors: expected personal impact and expected organizational gain.

First, resistance is largely determined by the expectation of personal impact by those who must pass through it. This means that there is no natural proportional relationship between a change and the resistance it provokes. Indeed, the size and significance of a change may be a poor indicator of the potential resistance it may cause. A small change—even what appears to be a trivial change—can ignite enormous resistance because it springs from how people perceive the impact rather than the size or importance of the change.

With Vernon, for example, leadership failed to appreciate the disruptive potential of moving him. In fact, they were surprised at his resistance. The change request was a small thing in absolute terms, but what management failed to do was examine the change from the perspective of personal impact to Vernon even though he was a linchpin opinion leader whose support was critical. To Vernon, an office move would strip him of his local network, social ties, power base, and channels of communication. The disruptive potential reflected the perceived personal cost to Vernon rather than some proportional reflection of the change.

In a contrasting example, a professional services firm on the verge of business failure was acquired by a financially strong firm. News of an acquisition can provoke strong resistance among affected employees, but there was no such reaction in this case. Despite the prospect of massive change, employees met the news and subsequent integration process with cooperation. Obviously they were happy to be rescued.

The second determining factor of resistance is that of organizational gain. A perception among employees that a proposed change will clearly benefit the organization can lessen what might otherwise be strong resistance. Unless employees are severely disaffected, an organization's strategy and goals matter to its employees at some level. So when employees understand how the organization stands to benefit from change, they become more willing to endure the personal impact of change if they feel convinced that it will contribute meaningfully to the organization's direction and success.

A billion-dollar software company was acquired by a competitor that was about the same size. The acquired company had grown up under the leadership of a benevolent founder, who had instilled a hardworking yet comfortable culture. Among the many symbols of this culture were the free soda and ice pops that filled the hundreds of refrigerators throughout the campus.

One of the first acts of leadership by the acquiring firm was to eliminate these low-cost perks. Certainly this change had almost no economic impact, but it was a deliberate attempt to signal a new culture and approach within the newly merged organization. According to management, the impact of this change created an estimated loss in productivity of 25 percent and dealt a powerful blow to initial attempts to merge the organizations. Employees saw no real organizational gain associated with the change. What they did see was bravado rather than judgment on the part of the new leaders. This perception of intent served only to intensify resistance to overall merger integration activities. Over the next eighteen months, merger integration efforts foundered until the acquired company was resold to another competitor. Certainly soda and ice pops weren't the sole cause of failure, but the change created a negative catalyst that prompted further resistance.

THE GAIN/IMPACT MATRIX

Major potential resistance may lurk under all kinds of small changes. There is no surefire way to measure it, but there is a degree of predictive power available to leaders who carefully evaluate the expected personal impact and organizational gain of individual change elements ahead of time.

After evaluating hundreds of small changes in an attempt to understand potential resistance better, I see a clear pattern around the two dimensions that I've discussed: (1) expected personal

FIGURE 8.1. GAIN/IMPACT MATRIX.

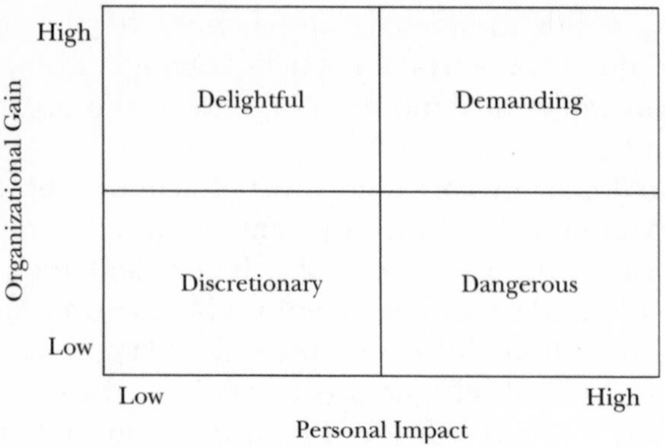

impact and (2) expected organizational gain. Combining these two dimensions distills four separate types of change. Employees seem instinctively to sort change elements along similar lines. The good news is that you can help avoid early or unexpected failure in your initiatives if you evaluate individual change elements in the same way before implementation.

Shown in Figure 8.1 are the two dimensions of expected personal impact and organizational gain organized into a two-by-two matrix, thus yielding four different kinds of change: discretionary, delightful, demanding, and dangerous.

DISCRETIONARY CHANGE

Discretionary changes are low in both expected organizational gain and personal impact. They are optional and nonessential. An organization can take or leave a discretionary change without causing either undue injury or the loss of significant value. Discretionary changes require little organizational preparation because they don't significantly disrupt the status quo. They may ruffle employees but not enough to provoke strong, broad-based resistance. Most discretionary changes are simply a matter of preference. Examples might include minor modifications to process,

FIGURE 8.2. DISCRETIONARY CHANGE.

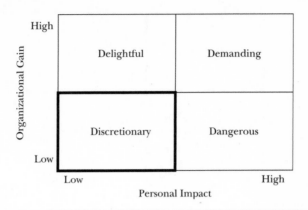

policy, or technology. Or they might include bigger changes that employees simply won't feel because they don't reach far enough to have an impact on them directly, such as with changing a minor supplier, an accounting policy, or a marketing campaign.

Figure 8.2 shows the gain/impact matrix with the lower left quadrant outlined in bold to represent discretionary change.

DELIGHTFUL CHANGE

Delightful changes are high in organizational gain but low in personal impact. In other words, they represent a significant return for a relatively small investment. They don't come around very often, so they are changes to relish. They usually represent a breakthrough in performance and release positive energy. If a delightful change fails on implementation, there is typically little disruption because delightful changes have little impact on the everyday lives of employees.

Dependent changes are less common because most major changes that are high in organizational gain have a deep impact on people. On occasion, however, there are important changes that don't cause great disruption to employees on a personal level. Examples are outsourcing the development of a new product,

FIGURE 8.3. DELIGHTFUL CHANGE.

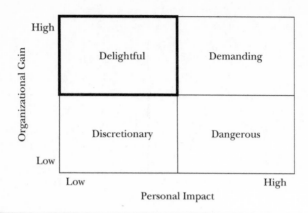

obtaining approval for a new patent, building a greenfield manufacturing facility, lobbying for and obtaining new legislation to
reduce taxes on major capital equipment expenditures, or gaining
a new round of funding for a start-up company. Each of these
changes carries high strategic importance yet exerts little direct
impact on employees.

Figure 8.3 shows the gain/impact matrix with the upper left
quadrant outlined in bold to represent delightful change.

DEMANDING CHANGE

Demanding changes are high in both organizational gain and
personal impact. They are necessary when an organization has to
learn to adapt and compete in a new way. They are critical to the
ongoing competitive advantage of organizations, yet they unavoid-
ably affect people in significant ways. Most major change initiatives
that organizations undertake fall into the demanding category.
They require a large investment of time and resources and, most
of all, energy. Without effective leadership, good planning, and
ample resources, demanding changes can't be implemented successfully. They aren't quick or easy. Rather, they usually require

significant preparation and time to produce desired results. Most significant changes to structure, process, systems, and roles and responsibilities represent demanding changes.

The difference between a demanding change and a dangerous change is that demanding changes is usually critical to the implementation of the major initiative due to their strategic importance. These are changes that can't be put off. For example, a biotechnology company decided to pursue a new direct sales model in which it would hire part-time sales professionals. This shift required the existing sales force to move to part-time status, which meant a significant reduction in base pay and benefits, or leave the organization. The change exacted a high personal cost on current employees, but it was fundamental to the new sales model and therefore of high strategic importance.

Figure 8.4 shows the gain/impact matrix with the upper right quadrant outlined in bold to represent demanding change.

DANGEROUS CHANGE

Dangerous change, or what I refer to as mice, combines low organizational gain with high personal impact. It offers little of real value yet brings with it significant personal disruption. This occurs because people normally resist the strongest those

FIGURE 8.4. DEMAND CHANGE.

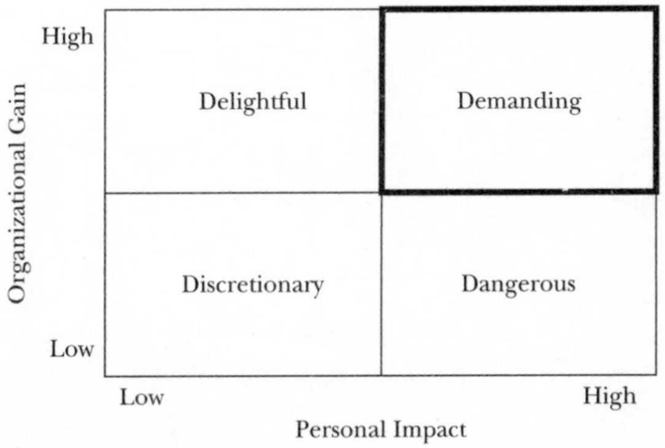

changes that threaten them with the greatest personal impact. The difference between a dangerous change and a demanding one is the perception and understanding of organizational gain. In other words, does the change really matter? Will it contribute to the strategy, growth, and success of the organization? Will it make a difference in helping the organization reach its goals?

A dangerous change, or mouse, is dangerous because the initial resistance that the change creates can spread and grow into something that puts a change initiative in jeopardy. It works according to the familiar concepts of catalyst, momentum, and critical mass but in a negative direction. Out of the expectation of high personal impact, a mouse may sire a lion of resistance—in other words, a disproportionately large amount of resistance that can build until the forces restraining change overtake the forces driving it. The mouse acts as a negative catalyst that creates reverse momentum. In some cases, the mouse can gain such strong and sweeping momentum that it eventually reaches critical mass in a negative direction and takes down the entire effort.

Figure 8.5 shows the gain/impact matrix with the lower right quadrant outlined in bold to represent dangerous change.

FIGURE 8.5. DANGEROUS CHANGE.

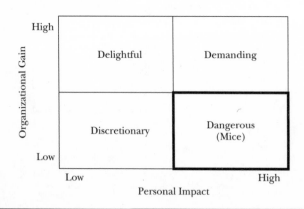

CATCHING MICE

Why do leaders fail to see and catch mice? It's not that they are heedless of the toll of change on their organizations or that they have an unguided impulse to initiate it. Many have good instincts about how to go about it. It's simply counterintuitive to focus on things that seem to be of lesser importance. You don't see mice if you're not looking for them. To most leaders, mice represent an unfamiliar category.

Mice are dangerous not only because they can create such exquisite disruption but also because they tend to be too small to attract attention in the first place. For example, a college president in a Great Lakes state had to make deep cuts to the operating budget because enrollment has decreased sharply and state funding was down by 15 percent. After trimming costs from the academic and administrative areas of the budget, there was another $300,000 that had to be cut from athletics. A task force of professors put forward the recommendation to cut the hockey program and close the ice rink. The board of trustees came together for a meeting to approve the measure. Members of the community, where hockey was deeply rooted in the culture, swarmed into the board meeting with hockey sticks and pounded them on the ground in angry protest until the board changed its decision. It took years to reestablish trust between the college and community. The president and faculty understood the cultural importance of hockey; they simply believed that every part of the college should have to share in the sacrifice. They never considered that there would be an outright revolt.

Once leaders understand the mice category, they can take a different approach to examining their major initiatives. To catch the mice that may be nesting in major initiatives, I suggest the following practical steps:

1. *Plan.* Break down the initiative into tasks. In the field of project management, this is called creating a work breakdown structure. Once you have the breakdown complete and documented, identify any elements that might be in the dangerous category. Prioritize them and determine the ones you consider

the biggest threats. Identify those elements that carry potential resistance by creating significant personal impact in the following areas:

- Formal authority and informal influence
- Relationships
- Communication of and access to information
- Compensation, benefits, and privileges
- Roles and responsibilities, both formal and informal
- Technical skill requirements

For each individual change element that will likely create significant personal impact, determine whether the element is essential to the success of the initiative. Put yourself in the place of employees and try to perceive the impact the way they would. Better yet, ask them. Gather as much information from members of the coalition or other sources of information about perceptions or potential perceptions of certain change elements. In the end, you will have to make educated judgments regarding the net impact.

2. *Analyze.* Elements that are nonessential to initiative success are potential mice. Ask yourself whether these elements can be eliminated, postponed, or modified. For essential elements that will create personal cost but are strategically important, determine if those elements can be piloted or implemented on a trial basis. Also determine how you can increase the perceived strategic importance of these elements among employees.

3. *Decide.* Decide on a course of action to:

- Eliminate this individual change element altogether.
- Postpone or delay the implementation of this change element.
- Modify the change element before you implement it to lessen its impact.
- Implement the change element as is, based on your determination that it is critical to overall success and that there is no way to eliminate, postpone, or modify the element. Do it with more planning, communication, and support with the idea that you will encounter resistance, but manage it as effectively as you can. You may be able to pilot or test the change element on a trial basis to better understand the likely success of the element but also the likely resistance you should anticipate.

4. *Monitor.* Monitor the ongoing pulse and morale, energy levels, and specific reactions and responses to new change elements as you introduce them.

You should always look first to the fundamental aspects of planning and wise resource allocation as critical to leading successful change. But given the disruptive potential of mice, you should look a second time to see if any are nesting in your initiative. Not catching a mouse can turn into a serious miscalculation of resistance that stops an important change initiative dead in its tracks.

Summary

Key Points

- The first five energy sources in the EPIC methodology are based on people, reputation, ideas, and emotion. At some point, every change effort must cross over to the realm of tangible evidence by generating actual results.
- The span of uncertainty is the length of time an individual is willing to give discretionary effort without seeing actual results.
- The immediate goal of the implementation stage of change is to achieve early results in order to replenish energy.
- One of the keys to achieving early results is setting goals that meet five important criteria. The goals should be truly achievable, outwardly visible, easy to measure, easy to communicate, and symbolically important.
- The implementation stage of change introduces more complexity and reduces the control of the leader, both of which increase the chance of failure.
- Resistance to change is not proportional to change. It is proportional to the expected personal impact of change.
- The amount of potential resistance associated with individual change elements within a larger initiative results from the interaction of two factors: expected personal impact and expected organizational gain.

- The gain/impact matrix is a model that reveals four types of change based on the possible combinations of organizational gain and personal impact. Discretionary changes are low in expected organizational gain and personal impact. They are nonessential or optional. Delightful changes are low in personal impact yet high in organizational gain. They represent a significant return on investment. Demanding changes are high in organizational gain and personal impact. They represent the vast majority of large-scale organizational change initiatives. Dangerous changes — or mice — combine low organizational gain with high personal impact. They offer little or no value to the organization yet result in significant personal disruption.
- Leaders should follow a systematic process to analyze the individual elements of a change initiative in order to identify potential mice. That process should begin in the planning stage.
- Once a leader identifies a potential mouse in the larger change initiative, he or she should decide on a course of action based on four options: (1) eliminate the individual change element altogether, (2) postpone or delay the implementation of the element, (3) modify the change element to lessen its impact, or (4) implement the change element based on a determination that it is necessary.

PART FIVE

CONSOLIDATE

Having sustained rather than temporary results is the goal of change. In the end, if you can't put something in place that lasts at least long enough to create new value during the next strategy cycle, all of your efforts will have been in vain. The tragedy about late-stage failure is that it's almost always preventable. It stems most often from one of two sources:

- A basic misunderstanding of the change process and what is required to make change stick
- The fundamental motivations and weaknesses of the change leader

In both cases, failure results because those who are guiding the effort either never understood or have lost sight of basic principles of organizational change. In the end, unless change can become firmly established within an organization, it remains partially or wholly reversible.

The word *consolidation* captures the final stage of the change process perhaps better than any other. It derives from Latin roots that literally mean "to bring together" and "to make solid."

Consolidate: Latin consolidatus: con, together + solidare, to make solid. To make or become solid, strong, stable, firmly established. In other words, to make change stick.

The reason consolidation is a separate stage of change is that it's quite different from the implementation stage with its thrust of effort and production of early results. Cases of failed change demonstrate repeatedly that the process is fragile, even after that process produces the intended positive results. Case after case proves that backsliding is a constant threat. Change can unravel at any time if it's not yet rooted in the organization.

The gradual descent of the power curve during consolidation indicates two important facts. First, the energy requirements for change begin to decrease as the amount of incremental change work drops. Second, the process of consolidation is slow. You can't artificially expedite the consolidation process within an organization. In the figure here, the arrow indicates the gradual descent of the consolidation stage.

THE GRADUAL DESCENT OF CONSOLIDATION.

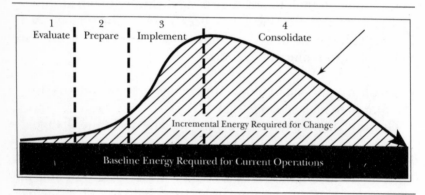

CHAPTER NINE

CONSOLIDATE WITH SUSTAINED RESULTS

Genius is the power to make continuous effort.
BENJAMIN DISRAELI, BRITISH PRIME MINISTER

CONSOLIDATE WITH SUSTAINED RESULTS.

EPIC Stage	1 Evaluate	2 Prepare	3 Implement	4 Consolidate
The Leader's Role	**Equilibrium Step** Supply energy for the ongoing evaluation of competitive reality, internal performance, and change alternatives.	**Ignition Step** Replenish energy to supply a gradual increase in work performed and stress absorbed during preparation.	**Refueling Step** Replenish energy to supply a significant increase in work performed and stress absorbed during implementation.	**Refueling Step** Replenish energy to supply a gradual decrease in work performed and stress absorbed during consolidation.
Energy Sources	**1. Agility**	1. Agility **2. Urgency** **3. Credibility** **4. Coalition** **5. Vision**	1. Agility 2. Urgency 3. Credibility 4. Coalition 5. Vision **6. Early Results**	1. Agility 2. Urgency 3. Credibility 4. Coalition 5. Vision 6. Early Results **7. Sustained Results**

A major teaching hospital had a balance of more than $300 million that patients, insurance companies, and government entities owed and hadn't paid. The mountain of delinquent receivables was growing at the rate of about $2 million a month. The hospital administrator had given directive after directive to collect the money. He had explained the importance of good cash flow and fiscal health. Someone told him that "what gets measured gets done," so he instituted new weekly reporting with more metrics going to more people who had a hand in the hospital's revenue cycle. He threatened the CFO's job and members of his staff if they didn't get collections under control. They didn't, so he fired the CFO.

Clearly understanding her charge to fix the problem, the new CFO commissioned a cross-functional team to figure out why this was happening and reverse the trend. The team consisted of several finance and accounting staff members, as well as the directors of patient access (registration), patient accounts, case management, and health information management (coding). After conducting a three-week assessment and digging into every aspect of the hospital's revenue cycle, the team found the following information:

- Nearly half of the $300 million that the hospital was owed was older than ninety days.
- One of every five of its claims was being denied by payers due to incorrect patient information.
- Its gross days in accounts receivables were over one hundred.
- Its bad-debt write-offs had increased by 27 percent from the previous year.

With the findings in hand, the CFO and her team set a goal to reduce collections by $10 million a year. They put in place several measures to address the root causes of the problem. After three months, cash collections started increasing by $1 million per month. At the end of the first year, the hospital's receivables balance was down $13 million from the prior year. The administrator, the CFO, and the rest of the administrative staff were elated with the progress. The next month, the CFO accepted a new position as administrator of a children's hospital in a different state, and a new CFO took over. Six months later, the hospital's receivables balance ballooned to more than $300 million once again.

What happened in this example is all too common. The organization was well on its way to accomplish its change objectives but then let it all slip away. Things went right back to the way they were because the change was never consolidated.

THE MILLION-DOLLAR DRAWER

I met with a CEO once who showed me a drawer in his filing cabinet. Pointing to the overstuffed folders that filled the drawer, he exclaimed with mock pride, "This is my million-dollar drawer." He went on to explain that the drawer was filled with plans for change initiatives that never materialized. Over the years, the organization had literally paid more than a million dollars to commission studies and draw up plans that were now doing nothing but gathering dust. All had been tried, and all had failed.

Many organizations have a million-dollar drawer. Either literally or figuratively, somewhere in the company is a drawer full of archived ideas that challenged the gospel of the status quo and lost. Everything in the drawer was at one time considered a good idea. What's also true is that invariably many of the ideas are perfectly sound and should have accomplished their aims, but they fell apart soon after implementation. There are many reasons for failure. But there is one human-side reason that we can't ignore because it happens so often: change often fails out of neglect before it has time enough to consolidate. This is primarily an execution failure in which leaders cease to manage the point of action.

Change uncoils when leaders cease to manage the point of action.

The point of action is where plans become real and tasks are performed. It's where leaders ensure that work gets done. It means holding people accountable to perform their assignments properly and on time. It's a spectacularly simple concept but not easy to do. Of course, failure is never intentional, but leaving the point of action can be. As a result, change unwinds before it consolidates.

WHY LEADERS FAIL TO CONSOLIDATE CHANGE

The moment you commit to a change imperative, the organization trades the carried risk of the status quo for unknown risk of change, and it's difficult to turn back. Once the boats are in the water and the planes are in the air, it's no small thing to turn them back to dock and landing strip. So the mere contemplation of major change should be done cautiously, with a full realization of what's on the table. You have to carefully weigh the risk of action against inaction. You need commitment firmly in hand before you set your course. Change demands extraordinary fidelity to the effort from beginning to end.

Starting and stopping change initiatives can become a business addiction and a serious organizational pathology. Some leaders grow fond of flitting to and fro among the vast array of glittering options for improvement and innovation. In my research, I asked, "Why do leaders take their hands off the wheel when change is progressing nicely and results are starting to appear?" I discovered that leaders are seduced into error for several reasons, all of which tend toward ill-conceived and ill-fated change. Let me review several pitfalls and then discuss what I believe are the proper motivations that should drive a change effort.

PITFALL 1: CONFUSING CRITICAL MASS WITH CONSOLIDATION

The most common reason leaders walk away from the point of action is they mistakenly believe that change will become self-executing because there is what appears to be irreversible momentum. The first appearance of results creates renewed energy that the change effort needs during the implementation stage. If positive results continue, they generate significant energy and relieve the leader of having to rely exclusively on the first five energy sources to keep the effort going.

At this point, change often crests at the top of the power curve, indicating critical mass, or what Malcolm Gladwell has popularized as the "tipping point."[1] With critical mass, the energy requirements for change start to decrease due to the momentum.

FIGURE 9.1.   CRITICAL MASS ON THE POWER CURVE.

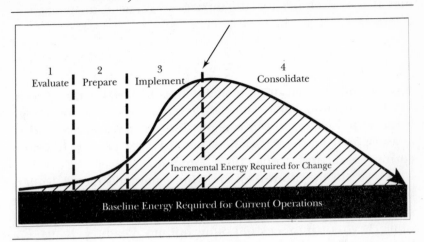

Sometimes the positive results of change are so energizing at the top of the power curve that it seems the change can slide effortlessly down the back side toward consolidation like a surfer ridding a wave. The arrow in Figure 9.1 indicates the top of the power curve, or crest, referring to critical mass.

But this is a false positive. Although change may now require less energy, it still needs direction, coordination, communication, and accountability. These basic leadership requirements never go away, yet leaders often naively behave as if the change process can run by itself. What they miss is that change is not yet rooted into the culture of the organization. It remains perilously fragile even though it has produced positive results.

> *Regardless of positive results, change remains fragile until it is rooted in culture.*

The distinction between consolidation and critical mass is essential to successful organizational change. Confusing the two leads to a false sense of success and completion and causes many to step away from the point of action.

PITFALL 2: TAKING ON TOO MUCH CHANGE

Taking on too much change at once can lead to outrunning your resources. In one case that I studied, a CEO attempted three mergers at one time. The merger integration work was so intense that it overwhelmed the organization's capacity to manage it. There are limits to change capacity.

PITFALL 3: GETTING DISTRACTED

Another pitfall is lacking the ability to concentrate and perform steady, unexciting labor, which is often the very essence of change leadership. Leaders in this category like to play with alternatives as a respite from the mundane. They start new projects based on curiosity and a way to quell their boredom.

Once they're drawn to something new, distracted leaders break with the previous affair, thinking the erstwhile interest will simply die a quiet, ignominious death of benign neglect while they return to seek out other options. Leading change is a labor-intensive, often inglorious affair. But for distracted leaders, it quickly loses its luster. To think that a change initiative can die quietly after an organization has been deliberately disturbed is a destructive fiction, but it happens all the time, leaving piles of false starts and beleaguered employees.

PITFALL 4: IMITATING THE COMPETITION

This pattern afflicts legions of unreflecting conformists. Those in this category, though possessed of good intentions, move into major change efforts without really understanding how they fit with long-term strategy. Me-too leaders imitate rather than innovate, free riding on the business models of the competition. They suffer not from bad motive but poor judgment and a susceptibility to touted results. They accept the latest management trends without thinking deeply about their own organizations, the real merit of an idea, or the fit between the two. When asked why they are embracing a new initiative, they often respond by cataloging the claims of its promoters and the testimonials of its poster executives as proof that it works. Those who can't resist the beckoning call of what's new end up suffering from flavor-of-the-month programmitis.

PITFALL 5: INCESSANT TINKERING

Another pitfall is incessant and needless tinkering—and not just at the margins but with the organization's core strategies, systems, and structure. Sparked with new ideas or smitten with technology, tinkering leaders experiment constantly. They start new projects before old ones reach fruition. They follow their muse, but this try-everything approach slowly erodes the agility of the organization.

You should foster a learning organization, an inclination for calculated risk taking, and an ethos of continuous improvement. Innovation and challenging conventional wisdom are the staples of progress. But the idea that probability will eventually reward you is the preserve of the research lab and not normally tolerable to the larger business entity that must spend most of its time trying to remove variability rather than introduce it. Change initiatives are not fungible. They don't contain interchangeable parts. They aren't clinical trials.

PITFALL 6: HOARDING

Leaders who hoard never learned that the essence of strategy is the reduction of alternatives. Hoarders are loath to foreclose an option and prone to mistake strategic opportunism for being all things to all people. They are acquisitive because they don't recognize the necessity of trade-offs. You can find them purposely putting themselves at sea and trolling for new ideas—not to exchange but to add to their already full nets. They catch but don't release. They refuse to cull the critical few from the trivial many.

PITFALL 7: CHANGE FATIGUE

Managing the point of action is tedious work, but it's critical to success. Change requires the grinding discipline of good execution, and there's no substitute for it. Unfortunately, resistance and inertia often win through a war of attrition. Especially with major change, you may underestimate the required commitment.

Fatigue becomes a factor especially when results are suspended and morale is low. Leading change almost always requires physical stamina and emotional drive. When you start feeling like a grief counselor and a triage nurse, understand that this *is* in your job description as a change leader.

A weary leader is prone to rationalize away the need to manage the point of action. Realizing that change is a long march, the tired leader is tempted to let go of the wheel and defend the absentee landlord approach with romantic notions like, "I manage the dream. I do strategy. I sponsor change." Tired leaders also have the habit of abdicating a change initiative early if they can save face and point to unintended consequences as the culprit.

When this happens repeatedly, all change initiatives take on an ad hoc quality. The leader becomes the bottleneck of commitment whose pace the organization cannot exceed. It's easy to forget that real change leadership requires endurance long after the emotion that surrounded the decision to launch dissipates.

PITFALL 8: STAYING IN FASHION

Another pitfall afflicts those who display an almost mindless devotion to hero worship. Out of a compulsive need to keep company with the larger-than-life CEOs of the day, fashionable leaders tend to mimic their admirers. They need attention and fear obscurity. They love and leave on the basis of popular opinion and the social mirror. If it doesn't appeal to the ego, move on. It's a titillating thing to accessorize with the best. Thus, fashionable leaders are all too quick to commit company resources to pursue yet another transitory fling based on infatuation.

PITFALL 9: PARANOIA

Those who become paranoid embrace change initiatives with abandon, fearing they will fall behind. They overcompensate to ensure that their organizations don't get stale and caught in the grip of debilitating inertia. They adhere to conventional wisdom as a way to stay competitive. They practice management-by-best-seller, reading hyperbolic business books that speak of revolutions, obliterating reality, and overthrowing the order of things, and then feel an unguided impulse to act. The paranoid are seduced out of fear and a belief that disaster lurks around the corner. But failure often comes as the consequence of too many course corrections.

PITFALL 10: UNBRIDLED PERSONAL AMBITION

Aspiring leaders often rearrange the furniture not because the organization needs it but because they want to prove something and promote their upward mobility. Driven by self-interest, they see organizational needs as incidental to hankering personal ambition and status aspiration. They become restless to gain notice. For someone who wants to be a hero, the organization is a facilitative instrument through which a career is advanced. People are second to adrenaline rush. With little concern for the costs incurred, an overaspiring leader engages in rivalry and contends for dominance. He or she sorts change options according to what appears personally lucrative because the organization is secondary to personal agenda.

CHECK YOUR MOTIVATION AND UNDERSTANDING

Organizational pathologies don't come from organizations; they come from leaders. All of the propensities just reviewed reveal leaders who lack the proper motivation to lead change. None of the motivations that I've outlined should be the driving force. Each is likely to fall short of generating the sustained energy required to secure institutional commitment and consolidate change. If you choose to pursue change outside of deep conviction and constancy of purpose, your effort will probably break down at some point in the process.

The most effective change leaders whom I have observed pursue change out of some combination of the following considerations:

- They view change as the last alternative.
- They understand the stakes organizationally and from a human perspective.

- Their express goal is to add value and increase competitiveness.
- They have expectations that the journey will be full of challenges, uncertainty, resistance, and possibly unintended consequences.
- They test their options.
- They cross a threshold of conviction before they begin.
- They clearly understand how change is linked to strategy.

If you move forward with change, do it with resolve—with slavish attention and rapt commitment to stay the course. Remember that leaders who truly understand change demonstrate a relentless commitment to see it through. Ask yourself the following questions?

- What is my current change agenda?
- Does it reflect a bias to change the least to get the most?
- Have any important change initiatives failed during the past year or two?
- Did any fail because leadership selected the wrong strategy?
- Did any fail because leadership didn't have the skills to execute change properly?
- Did any fail because leadership lacked the proper motivation?

Understanding Consolidation

To achieve consolidation, it's helpful to understand the way change roots itself within an organization. Consolidation occurs as change sinks, level by level, into the organizational soil. There are three levels of change that a change effort must pass through before it reaches consolidation. If the leader fails to manage the point of action for any reason before change reaches the third level, there is always the chance that change will unravel. To explain the three levels of change, I will use the example of installing a major computer system.

Level 1: Structural Change

The first level of change is structural. Structural change occurs when the nonbehavioral aspects of change are prepared. Nonbehavioral aspects of change relate to structure, systems, process, technology, and legalities. In the example of a major systems implementation, structural change is accomplished when the necessary hardware is procured, the system configured and installed, and the system brought online. Structural change implies that all of the resources, tools, and conditions are made ready for implementation.

Level 2: Behavioral Change

Change moves to the behavioral level when people begin to behave differently under new conditions and with the aid of new or different resources. For a major systems implementation, when people have access to learn and use the system and begin doing so, there is behavioral change, but that behavioral change is only compliance based. There are still many obstacles to overcome. For example, people may not like the new system, or they may not understand how to use it very well, or the system may or may not be better than the old one. When change progresses to the behavioral level, the behavior given to support change may or may not be willing behavior. It certainly isn't behavior that has become routine. Finally, with behavioral change, the results of change often result in higher frustration and lower productivity, so there is no outwardly confirming evidence that change has made things better. In the short term, the organization might be worse off, a situation that only strengthens any resisting forces.

In one accounting systems implementation that I studied, accounting personnel were trained in the new system, but it took three months before they felt comfortable using it. In the meantime, they had to run the old and new accounting systems on parallel tracks until they were confident that they had removed the bugs from the new system and that people were proficient enough to leave the old system behind. All the while, several staff accountants were frustrated and wanted to go back to the old system. It was especially taxing at the end of the month when the department had to close the accounting books in both systems. The change had created a great deal of incremental work and stress. At any point during implementation, neglecting the point of action would almost surely have guaranteed implementation failure.

LEVEL 3: CULTURAL CHANGE

Business author and editor Thomas Stewart makes the point that "for change to be anything but superficial and temporary, it must be systemic."[2] But what makes it systemic? Beyond being written into the business rules of a new IT system, the answer is "culture." Unless change finds purchase in the elements of culture, it won't last. The principle of cultural change acknowledges that it's not only possible but also common to change behavior before we change minds. Cultural change occurs when the culture supports change. By *culture* I mean the held norms, habits, assumptions, attitudes, beliefs, and values of an organization. This is clearly the most difficult part of change. Culture changes last.[3] It's the most stubborn element in any change effort because it takes people time to internalize, accept, and support change even though they may already be supporting it behaviorally. People want and need time to verify the need for change-based confirming evidence. They want time to internalize change and make it their own, especially if they had nothing to do with its design. They need time to psychologically adjust to a new reality because "thinking within the organization gets grooved."[4] It takes time to carve new grooves and overcome the artifacts of the past.

Table 9.1 summarizes the three layers of change based on the example of a major systems implementation I've described.

Almost without exception, leaders who engineer organizational transformations are quick to acknowledge the primacy of culture. Commenting on his quest to revamp the medical systems giant McKesson, CEO John Hammergren said,

> The first, very quickly, was the realization that this was going to be a long march—not one of those quick-turnaround stories. In my experience, quick turnarounds are usually financial rather than cultural and performance turnarounds. And a quick turnaround, typically involving some kind of financial engineering, doesn't necessarily position a company for success. McKesson has been around for 172 years, so my goal was to make sure it could sustain itself for another 172. I knew that the turnaround was going to take years, not months, and I needed to get that point across.[5]

TABLE 9.1. THE THREE LAYERS OF CHANGE.

Level	Definition	Example
Level 1: Structural change	A condition in which the nonbehavioral aspects of change are prepared	The configuration and installation of a new software system
Level 2: Behavioral change	A condition in which there is compliance-based behavioral support for change	The use of the new software, which may or may not produce performance improvement
Level 3: Cultural change	A condition in which the organization's culture—held norms, habits, assumptions, attitudes, beliefs, and values—supports change[a]	The acceptance, familiarity, comfort, and proficiency of users in using the new software system[b]

[a]Edgar Schein defines *culture* as "a basic set of assumptions that defines for us what we pay attention to, what things mean, how to react emotionally to what is going on, and what actions to take in various kinds of situations." *Organizational Culture and Leadership*, 3rd ed. (San Francisco: Jossey-Bass, 2004), p. 32.

[b]Gene W. Dalton, "Influence and Organizational Change," in Kurt Sandholtz (ed.), *Insight and Responsibility* (Provo, Utah: Novations Group, 2000). Dalton emphasizes the idea that consolidation comes through personal internalization of change, which comes by "verification through experience," meaning that the positive results have a confirming effect that induces personal ownership.

Another successful change leader, Louis Gerstner, the former chairman of IBM, summed up his experience this way: "The hardest part was neither the technological nor economic transformations required. It was changing the culture—the mindset and instincts of hundreds of thousands of people."[6]

Based on the three levels of change, it becomes clear why so many change initiatives fail to achieve consolidation after they achieve results.[7] Most initiatives show results long before consolidation because change has progressed through the structural and behavioral levels of the process. But real consolidation may still be a distance off. Until the roots of change sink into the culture of the organization, you should assume that the culture will be working against you. As John Ehrenfeld, the executive director of the International Society for Industrial Ecology, concludes, "In the final analysis, underlying cultural values will always trump technology and design in determining behavior."[8]

FEEDING AND STARVING

How do you embed change in the culture to achieve consolidation? Again, the answer is to manage the point of action. Specifically, the key to success is to feed the sources of energy and starve the sources of resistance at the tactical and operational levels.[9] When leaders do this consistently over time, change gradually embeds itself into the culture, providing the opportunity to unleash the power of the seventh and final energy source: sustained results.

Getting to consolidation is seldom easy: you can usually count on some unanticipated challenges to come your way, you may not see results for a long time, you may encounter resistance from new stakeholders, you may face unintended consequences. A host of things could go wrong. Given the things that can and will go wrong, the only way to consolidate change is to manage the point of action and constantly feed and starve the effort. Ask yourself and others:

> *Sustained results are the only energy source strong enough to consolidate change.*

- What factors are driving change? How can I feed them?
- What factors are resisting change? How can I starve them?

To help you be systematic in your approach, ask these questions in reference to the following eight areas:

People

- Who is energizing the change?
- Who is de-energizing the change?

- Are there people whose long-term support is essential to consolidate change?
- Are there people who will seriously threaten success along the way?
- What can you do to feed the energizers and starve the de-energizers?[10]

Structure, Roles, and Responsibilities

- Is organizational structure promoting the coordination and communication necessary for change, or is it getting in the way?
- Are people's roles and responsibilities clearly established?
- Is there clear ownership and accountability for various aspects of the change project, or are there areas of confusion?

Behavior and Skills

- Are leaders modeling the proper behavior to move change forward?
- Are some becoming a stumbling block?
- Do people possess the necessary skills to embrace change and make it work?
- Are there skill requirements that threaten the success of change?

Process and Systems

- Do current processes and systems support change or get in the way?
- Are new processes and systems being put in place that will support change if the current ones are inadequate?
- Which specific processes and systems are creating obstacles for change?

Policy and Procedures

- Do current policies and procedures support change or get in the way?
- Are the necessary changes to policies and procedures being made to support change?
- What are the biggest potential obstacles?

Tools and Technology

- Do you have the right tools and technology to enable change?
- What tools and technology are working to promote change?
- What tools and technology are getting in the way?
- Will tools and technology require behavioral compliance in support of change before the culture can catch up?

Time and Resources

- Do you have enough time and resources to accomplish change?
- If not, what can you do to extend what you have or use it more efficiently?

Culture (Values, Habits, Beliefs, and Assumptions)

- What aspects of the organization's culture are supportive of change?
- What aspects are unsupportive?
- Does culture dangerously threaten the change initiative?
- If so, what can you do about it?

If you consistently feed and starve the right things, change will become consolidated. It will become embedded and internalized in the culture and yield sustained results. With sustained results, the organization enters into a virtuous cycle in which the results support the new behavior and the behavior supports the new results. Over time, this dynamic recasts the organizational culture until the organization won't spring back to past.

Exhibit 9.1 is a simple template to guide your analysis and planning.

AFTER THE EXCITEMENT IS GONE

I have yet to meet a single leader who hasn't, at one time or another, left the point of action too soon. Accounts of change unraveling instead of proceeding on to consolidation are found in every organization. Leaving the point of action before consolidation usually erases all of the gains and turns the entire initiative into a complete waste of time and effort.

EXHIBIT 9.1. FEEDING AND STARVING TEMPLATE.

Driving Force	Feeding Plan
1.	
2.	
3.	
Restraining Force	Starving Plan
1.	
2.	
3.	

I've rehearsed some of the pitfalls that explain why this happens, such as getting bored, or tired, or busy. Without exception, leaders tell me that it happens frequently. More than anything else, consolidation is about feeding and starving and continuing to manage the point of action. Embedding change into the culture requires stamina and concentration. You must continue to feed driving forces and starve restraining forces.

Even after change is implemented and providing the hoped-for benefits, there are usually pockets of resistance and ongoing obstacles. Restraining forces are many times starving but not dead. They can reassert themselves powerfully if given the chance. For the long term, consolidation results from continuously:

- Feeding and starving
- Measuring
- Adjusting
- Communicating
- Reinforcing, rewarding, and recognizing

Summary

Key Points

- The final stage of the EPIC process is consolidation, which implies making change solid, strong, stable, and firmly established — in other words, making change stick. During consolidation, the energy requirements for change decrease as the requirements for change work decline, indicated by the gradual descent of the power curve.
- Change can unravel after it produces initial results unless it is deeply rooted in the organization. Most late-stage failures relate to unconsolidated change.
- Leaders must manage the point of action in order to consolidate change. There are several reasons leaders fail to do this, the most common of which is confusing consolidation with critical mass. Critical mass indicates only the beginning of the consolidation process. It is the point at which change gains significant momentum through early results and begins to consume less energy than it did during implementation.
- If a leader steps back from the point of action when change reaches critical mass, the effort will likely fail because it still requires direction, coordination, communication, and accountability.
- Leaders should assess their understanding and motivations concerning organizational change before they launch an initiative in order to reduce the risk of failure. Successful change requires deep conviction and constancy of purpose.
- Change consolidates by progressing through three separate levels of change: structural, behavioral, and cultural. Structural change is a

condition in which the nonbehavioral aspects of change are prepared. Behavioral change is a condition in which there is compliance-based behavioral support for change. Cultural change is a condition in which the organization's culture supports change.

- Consolidation requires that leaders tactically and systematically feed the factors that drive change and starve the factors that resist change. Feeding and starving activity should address the following eight areas of the organization: people; structure, roles, and responsibilities; behavior and skills; process and systems; policy and procedures; tools and technology; time and resources; and values, habits, beliefs, and assumptions (culture).

- The final requirement of consolidation is stamina. The leader must continue feeding and starving to allow change to progress through the structural, behavioral, and cultural levels. Until change moves to the cultural level, the restraining forces of the status quo can reassert themselves and reverse the gains.

CHAPTER TEN

CONCLUSION

There is nothing stable in the world—uproar's our
only musick.
JOHN KEATS

On one occasion, British prime minister Harold Macmillan was asked what his greatest challenge was. He responded, "Events, my dear boy, events." That is the precise nature of the challenge that leaders face in the global age. You don't know what kind of events will present themselves, and you don't know exactly when. But what you do know with absolute certainty is that they will come. In the meantime, to prevent events from overtaking you, it makes eminently good sense to prepare your response for their arrival. More than ever before, this means becoming a student of organizational change and understanding the underlying principles. Whether you consider it a curse or fortune of circumstance, you have been asked to lead in the global age. The environment is faster and more turbulent than anything of the past, and I think there will be no spontaneous return to order.

I began this book by making the argument that accelerating environmental change is challenging leaders in unprecedented ways and creating a rising tide of incompetence—not because leaders are less capable but because new requirements are being thrust on them. Unless you can learn how to lead change, the environment will expedite your ineptitude and push you out as a casualty of the Peter principle—a principle that says people rise to the level of their incompetence. What compounds the problem is that the broader shortage of leadership talent is kicking managers upstairs even faster. The talent crunch is tapping thousands of young leaders very early and asking them to lead sooner than they expected.

In addition to the EPIC methodology that I have laid out in the previous chapters, I raise two additional questions: First, does your leadership style matter? Second, if culture is both friend and foe in organizational change, what should you do about it?

A CALL FOR OPENNESS

I have worked with highly successful leaders who are unimaginative, boring, and stale. I've worked with others who don't think strategically, can't comprehend operations, or don't have a technical bone in their body. Of course, every leader possesses a different constellation of skills, but I have yet to meet a truly outstanding change leader who was an interpersonal disaster. If there are any stylistic demands of a change leader in the global age, there is at least one that has to do with openness. Leaders who haven't moved with the times on this issue possess a clear liability. Some leaders are too withdrawn for people to go at risk with them. Others live on the dark side of charisma, leading with a false sense of openness that repels people for different reasons. In each case, lack of openness poses a challenge to effective change leadership.

Numerous studies find that a variety of leadership styles can yield results. I agree, albeit with the caveat that the leader remains fundamentally open to other people's views, feelings, and aspirations. This stylistic variable is critical because the global age demands collaboration in order to maintain competitive advantage. Leading change is not a solo act. It's not a function of individual brilliance or skillful manipulation or cunning. The enduring truth is that change leadership is mostly about people. What an avalanche of data confirm is that an open, collaborative, transparent, and approachable style is far more successful in generating and replenishing energy in exchange for discretionary effort than any species of a closed, rigid, paternalistic, or authoritarian approach.

Can you be an unassuming or introverted personality and succeed? Of course you can, provided that at some level and in some way, you are able to express genuine concern for people, invite them to challenge you, reveal your motives, and demonstrate emotional control under pressure. The way you manifest openness can vary, but it must be present and discernable to others.

Consider that leaders generally begin the work of leading change in a deficit position. For example, the Edelman Trust Barometer 2007 reports that only 22 percent of respondents in the United States trust CEOs generally. And it doesn't get much better if you're not a CEO: only 36 percent trust rank-and-file employees.[1] So whether you're a CEO or a frontline supervisor, you face an uphill battle to build trust and pull energy out of the organizational system.

What does style have to do with these findings? In the same Edelman study, Nancy Turett, the chair of Edelman in Canada and Latin America, makes the observation that "openness trumps an image of perfection."[2] This doesn't mean that credibility comes from showcasing your weaknesses, but it does say that people want to see that you are willing to be accountable and that you won't try to hide your shortcomings. People still hold their leaders to higher standards than they hold themselves, but when a mistake has been made, people want their leaders to square up to the truth. They want to see that their leaders are trying to manage reality rather than an image. Leaders who are transparent have an advantage: they gain credibility faster and keep it longer in the face of adversity. Openness puts people at ease. Can you name a leader who in recent years has been convicted in a corporate scandal who had a truly open style? It doesn't work. You can't create and conceal an edifice of corruption if you're open.

In the past, leaders often expected people to support them out of duty. General George C. Marshall summarized the old conventional wisdom this way: "Enlisted men may be entitled to morale problems, but officers are not. I expect all officers in this department to take care of their own morale. No one is taking care of my morale."[3] That approach may have worked in the past, but in the global age, it comes across as glib, detached, and flippant. If you're the leader asking others to go at risk with you, people want to know that you are human, that you will shoulder your share of the sacrifice, and that you are vulnerable to loss as much as they are. They also want to see evidence that you have what it takes to lead. Openness conveys that you acknowledge the reality of your own strengths and limitations, your dependence on others, and the reality of the challenges you face. It presents your values and motives for examination.

Burn the Houses, Save the Nails

Now the second point: if we know anything about culture in organizations, we know that it matters. It exerts an autonomous influence on performance, competitiveness, and contribution. It is relevant to every aim and a factor in every outcome.[4] Those who dismiss it as a residual category deny reality and need to take a closer look.

Cultures do nothing suddenly. So here's the problem: If culture is the hardest and slowest thing to change, how should you address it? If we change the culture, we may be sowing the seeds of our greatest resistance in the future. But if we want to consolidate change and reap its full benefit, we need culture to hold change in place. Someday the new culture may become obsolete and the biggest obstacle to ongoing competitiveness in the next strategy cycle. Once new culture cures around change, it holds the change in place and makes it sustainable. Recasting the culture therefore is bound to be an intractable problem. This raises some interesting questions:

- If culture change is slower than the average strategy cycle, how can you implement change and reap the benefits if the culture never has time to consolidate?
- Can or should you try to effect organizational change at the structural and behavioral levels and simply avoid trying to consolidate it all the way to the cultural level?
- From a cultural standpoint, is there a way to keep change shallow and unhabituated? In other words, should you avoid driving the piles of change as deep so you can pull them out again and place them somewhere else more easily? Is there a transitional formlessness that organizational culture can or should take on so it doesn't work against you?

If you review early American history, there's an interesting parallel between building a house then and building a modern organization today. In colonial times, pioneers pushed out the western frontier. They would find a spot to settle, build their homes, and stay until the prospect of better land, better conditions, and a brighter future appeared. Often when settlers moved west, they burned their houses to reclaim the nails. The hand-forged nails were so rare and valuable that they represented the one thing they would not leave behind.

Metaphorically speaking, it should be the same today. In the global age, you must stand ready to abandon almost any aspect of an organization in order to press forward to more fertile fields. I agree with the assessment made by Deloitte consultants that leaders should not take "culture as a given, but rather as part of the business model to shape and form to help achieve their strategic objectives and capture financial returns."[5]

In almost every organization I studied, senior leaders readily acknowledged that nothing is sacrosanct, that anything can change at any time. But there was one exception: values. When it comes to changing culture, the cutting point is between values and everything else. Values are the one element of an organization that should endure through transformational change. Values represent precious, freestanding assets that should be independent of strategy. They provide continuity and identity when everything else becomes expendable.[6] Leaders should intentionally shape and manage culture as part of the strategy but look on values as part of the unchanging soul of the organization.

Values constitute the core element of culture that should stay in place. Let the strategy, structure, process, and systems go if need be, but keep the values. Cases in which leaders have successfully remodeled an entire enterprise represent organizational change in its comprehensive and supreme category. We learn from these cases that retaining values through the process of change is not only possible but necessary to provide continuity. In fact, values are the deepest source of identity that an organization can have. Ironically, perhaps, organizations with the strongest values often have the highest adaptive capacity because people attach themselves to the values and understand that everything else is on the table.

Research Appendix

As the basis of research for this book, I selected fifty-three cases of organizational change for study. The cases involved minor, mid-range, and major change and represented business, education, health care, government, and nonprofit organizations in small, midsized, and large organizations. All cases were taken from U.S.-based organizations or foreign-based organizations with U.S. operations. Cases were also selected to represent a cross section of major categories of change:

- Institutional mission, vision, and values

  - Major shift in institutional mission
  - Definition and implementation of new values
  - Shift in institutional mission

- Strategy, business model

  - Major shift in strategy or business model

- Human resources

  - Competency development, promotion, and training
  - Diversity initiative
  - Creation of a succession planning system
  - Transition of chief executive

- Mergers, acquisitions, and divestures

  - Major organizational structure and cost reduction
  - Centralization of functions
  - Creation of shared service organization
  - Major process or function outsourcing
  - Major reductions in force/layoffs
  - Chapter 11 bankruptcy and reorganization

- Business process redesign

  - Revenue and billing cycle improvement
  - Procurement process redesign
  - Sales forecasting redesign
  - Shorten product development cycle
  - Improve efficiency of supply chain
  - Reduce inventory
  - Reduce manufacturing costs

- Information technology systems implementation

  - Enterprise resource planning systems
  - Customer relationship management systems
  - Learning management systems
  - Human resource systems

RESEARCH AND INTERVIEW QUESTIONS

I conducted semistructured, in-depth interviews with leaders directly responsible for the change initiatives as well as other members of the organizations at lower levels who were involved at some level to implement the change initiatives. The qualitative interviewing format was based on a standard interview protocol, consisting of the following question categories and items:

Background

- What was the rationale for change? Why did you do it? Where did the idea or impetus for change originate? Were you reacting to a need or responding to an opportunity?
- Was the change minor, medium, or major? How deep and how broad was the impact?
- Was the change performance or compliance based? In other words, did it require people to behave, work, and perform differently, or did it merely require people to accept or comply with something new such as a policy?
- What areas of the organization were affected the most by the change?

  - Mission, vision, values
  - Major strategy

- Structure, roles, responsibilities
- Tools, equipment, technology
- Policies and procedures
- Processes and systems
- Skills and competencies
- Culture
- Specific personnel

- Did you design, develop, or decide on the change, or did you inherit the change from higher levels in the organization?
- What was your personal role in implementing the change?

Preparation

- What role did organizational history play? Were there legacies of the past that helped or hindered change?
- What is the organization's track record with organizational change? How did this affect the process and outcome?
- How would you rate your organization's overall agility or change-readiness level when you started the change process? What factors explain your rating? Did you think about this before you launched change?
- What was the level of urgency associated with the change before implementation? Was there a visible threat or crisis? Explain. Did you do anything to try to increase urgency?
- What role did other organizational attributes such as size, age, institutional complexity play?
- Was culture a net asset or liability? Why?
- How prepared was the organization for change? Explain.
- Are there other elements of past performance that were relevant to the outcome, either positive or negative?
- Did leadership try to prepare the organization for change in advance? If so, how? Did this make a difference? What did you learn from this?

Structure

- Was there a steering team responsible for implementing change? Did it consist of full-time or part-time resources? Who was on the team? What authority did they have? Whom did they report to? How did you select the members?

- What process did the team follow?
- What were the specific responsibilities of the team?
- What metrics did the team define and track?
- Did the team use incentives? How?
- How did the team hold people accountable?
- Did you formally disband or decommission the team?

Process

- Was there a formal planning process for change? Did you establish a formal budget, schedule, milestones?
- How long did the planning and preparation last?
- How was the implementation stage of change initiated? Was it formal or informal?
- Were there clearly established and communicated goals? Were there short-term versus long-term goals?
- Was there a broader vision for change? How did change tie to mission, vision, and strategy? Did people understand it? How do you know that?
- How was change communicated? What channels were used?
- How was progress tracked and communicated? How well did it work?
- Was there a formal communications process for change?
- Were there discernable stages to the change process? What were they? How long did each stage last?
- Did the effort stall or dip into a failure at any point in the process? Why?
- If the effort started to fail, did the effort recover? How and why? Were there points along the way when people doubted or gave up hope?

Technical Resources

- What internal technical resources did you use to support the change process? How reliant were you on these resources? How did they perform?
- What outside technical resources did you use to support the change process? How reliant were you on these resources? How did they perform?

Barriers and Resistance

- What barriers did you encounter? Did you overcome them? How? Did you predict or anticipate the resistance?
- What resistance did you encounter? Where did it come from? Why? How did you address it? Did you predict or anticipate the resistance?
- What degree of support did you have at the beginning? What made it increase or decrease over time?

Leadership

- What role did senior leadership play? What were the main strengths and weaknesses of senior leadership?
- Was leadership considered credible? How and why? Did leadership have enough credibility at the beginning to assemble a coalition?
- How committed was top leadership to the change?
- Was there an executive sponsor?
- Was there a supportive coalition? What stakeholder groups were part of the coalition? What did they care about? What assets did they have? How did they use them? Did leadership actively recruit members of the coalition?
- When did leadership matter the most? How was it manifest?
- What attributes of leadership were most important?

Outcome

- How did you define success?
- Do you consider the change an overall success or failure? Why?
- What original objectives did you meet? What original objectives did you miss?
- If it failed, why? Did the change generate positive results before it failed?
- What were the technical causes of failure?
- What were the nontechnical or human causes of failure?
- Did the change reach consolidation? Do you still have the benefits of change today?

- Is the change firmly rooted in the culture?
- Did the change ever unravel partially or completely at any time in the process?
- What are the most important lessons that you learned from the experience?

Notes

Chapter One

1. Carlos Frias and William M. Hartnett, "Heavy Pressure: NFL Players Struggle with Weight Game." *Palm Beat Post*, Oct. 29, 2006.
2. Retrieved Feb. 6, 2007, from www.nba.com/players/international_player_directory.html.
3. Burson Marsteller; retrieved Jan. 10, 2007, from http://www.ceogo.com/pages/home.
4. See Liberum Research's report for management changes in 2006 of North American public companies at http://www.liberum.twst.com.
5. Conference Board, *CEO Challenge: Top 10 Challenges* (New York: Conference Board, 2004).
6. See www.leadershipiq.com/news_mismanagement.html, June 27, 2005; retrieved January 11, 2007. See also Conference Board, "CEO Challenge, p. 3.
7. Peter Cheese, "Disturbing the System." *Accenture Outlook Journal*, June 2004, p. 1. See also Michael Beer and N. Nohria, "Cracking the Code of Change," *Harvard Business Review*, 2000, *78*, 133–141. Beer and Nohria cite a failure rate of two-thirds.
8. Robert J. Grossman, "IBM's HR Takes a Risk," *HRMagazine*, Apr. 27, 2007, p. 57.
9. Bill George, Peter Sims, Andrew N. McLean, and Diana Mayer, "Discovering Your Authentic Leadership," *Harvard Business Review*, Feb. 2007, p. 138.
10. Dov Frohman, "Leadership Under Fire,"*Harvard Business Review*, Dec. 2006, p. 126. I agree with Frohman's statement that "the primary task of a leader is to ensure the survival of the organization."
11. Ronald A. Heifetz and Donald L. Laurie, "The Work of Leadership," *Harvard Business Review*, Jan.–Feb. 1997, p. 124. They also state, "The new role of a leader is to help people face reality and mobilize them to make change." See William C. Taylor, "The Leader of the Future," *Fast Company*, June 25, 1999, p. 130.

12. John S. McClenahen, "The Effective Executive," *IndustryWeek*, June 7, 1999, p. 100.
13. Warren Bennis, "Leaders: Don't Go It Alone," *Harvard Management Update*, Dec. 2006, p. 9.
14. Paul Michelman, "What Leaders Allow Themselves to Know: Warren Bennis Unveils Some New Thinking on the Filters That Govern Decision Making," in *Mastering the Challenges of 21st Century Leadership* (Boston: Harvard Business School Press, 2004), p. 4.
15. Phil Rosenzweig, "The Halo Effect, and Other Managerial Delusions," *McKinsey Quarterly*, 2007, no. 1, 83, 84.
16. Retrieved Feb. 22, 2007, from blog.guykawasaki.com.
17. U.S. Department of Commerce, Bureau of Economic Analysis; retrieved Mar. 6, 2007, from http://www.bea.gov/briefrm/saving.htm.
18. Marc Gunther, "Going Green," *Fortune*, Apr. 2, 2007, p. 44.
19. Alan Deutschman, "Why Is This Man Smiling?" *Fast Company*, Apr. 2007, p. 63.
20. See Patricia M. Lines, *Homeschoolers: Estimating Numbers and Growth* (Washington, D.C.: National Institute on Student Achievement, Curriculum, and Assessment, Office of Educational Research and Improvement, U.S. Department of Education, Web edition, spring 1999); retrieved Feb. 7, 2007, from http://www.ed.gov/ offices/OERI /SAI/homeschool/index.html. *Homeschooling in the United States: 2003* (Washington, D.C.: National Center for Education Statistics, U.S. Department of Education, 2004); retrieved Feb. 22, 2007, from http//ncesed.gov/publs2006/homeschool/.
21. "Face Value: Nasdaq's Nemesis," *Economist*, Mar. 17, 2007, p. 74.
22. Steven Rattner, "Red All Over," *Wall Street Journal*, Feb. 15, 2007, p. A19.
23. Ilan Brat and Bryan Gruley, "Global Trade Galvanizes Caterpillar," *Wall Street Journal*, Feb. 26, 2007, p. B1.
24. Ram Charan, *Know-How: The Eight Skills That Separate People Who Perform from Those Who Don't* (New York: Crown Business, 2007), p. 55.
25. Brian Wallace, "Don't Get in a Rut," *Deseret News*, Jan. 12, 2007, p. D9.
26. For a good summary of innovation and trend sorting practices, see John F. Engel, Anita M. Thompson, Paul F. Nunes, and Jane C. Linder, "Innovation Unbound," *Outlook Journal*, Jan. 2006; retrieved Apr. 18, 2007, from http://www.accenture.com/Global/Research_ and_Insights/Outlook/By_Issue/Y2006/Innovation.htm.

27. Clive Thompson, "A Head for Detail," *Fast Company*, Nov. 2006, p. 72.

28. See the top countries or region of origin using PCT: www.wipo.int/ipstats/en/statistics/patents/top_countries.html.

29. "By the Numbers," *Fast Company*, July–Aug. 2006, p. 86.

30. Ian Davis and Elizabeth Stephenson, "Ten Trends to Watch in 2006," *McKinsey Quarterly*, Feb. 23, 2006; retrieved Mar. 14, 2007, from http://www.mckinseyquarterly.com/article_page.aspx?ar=1734.

31. Sourceforge.com alone reports that it is now hosting 136,000 such programs; retrieved Feb. 15, 2007, from http://sourceforge.net.

32. Andrew Zoll, "Demographics: The Population Hourglass," *Fast Company*, Mar. 6, 2006, p. 63.

33. U.S. Bureau of Labor Statistics, retrieved from www.bls.gov.

34. Jeffrey Pfeffer, "Why Free Agents Don't Feel Free," *Business 2.0*, Oct. 2006, p. 78.

35. David Kirkpatrick, "Making Connections," *Fortune*, Aug. 7, 2006, p. 31.

36. Steven Ike, "Russia's Population Falling Fast," BBC News, June 7, 2006. Demographers have established that the total fertility rate (the number of births to the average woman over her lifetime) must be at least 2.1 in order to prevent population decline, assuming no immigration. See Gary S. Becker, "Missing Children," *Wall Street Journal*, Sept. 1, 2006, p. A14.

37. Charles Fishman, "Message in a Bottle," *Fast Company*, July/Aug. 2007, p. 113.

38. Davis and Stephenson, "Ten Trends to Watch in 2006."

39. Diana Farrell, Martha A. Laboissiere, and Jaeson Rosenfeld, "Sizing the Emerging Global Labor Market," *McKinsey Quarterly*, no. 3, 2005; retrieved Dec. 7, 2007, from http://www.mckinseyquarterly.com/article_page.aspx?ar=1635.

40. Maurice R. Greenberg, "Regulation, Yes. Strangulation, No," *Wall Street Journal*, Aug. 21, 2006, p. A10.

41. *Global Facts and Forecasts: World Press Trends 2005* (London: ZenithOptimedia, 2006).

42. Michael Mandel, "Can Anyone Steer the Economy?" *BusinessWeek*, Nov. 20, 2006, p. 58.

43. Adam Segal, "Is America Losing Its Edge?" *Foreign Affairs*, Nov.–Dec. 2004; retrieved Jan. 19, 2007, from http://www.foreignaffairs.org/20041101facomment83601/adam-segal/is-america-losing-its-edge.html.

44. Michael R. Bloomberg. "Flabby, Inefficient, Outdated," *Wall Street Journal*, Dec. 14, 2006, p. A20.
45. Jonathan D. Glater and Alan Finder, "In Tuition Game, Popularity Rises with Price," *New York Times*, Dec. 12, 2006.
46. Organization for Economic Co-operation and Development, *Education at a Glance—OECD Indicators 2004* (Paris: Organization for Economic Co-operation and Development, 2005).
47. "Education Online," *US News & World Report*, Oct. 16, 2006, p. 61.
48. Maria Cheng, "AIDS to Be Third Leading Cause of Death," CBSNews.com, Nov. 29, 2006.
49. Matthew Herper and Robert Langreth, "Dangerous Devices," *Forbes*, Nov. 27, 2006, p. 96.
50. Marc Kaufman and Rob Stein, "Record Share of Economy Spent on Healthcare," *Washington Post*, Jan. 10, 2006, p. A1.
51. Steven Kurtz and others, "The Future Burden of Hip and Knee Revisions: U.S. Projections from 2005 to 2030" (paper presented at the Seventy-Third Annual Meeting of the American Academy of Orthopaedic Surgeons, Chicago, Mar. 22–26, 2006).
52. Thomas L. Friedman. *The World Is Flat* (New York: Farrar, Straus and Giroux, 2005). Similarly, American and British companies are outsourcing basic legal work to lawyers in India. See Eric Bellman and Nathan Koppel, "More U.S. Legal Work Moves to India's Low-Cost Lawyers," *Wall Street Journal*, Sept. 28, 2005, p. B1. Outsourced legal work mainly consists of patent applications, divorce papers, and legal research.
53. Daniel Larkin, "Meet Cyberspace's Head Fed," *BusinessWeek*, May 30, 2005, p. 77. Cyber- or e-crime includes virus attacks, computer break-ins, online scams, auctioning stolen merchandise, and identity theft.
54. C. Raja Mohan, "India and the Balance of Power," *Foreign Affairs*, July–Aug. 2006; retrieved Dec. 14, 2006, from http://www.foreign-affairs.org/20060701faessay85402/c-raja-mohan/india-and-the-balance-of-power.html.
55. Ben W. Heineman Jr. and Fritz Heimann, "The Long War Against Corruption," *Foreign Affairs*, May–June 2006; retrieved Dec. 14, 2006, from http://www.foreignaffairs.org/20060501faessay85305/ben-w-heineman-jr-fritz-heimann/the-long-war-against-corruption.html.
56. N. Gregory Mankiw and Phillip L. Swagel, "Anti-Dumping: The Third Rail of Trade Policy," *Foreign Affairs*, Dec. 2005; retrieved

Dec. 14, 2006, from http://www.foreignaffairs.org/20051201faessay-84708/n-gregory-mankiw-phillip-l-swagel/antidumping-the-third-rail-of-trade-policy.html.

57. Tim Kane, Kim R. Holmes, and Mary Anastasia O'Grady, *2007 Index of Economic Freedom* (Washington, D.C.: Heritage Foundation and Dow Jones, 2007).

58. Boris Worm and others, "Impact of Biodiversity Loss on Ocean Ecosystem Services," *Science*, Nov. 3, 2006, pp. 787–790.

59. William K. Caesar, Jens Riese, and Thomas Seitz. "Betting on Biofuels." *McKinsey Quarterly*, no. 2. 2007.

60. Victoria Markham, *U.S. National Report on Population and the Environment* (New Canaan, Conn.: Center for Environment and Population, Fall/Winter 2006), p. 8.

61. "Record Year for Wind Energy," press release, Feb. 17, 2006; retrieved Dec. 16, 2006, from http://www.gwec.net/index.php?id=30&no_cache=1&tx_ttnews%5Btt_news%5D=21&tx_ttnews%5BbackPid%5D=4&cHash=d0118b8972.

62. Gregory Mock, "How Much Do We Consume?" *World Resources*, June 2000; retrieved Dec. 17, 2006, from http://earthtrends.wri.org/features/view_feature.php?fid=7&theme=6.

63. Charles Handy, *The Age of Unreason* (Boston: Harvard Business School Press, 1989), p. 4.

64. Bill Breen. "C. K. Prahalad: Pyramid Schemer," *Fast Company*, Mar. 2007, p. 79.

65. Ray Kurzweil, "The Law of Accelerating Returns." 2001; retrieved Jan. 22, 2007, from http://www.kurzweilai.net/articles/art0134.html?printable=1.

66. Robert J. Samuelson, "The Next Capitalism," *Newsweek*, Oct. 30, 2006, p. 45.

67. Geoffrey Colvin, "Who Wants to Be the Boss?" *Fortune*, Feb. 20, 2006, pp. 76–77.

68. William H. Gates III, *Business at the Speed of Thought* (New York: Warner Books, 1999), introduction.

69. Louis V. Gerstner Jr., *Who Says Elephants Can't Dance?* (New York: HarperBusiness, 2002), p. 214.

70. Larry Bossidy and Ram Charan, *Confronting Reality: Doing What Matters to Get Things Right* (New York: Crown Business, 2004), p. 7.

71. See James MacGregor Burns and Georgia J. Sorenson, *Dead Center: Clinton-Gore Leadership and the Perils of Moderation* (New York: Scribner, 2000).

72. Accelerating change requires a shift in several leadership competencies. For example, because of an increasingly complex and demanding environment, leaders have to be more collaborative and less directive, more emotionally aware, more cross-culturally fluent, and more flexible in every aspect. See, for example, Marshall Goldsmith, Cathy L. Greenbert, Alistair Robertson, and Maya Hu-Chain, *Global Leadership: The Next Generation* (Upper Saddle River, N.J.: Prentice Hall, 2003). See also Morgan W. McCall Jr. and George P. Hollenbeck, *Developing Global Executives* (Boston: Harvard Business School Press, 2002).

73. "Letter from the Editor," *Fast Company*, June 2006, p. 12.

74. Sven Behrendt and Parag Khannna, "Geopolitics and the Global Corporation," *Strategy + Business*, 2003, *32*, 69–75. The authors note that the instability of the global environment is one of system discontinuity. The implication is that adaptive challenges are now totally beyond our ability to predict.

75. Roger L. Boehm, "The Future of the Global Workplace: An Interview with the CEO of Manpower," *McKinsey Quarterly*, Mar. 20, 2006; retrieved Dec. 11, 2007, from http://www.mckinseyquarterly.com/article_page.aspx?ar=1709. Jeff Joerres, the CEO of Manpower, states, "Today hot jobs turn cold almost as fast as a product's life cycle changes. So if the cycle used to be three years, now it's nine months. Every industry has its own speed of compression, of course, but underneath the compression is a never-ending treadmill of improving your skills, and it's quite sobering for people to find themselves on the cold list when 12 months before they were on the hot list."

76. Gerstner, *Who Says Elephants Can't Dance?* p. 235.

77. Abraham Lincoln, Second Annual Address to Congress, Dec. 1, 1862; retrieved Dec. 5, 2007, from http://www.presidency.ucsb.edu/ws/index.php?pid=29503.

78. Peter Senge, *The Fifth Discipline: The Art and Practice of the Learning Organization* (New York: Doubleday, 1990), p. 114.

CHAPTER TWO

1. Tim Breene, Walter E. Shill, and Paul F. Nunes, "Transformation: Changing Ahead of the Curve," *Outlook Journal*, Jan. 2007, p. 4.

2. The term *punctuated equilibrium* was coined by Niles Eldredge and Stephen Jay Gould in a landmark paper written in 1972. The theory, out of evolutionary biology, submits that species are relatively

stable for long periods of time. I'm not suggesting that this theory resembles the cycles of continuity and discontinuity that characterize commercial markets. Markets vary. Some do resemble this pattern, and others resemble something more along the lines of chaotic disequilibrium because there seem to be few, if any, periods of stability. See Eldredge and Gould. "Punctuated Equilibria: An Alternative to Phyletic Gradualism," in T.J.M. Schopf (ed.), *Models in Paleobiology* (New York: Freeman, 1972).

3. The reality of many organizations, especially those that are being tossed by dramatic external changes, is that they cycle through periods of stability and instability based on external threats and upheavals. See Connie J. G. Gersick, "Revolutionary Change Theories: A Multilevel Exploration of the Punctuated Equilibrium Paradigm," *Academy of Management Review*, 1991, *16*, 10–36. Gersick writes that "within equilibrium periods, the system's basic organization and activity patterns stay the same, and the equilibrium period consists of maintaining and carrying out these choices" (p. 16). In order to perform operational work and provide current products or services, an organization's internal systems must be in a state of relative equilibrium.

4. Rosabeth Moss Kanter, "Managing Through the Miserable Middle," *Business 2.0*, Nov. 2001.

5. The McKinsey 7-S model makes the distinction between hard S's (strategy, structure, and systems) and soft S's (skills, staff, style, and shared values). The model, developed by Richard Pascale, Anthony Athos, Tom Peters, and Robert Waterman in 1978, was first included in Pascale and Athos's book, *The Art of Japanese Management* (New York: Warner Books, 1981), and then in Tom Peters and Robert Waterman's book, *In Search of Excellence* (New York: Warner Books, 1982).

6. Harold L. Sirkin, Perry Keenan, and Alan Jackson, "The Hard Side of Change Management," *Harvard Business Review*, Oct. 2005, p. 110. Despite the authors' contention, the "Dice" model, which includes the factors of duration, integrity, commitment, and effort, is not primarily a model of hard factors. Clearly two of those factors, commitment and effort, are indisputably soft in the literature of change management, and a third factor, integrity, which means the skills and capability of team members, is also arguably soft in many respects, unless we are talking about technical expertise. The Boston Consulting Group's Dice framework is a helpful explanatory model, but it is not a prescriptive model. In other words, it does not help leaders know how to increase the factors that it attempts to measure.

In the end, it appears that the framework simply underscores the basic principle that obvious hard factors, such as time and technical resources, are important to success but that the elusive soft factor of energy will often be the determining factor of success, assuming hard factors are in place.

7. Generally the use of hard-side resources should be based on the risk level of the change, which is generally proportional to the scope of the change. See Cisco Systems, *Change Management: Best Practices White Paper* (San Jose, Calif.: Cisco Systems, 2006).

8. There is substantial research supporting the claim that the human side is the most challenging aspect of leading change. For example, in a recent study by the Conference Board, respondents rated organizational resistance as the biggest challenge to implementing successful change. See *Effecting Change in Business Enterprises* (New York: Conference Board, 2005), p. 18. In an interview, Paul Allaire, CEO of Xerox, said, "The hardest stuff is the soft stuff." See Robert Howard, "The CEO as Organizational Architect: An Interview with Xerox's Paul Allaire," *Harvard Business Review*, Sept.–Oct. 1992, pp. 106–121. See also Robert Kegan and Lisa Laskow Lahey, "The Real Reason People Won't Change," *Harvard Business Review*, Nov. 2001, pp. 85–92. Jeanie Daniel Duck from the Boston Consulting Group states that "change is fundamentally about feelings; companies that want their workers to contribute with their heads and hearts have to accept that emotions are essential to the new management style." She further states that "the most successful change programs reveal that large organizations connect with their people most directly through values—and that values, ultimately, are about beliefs and feelings." See "Managing Change: The Art of Balancing,"*Harvard Business Review*, Nov.–Dec. 1993, p. 32.

9. See *Results Oriented Cultures: Implementation Steps to Assist Mergers and Organizational Transformations* (Washington, D.C.: U.S. General Accounting Office, July 2003), p. 1. There are also a host of studies that have analyzed the challenges of mergers and acquisitions, including recent studies by WatsonWyatt, PriceWaterhouseCoopers, A. T. Kearny, and Hewitt Associates. In every case, people or culture is cited as the biggest challenge to merger integration success.

10. Capgemini, Financial Services Practice, "Sales and Service Innovations"; retrieved Jan. 4, 2007, from http://www.answers.com/topic/capgemini.

11. David A. Nadler, *Champions of Change* (San Francisco: Jossey-Bass, 1998), p. 131.

12. Gautum Kumra, "Leading Change: An Interview with the Managing Director of Tata Motors," *McKinsey Quarterly*, Jan. 2007; retrieved Jan. 22, 2007, from http://www.mckinseyquarterly.com/article_page .aspx?ar=1908.

13. Ken Iverson, the former longtime CEO of Nucor Steel, now the largest steel company in the United States, observed at the end of his career: "Concede once and for all that employees, not managers, are the true engines of progress, and dedicate your management career to creating an environment in which employees can stretch for higher and higher levels of performance." See Ken Iverson, *Plain Talk: Lessons from a Business Maverick* (Hoboken, N.J.: Wiley, 1998), p. 98.

14. James K. Clifton, *Gallup Summit on Q12 Economics* (Washington, D.C.: Gallup Press, 2001), p. 1.

15. Marc Vinson, Caroline Pung, and Javier Muniz Gonzalez-Blanch, "Organizing for Successful Change Management: A McKinsey Global Survey," *McKinsey Quarterly*, July 2006; retrieved Jan. 19, 2007, from http://www.mckinseyquarterly.com/article_page.aspx?L2= 18&L3=27&ar=1809&pagenum=1. It is noteworthy that the authors begin their review of survey results by stating, "The most successful transformations of business performance occur when executives mobilize and sustain energy within their organizations." See also Heather A. Haveman, "Between a Rock and a Hard Place: Organizational Change and Performance Under Conditions of Fundamental Environmental Transformation," *Administrative Science Quarterly*, 1992, *37*, 51.

16. John P. Kotter, "What Leaders Really Do," in *Harvard Business Review on Leadership* (Boston: Harvard University Press, 1990), p. 48.

17. Roger Dickout, Michael Denham, and Norman Blackwell, "Designing Change Programs That Won't Cost You Your Job," *McKinsey Quarterly*, 1995, no. 4, p. 105. It is also interesting that in their research of twenty-five corporate transformations, the authors observe that "understanding how to energize transformation is a neglected area in the change literature, but one that lies at the heart of successful change." See also Roger Dickout, "All I Ever Needed to Know About Change Management I Learned at Engineering School," *McKinsey Quarterly*, 1997, no. 2, p. 119, in which the author states, "If it is to drive continuing change, a change effort must build sources of energy as well producing results." He further states, "You must achieve results and build energy for more change. If you do not go forward, you will slip back."

18. See Pierre Bourdieu, "The Forms of Capital," in John G. Richardson (ed.), *Handbook of Theory and Research for the Sociology of Education* (Westport, Conn.: Greenwood Press, 1986). James S. Coleman, "Social Capital in the Creation of Human Capital," *American Journal of Sociology*, 1988, *94*, S95–S120. See also Rob Cross, Jane Linder, and Andrew Parker, "Charged Up: Managing the Energy That Drives Innovation" (Accenture and Network Roundtable, Mar. 2006); retrieved Feb. 8, 2007, from http://www.accenture.com/Global/ Research_and_Insights/Institute_For_High_Performance_Business /By_Publication_Type/Bylined_Articles/AllChargedUp.htm.

19. Deborah Steinborn, "Creating Better Business Leaders," *Wall Street Journal*, Mar. 30, 2006. The concept of creating and replenishing energy to move up and down the power curve is consistent with what John Alexander, president of the Center for Creative Leadership, explains in Steinborn's article as the second of the three tasks of a leader: "We like to say there are three leadership tasks. The first is setting direction or creating a vision for the future, followed by creating alignment in the organization. The third thing is gaining commitment from a team, group or organization to support the alignment or movement in a certain direction. Those are the basic tasks of leadership." Similar to "gaining commitment" is Chester I. Barnard's observation to "secure essential efforts" included in his seminal work, *The Functions of the Executive* (Boston: Harvard University Press, 1938), p. 217. He writes, "The essential executive functions are first, to provide the system of communication; second, to promote the securing of essential efforts; and third, to formulate and define purpose."

PART TWO: EVALUATE

1. Andrew S. Grove, *Only the Paranoid Survive* (New York: Currency Doubleday), 1996, p. 107.
2. "Globalisation's Offspring," *Economist*, Apr. 7, 2007, p. 11.

CHAPTER THREE

1. Richard T. Pascale, "Transformation," BBC Interview, Oct. 1991.
2. Gloria Macias-Lizaso and Kiko Thiel, "Building a Nimble Organization: A McKinsey Global Survey," *McKinsey Quarterly*, June 2006; retrieved Sept. 25, 2007, from http://www.mckinseyquarterly.com/

article_page.aspx?ar=1808. In the study, the researchers operationalize the definition of *agility* as "the ability to change tactics or direction quickly—that is, to anticipate, adapt to, and react decisively to events in the business environment."

3. Stephen J. Wall, "The Protean Organization: Learning to Love Change," *Organizational Dynamics*, 2005, *34*(1), 37–46. Wall argues that agility results from a "continuous, dynamic process of strategy making."

4. Stan David and Christopher Meyer, *Blur: The Speed of Change in the Connected Economy* (New York: Warner Books,), p. 126.

5. Larry Bossidy and Ram Charan, *Confronting Reality: Doing What Matters to Get Things Right* (New York: Crown Business, 2004), p. 169. See also by the same authors *The Essential of Managing Change and Transition* (Boston: Harvard University Press and Society for Human Resource Management, 2005), p. 51.

6. Mary Lynn Pulley and Michael Wakefield, *Building Resiliency: How to Thrive in Times of Change* (Greensboro, N.C.: Center for Creative Leadership, 2001), p. 11. Betsy Morris also notes that agility is becoming more important than scale, which is typically the strength of large organizations. See "New Rule: Agile Is Best; Being Big Can Bite You," *Fortune*, July 11, 2006; retrieved Oct. 3, 2006, from http://money.cnn.com/2006/07/10/magazines/fortune/rule1.fortune/index.htm.

7. The Center for Creative Leadership cites the research of Steve Zaccaro at George Mason University in which he describes adaptability as having three elements: cognitive, emotional, and dispositional. See Allan Calarco and Joan Gurvis, *Adaptability: Responding Effectively to Change* (Greensboro, N.C.: Center for Creative Leadership, 2006), p. 13. I find no material difference between the emotional and the dispositional elements they put forward as they describe dispositional adaptability to be "the ability to remain optimistic and at the same time realistic," which I consider part of emotional adaptability. From my perspective, there is a glaring gap in the model: the physical element, which becomes important especially in the course of pursuing complex, large-scale change.

8. Paul R. Bernthal and others, *ASTD Competency Study: Mapping the Future* (Alexandria, Va.: ASTD Press, 2004), p. 62. The ASTD competency model, which outlines competencies for workplace learning and performance professionals, is helpful in its definition of a competency termed demonstrating adaptability, in which it states, "Adjusts behavior—Quickly modifies behavior to deal effectively

with changes in the work environment; acquires new knowledge or skills to deal with the change; does not persist with the ineffective behaviors; shows resiliency and maintains effectiveness even in the face of uncertainty or ambiguity."

9. Elizabeth Kübler-Ross, *On Death and Dying* (New York: Scribner Classics, 1997). The stages of her five-phase model are denial, anger, bargaining, depression, and acceptance.

10. Michael Porter, *Competitive Advantage* (New York: Free Press, 1985). See also Jack Welch's characterization of strategy in which he uses the terms *high value* and *commodity* to represent the same two poles of strategic choice: Jack Welch, *Winning* (New York: HarperBusiness, 2005). These two choices do allow for successful strategies in the middle. Strategies in the middle, however, must create a successful combination of value and low cost.

11. W. Chan Kim and Renée Mauborgne, *Blue Ocean Strategy* (Boston: Harvard Business Review, 2005).

12. Geoffrey Colvin, "The Bionic Manager," *Fortune*, Sept. 19, 2005, p. 98.

13. Robert K. Wiggins and Timothy W. Ruefli, "Sustained Competitive Advantage: Temporal Dynamics and the Incidence and Persistence of Superior Economic Performance," *Organization Science*, 2002, *13*(1), 81–105. See also by the same authors, "Schumpeter's Ghost: Is Hypercompetition Making the Best of Times Shorter?" *Strategic Management Review*, 2005, *26*(10), 887–911.

14. Peter Drucker often gets credit for the term *planned abandonment*. In Peter Drucker, *Management Challenges for the Twenty-First Century* (New York: Harperbusiness, 1999), the idea of planned abandonment is a theme that runs throughout. But we must acknowledge the original and related concept of "creative destruction" that economist Joseph Schumpeter put forward in 1942. See Joseph A. Schumpeter, *Capitalism, Socialism and Democracy* (New York: HarperCollins, 1975). The most successful CEOs of the twentieth century collectively demonstrated a planned abandonment mentality. Noteworthy among them is Andy Grove, who led Intel for many years and titled his well-known memoir *Only the Paranoid Survive* (New York: Currency Doubleday, 1996), which is clearly a reflection of the same principle of elusive competitive advantage.

15. Gary Hamel, "Management à la Google," *Wall Street Journal*, May 26, 2006. I note Hamel's statement: "The capacity to evolve is the greatest advantage."

16. W. Chan Kim and Renée Mauborgne, "Tipping Point Leadership," *Harvard Business Review*, June 2002, pp. 76–83. The authors point

out that numbers alone won't build a case for change; dialogue is necessary to help people identify needs and opportunities. The need for change is often not self-evident. They write, "In many turnarounds, the hardest battle is simply getting people to agree on the causes of current problems and the need for change."

17. Frank Ostroff, "Change Management in Government," *Harvard Business Review*, May 2006, pp. 141–147. I agree with the fundamental point that for most organizations outside the public sector, change is mostly about achieving institutional mission rather than about generating profits or increasing shareholder return. However, both aims depend on similar aspects of competitiveness and performance.

18. Lester C. Thurow, "Building Wealth," *Atlantic Monthly*, 1999, *283*(6), 57–69.

19. The distinction between operational and change work is similar to the fundamental difference that defines leadership versus management. Two seminal articles address this issue. The first is Abraham Zaleznik, "Managers and Leaders," *Harvard Business Review*, May–June 1977, pp. 126–135. The other is John Kotter, "What Leaders Really Do," *Harvard Business Review*, May–June 1990, pp. 37–60. A similar distinction is also made by James MacGregor Burns in which he compares transformational leaders to transactional leaders, although there are differences in his conception. See James MacGregor Burns, *Leadership* (New York: HarperCollins, 1978). Another similar distinction is that made between operational work and projects. See *A Guide to the Project Management Body of Knowledge*, 3rd ed. (Newtown Square, Pa.: Project Management Institute, 2004). I would argue that the difference between operational and change work is even more fundamental. Change work is anything done to alter current operations, which includes many activities that are not and should not be converted into a project.

20. Eric D. Beinhocker, "The Adaptable Corporation," *McKinsey Quarterly*, 2006, no. 2, 76–87.

21. Charles Handy, *The Age of Unreason* (Boston: Harvard Business School Press, 1989).

22. Robert E. Quinn, "Moments of Greatness: Entering the Fundamental State of Leadership," *Harvard Business Review*, July–Aug. 2005, pp. 75–83. Quinn explains that people tend to defend the status quo with "self-protection and self-deception," and he makes the point that people usually won't move from it unless forced.

23. It can even get to the point of seemingly irrational behavior in which people become immobilized. Although they face a serious risk in

not pursuing change, they fear change so much that they conclude that the risk of change is too high to take a risk.

24. Kerry A. Bunker, "Coaching Leaders Through Change and Transition," in Sharon Ting and Peter Scisco (eds.), *The CCL Handbook of Coaching* (San Francisco: Jossey-Bass, 2006).

25. Les Worrall and Cary Cooper, "Short Changed," *People Management*, June 29, 2006, p. 36.

26. Association of Governing Boards of Universities and Colleges, *The Leadership Imperative: The Report of the AGB Task Force on the State of the Presidency in American Higher Education* (Washington, D.C.: Association of Governing Boards of Universities and Colleges, 2006), p. 27.

27. Michael T. Hannan and John Freeman, "Structural Inertia and Organizational Change," *American Sociological Review*, 1984, *49*(2), 149–164. As the authors point out, the most important factors contributing to structural inertia, and therefore increasing the risk of failure associated with change, are the age of the organization, the complexity of the organization, the size of the organization, and the duration of the change. As far as overall agility is concerned, however, the organization's history, industry characteristics, and leadership are also predictive of agility levels. On the factors of complexity, see Stuart Kauffman, *At Home in the Universe: The Search for the Laws of Self-Organization and Complexity* (New York: Oxford University Press, 1995).

28. Betsy Morris, "The New Rules," *Fortune*, July 24, 2006, p. 80.

29. The concept of total agility defined as the ability to deploy resources in the moment of need was developed by Conrad Gottfredson, an international expert in knowledge management systems. Interview with Gottfredson, Mar. 23, 2007.

30. Gautam Naik, "A Hospital Races to Learn Lessons of Ferrari Pit Stop," *Wall Street Journal*, Nov. 11, 2006, pp. A1, A10.

31. Diane Brady, "Secrets of an HR Superstar," *BusinessWeek*, Apr. 9, 2007, p. 66.

32. Google allows its engineers to spend up to 20 percent of their time working on "off-budget, out of scope" projects to provide "seed corn" for the future. See Hamel, "Management à la Google."

33. Among the group process techniques that can create significant intellectual and emotional agility in an organization, one of the best is the "future search" process, which is a longer and more comprehensive approach. See Marvin R. Weisboard and Sandra

Janoff, *Future Search: An Action Guide to Finding Common Ground in Organizations and Communities* (San Francisco: Barrett-Koehler, 2000).

34. Eric Abrahamson points out that Lou Gerstner did this constantly during his tenure at IBM. See Eric Abrahamson, "Change Without Pain,"*Harvard Business Review,* July–Aug. 2000, p. 78.

35. Tsun-Yan Hsieh and Dominic Barton, "Young Lions, High Priests, and Old Warriors," *McKinsey Quarterly*, 1995, no. 2, pp. 62–74. The authors point out that slowing down or not launching as many initiatives versus pursuing "one heroic charge" is a way to preserve resilience and avoid fatigue when there are clear shortages of leadership capacity. Another strategy is to sequence initiatives carefully and launch the most critical first.

CHAPTER FOUR

1. Peggy Pelt, *The Liberty Ship: Unique Cargo Ship of World War II.* 1994; retrieved Feb. 22, 2007, from http://organizations.ju.edu/fch/ 1994pelt. See also L. A. Sawyer and W. H. Mitchell, *The Liberty Ships,* 2nd ed. (London: Lloyd's of London Press, 1985).

2. James R. Chiles, "The Ships That Broke Hitler's Blockage,"*Invention and Technology Magazine,* Winter 1988, *3;* retrieved Feb. 22, 2007, from http://www.americanheritage.com/articles/magazine/it/1988/3/ 1988_3_26.shtml.

3. See Michael Beer, "Leading Change,"*Harvard Business Review,* Jan. 1988, p. 1. Beer states, "Dissatisfaction that leads to such loss of confidence is essential because it is the source of energy or motivation for the change and major organizational change requires an enormous amount of energy." Edgar Schein explains that we are willing to undertake change when "survival anxiety" is greater than "learning anxiety." See Edgar H. Schein, *The Corporate Culture Survival Guide* (San Francisco: Jossey-Bass, 1999), p. 121.

4. Jay A. Conger, Gretchen M. Spreitzer, and Edward E. Lawler III,*The Leader's Change Handbook* (San Francisco: Jossey-Bass, 1999).

5. Paul Hemp and Thomas A. Stewart, "Leading Change When Business Is Good: An Interview with Samuel J. Palmisano," *Harvard Business Review,* Dec. 2004, p. 66.

6. See*GE Annual Reports,* 1994, 1995. Jack Welch, *Jack: Straight from the Gut* (New York: WarnerBusiness, 2001).

7. Jack Welch, *Winning* (New York: HarperBusiness, 2005), p. 246.

8. See Chapter One of John P. Kotter and Dan C. Cohen, *The Heart of Change* (Boston: Harvard Business School Press, 2002). The gap in the authors' analysis is that it does not account for changes that possess little natural or inherent urgency and for which little more can be generated, especially changes based on opportunity. Their prescription fails to include the energy source of credibility, which must be used in combination with urgency to create enough overall energy to provide ignition to prepare for change.

9. Andrew S. Grove, *Only the Paranoid Survive* (New York: Bantam Doubleday, 1996), p. 3.

10. Bert A. Spector, "From Bogged Down to Fired Up: Inspiring Organizational Change," *Sloan Management Review*, 1989, *29*, 29–35.

11. "Business Prophet: How Strategy Guru C. K. Prahalad Is Changing the Way CEOs Think," *BusinessWeek*, Jan. 23, 2006, pp. 26–27; retrieved Dec. 12, 2006, from http://www.businessweek.com/magazine/content/06_04/b3968089.htm.

12. Gautum Kumra, "Leading Change: An Interview with the Managing Director of Tata Motors," *McKinsey Quarterly*, Jan. 2007; retrieved from http://www.mckinseyquarterly.com/article_page.aspx?ar=1908.

13. Louis Gerstner, *Who Says Elephants Can't Dance?* (New York: HarperBusiness, 2002).

14. Carolyn B. Aiken and Scott P. Keller, "The CEO's Role in Leading Transformation," *McKinsey Quarterly*, Feb. 2007; retrieved from http://www.mckinseyquarterly.com/article_page.aspx?ar=1912&L2=18&L3=0.

15. Alan Deutschman, "Making Change," *Fast Company*, May 2005, p. 55.

16. Justin Menkes, "The Leadership Difference: Executive Intelligence," *Leader to Leader*, Spring 2006, p. 51.

17. Norihiko Shirouzu, "As Rivals Catch Up, Toyota CEO Spurs Big Efficiency Drive," *Wall Street Journal*, Dec. 9–10, 2006, pp. A1, A6.

18. Joann Muller, "The Impatient Mr. Ghosn," *Forbes*, May 22, 2006, p. 106.

CHAPTER FIVE

1. Peter Drucker, *The Practice of Management* (New York: HarperCollins, 1954).

2. See Mark H. Moore, *Creating Public Value: Strategic Management in Government* (Cambridge, Mass.: Harvard University Press, 1995).

3. James M. Kouzes and Barry Z. Posner, *The Leadership Challenge*, 3rd ed. (San Francisco: Jossey-Bass, 2002). They write, "Credibility is the foundation of leadership," p. 37.
4. Rodger L. Boehm. "Leading Change: An Interview with the CEO of Deere & Company." *McKinsey Quarterly*, Dec. 2006; retrieved Jan. 12, 2007, from http://www.mckinseyquarterly.com/article_abstract .aspx?ar=1888.
5. Warren Bennis and Burt Nanus, *Leaders: The Strategies for Taking Charge* (New York: HarperCollins, 1985).
6. Marcus Buckingham and Curt Coffman, *First, Break All the Rules* (New York: Simon & Schuster, 1999), p. 155.
7. James O'Toole, *Leading Change: The Argument for Values-Based Leadership* (San Francisco: Jossey-Bass, 1995), p. 37.
8. Russell Hardin, "The Street-Level Epistemology of Trust," *Politics and Society*, 1993, *4*, 212–229.
9. Michael S. Malone, "The Un-Carly," *Wall Street Journal*, Apr. 14, 2007, p. A9.
10. Peggy Noonan, "Ronald Reagan: Fortieth President of the United States," in Robert A. Wilson (ed.), *Character Above All* (New York: Simon & Schuster, 1995), pp. 202–223.
11. See Robert E. Quinn's definition of the normal state as "comfort centered, externally directed, self focused, and internally closed," all of which combine to create a highly reactive condition. "Building the Bridge as You Walk on It," *Leader to Leader*, Fall 2004, pp. 21–26.
12. See David K. Carr, Kelvin J. Hard, and William J. Trahant, *Managing the Change Process* (New York: McGraw-Hill, 1996). The authors describe several characteristics that define an effective change sponsor.
13. Daryl R. Connor, *Managing at the Speed of Change* (New York: Villard Books, 1992), p. 122.

CHAPTER SIX

1. Monica Langley, "Inside Mulally's War Room: A Radical Overhaul of Ford," *Wall Street Journal*, Dec. 22, 2006, p. A10.
2. David Magee, *Turnaround: How Carlos Ghosn Rescued Nissan* (New York: HarperBusiness, 2003).
3. Gary Hamel, *Leading the Revolution* (Boston: Harvard Business School Press, 2000).
4. W. Chan Kim and Renée Mauborgne, "Tipping Point Leadership," *Harvard Business Review*, Apr. 2003, p. 28.

5. Richard Tanner Pascale and Jerry Sternin, "Your Company's Secret Change Agents," *Harvard Business Review*, May 2005, p. 74.
6. See Jonathan D. Day and Michael Jung, "Corporate Transformation Without a Crisis," *McKinsey Quarterly*, 2000, no. 4, p. 123. The authors note the dilemma in explaining that transformation requires central control and definition yet also a conversion of every individual through personal experience and participation.
7. Rosabeth Moss Kanter, "How Leaders Gain and Lose Confidence," *Leader to Leader*, Summer 1999, no. 13; retrieved Oct. 12, 2007, from http://www.leadertoleader.org/knowledgecenter/L2L/winter2005/kanter.html.

CHAPTER SEVEN

1. Peter Senge, *The Fifth Discipline: The Art and Practice of the Learning Organization* (New York: Doubleday, 1990), p. 153.
2. See *Employee Engagement: How to Build a High-Performance Workforce* (London: Melcrum Publishing, 2005).
3. Keith H. Hammonds, "Here Is How Michael E. Porter Regards the Business Landscape," *Fast Company*, Mar. 2001, p. 154.
4. Jim Collins, *Good to Great* (New York: HarperBusiness, 2001), p. 202.
5. Timothy R. Clark, "Vision in a Change-Battered Organization," HR.com, Jan. 2004.
6. Robert S. Kaplan and David P. Norton, "The Office of Strategy Management," *Harvard Business Review*, Oct. 2005, p. 72.
7. Quentin Hardy, "We Did It," *Forbes*, Aug. 11, 2003; retrieved Nov. 29, 2007, from http://www.forbes.com/forbes/2003/0811/076_print.html.
8. Quentin Hardy, "The UnCarly," *Forbes*, Mar. 12, 2007, pp. 82–89.
9. Giancarlo Ghislanzoni and Julie Shearn, "Leading Change: An Interview with the CEO of Banca Intesa," *McKinsey Quarterly*, Nov. 15, 2006; retrieved Nov. 30, 2007, from http://www.mckinseyquarterly.com/article_abstract.aspx?ar=1629.
10. James A. Phills Jr., "Leadership Matters—or Does It?" *Leader to Leader*, Spring 2005, p. 49.
11. Joseph L. Bower and Clark K. Gilbert, "How Managers' Everyday Decisions Create or Destroy Your Company's Strategy," *Harvard Business Review*, Feb. 2007, p. 79.

12. See Ghislanzoni and Shearn, "Leading Change."
13. Roger D'Aprix, *Communicating for Change* (San Francisco: Jossey-Bass, 1996).
14. See Athena D. Merritt, "Getting Company Message Across Is Hard, Firms Say," *Philadelphia Business Journal*, Sept. 13, 2005; retrieved Nov. 15, 2007, from http://philadelphia.bizjournals.com/philadelphia/stories/2005/09/12/daily22.html. In the survey of 472 organizations worldwide, 63 percent of the firms that responded said they considered aligning employees to the strategy of their business as their top employee communication goal, but just 37 percent said these efforts were successful.
15. See Boyd Clark and Ron Crossland, *The Leader's Voice* (New York: Select Books, 2002). According to their research, messages communicated informally break down at about the one-hundred-person mark.
16. Achieving and maintaining clarity of message becomes more difficult as more people become involved in change. From a communications standpoint, the number of interactions increases exponentially as more people get involved. Note, for example, the following equation, where I represents the number of interactions and N represents the number of people involved: $I = N (N - 1)/2$. According to this formula, three people have three possible interactions, five people have ten possible interactions, and ten people have forty-five possible interactions. This mathematically explains the basis for Colin Powell's borrowed statement from Michael Korda: "Great leaders are almost always great simplifiers, who can offer a solution everybody can understand." In Oren Harari, *The Leadership Secrets of Colin Powell* (New York: McGraw-Hill 2002), p. 260.
17. See Andrew S. Grove, *Only the Paranoid Survive* (New York: Bantam Doubleday, 1996) p. 140, in which he states, "To make it through the valley of the death successfully, your first task is to form a mental image of what the company should look like when you get to the other side. This image not only needs to be clear enough for you to visualize but it also has to be crisp enough so you can communicate it simply to your tired, demoralized and confused staff."
18. Bill Breen, "The Clear Leader," *Fast Company*, Mar. 2005, p. 65.
19. Blaise Pascal, *1660 Provincial Letters*, trans. Thomas M'Crie, Letter 16, Dec. 4, 1656; retrieved Mar. 23, 2007, from http://oregonstate.edu/instruct/phl302/texts/pascal/letters-contents.html.

20. "P&G: New and Improved," *BusinessWeek*, July 7, 2003; retrieved Mar. 20, 2007, from http://www.businessweek.com/magazine/content/03_27/b3840001_mz001.htm.

21. Alex Taylor, "Advice from a Fellow Outsider," *Fortune*, Apr. 4, 2005; retrieved Dec. 14, 2007, from http://money.cnn.com/magazines/fortune/fortune_archive/2005/04/04/8255919/index.htm.

22. Noel M. Tichy and Stratford Sherman, *Control Your Destiny or Someone Else Will* (New York: Doubleday, 1993), p. 48.

23. Interview with George Wright, Mar. 3, 2007.

24. For a good explanation of the attributes that tend toward stickiness, see Chip Heath and Dan Heath, *Made to Stick* (New York: Random House, 2007).

25. See James O'Toole, *Leadership A to Z: A Guide for the Appropriately Ambitious* (San Francisco: Jossey-Bass, 1999).

26. "Gadget Freak," *Fast Company*, Apr. 2007, p. 36.

27. Herbert A. Simon, "Designing Organizations for an Information-Rich World," in Martin Greenberger (ed.), *Computers, Communication, and the Public Interest* (Baltimore, Md.: Johns Hopkins University Press, 1971), pp. 40–41.

28. See Barbara Minto, *The Minto Pyramid Principle* (London: Minto International, 2003). Minto has perfected a methodology for sequencing messages according to the natural assimilation process of the human brain. Her point is to presort messages according to the way the brain wants them in the first place. This will facilitate assimilation, comprehension, and memory.

29. Deborah Ancona, Thomas W. Malone, Wanda J. Orlikowski, and Peter M. Senge, "In Praise of the Incomplete Leader," *Harvard Business Review*, Feb. 2007, pp. 92–100.

30. Association of Governing Boards of Universities and Colleges, *The Leadership Imperative: The Report of the AGB Task Force on the State of the Presidency in American Higher Education* (Washington, D.C.: Association of Governing Boards of Universities and Colleges, 2006), p. 6.

31. Communication is the most important principle in successful implementation. The syllogistic logic behind the premise is that implementation is based on motivation, motivation is based on understanding, understanding is based on communication, and therefore implementation is based on communication.

CHAPTER EIGHT

1. Research interview with Juliet Garcia, Apr. 3, 2007. The entire account cited at the beginning of this chapter is based on this interview.
2. Karl E. Weick, "Small Wins: Redefining the Scale of Social Problems," *American Psychologist*, 1984, *39*(1), 40–49.
3. Jim Collins, *Good to Great* (New York: HarperBusiness, 2001), p. 178.
4. See James Q. Wilson and George L. Kelling, "Broken Windows," *Atlantic Monthly*, Mar. 1982, pp. 29–38. The theory of early wins is similar to the broken window theory of crime put forward by Wilson and Kelling, with the difference being that one is a negative chain reaction and the other positive. In both instances, an event generates energy that leads to the next energy-generating event.
5. Rudolph W. Giuliani, *Leadership* (New York: Hyperion, 2002).
6. See Ellen Byron, "Call Me Mike!" *Wall Street Journal*, Mar. 27, 2006, p. B1.
7. See Jennifer A. LaClair and Ravi P. Rao, "Helping Employees Embrace Change," *McKinsey Quarterly*, 2002, no. 4; retrieved May 29, 2007, from http://www.mckinseyquarterly.com/article_page .aspx?ar=1225. The authors cite both financial and nonfinancial factors as critically important to successful change, especially among senior managers.
8. See Robert K. Merton, "The Unanticipated Consequences of Purposive Social Action," *American Sociological Review*, 1936, *1*, 894–904.
9. Peter Senge, *The Fifth Discipline: The Art and Practice of the Learning Organization* (New York: Doubleday, 1990), p. 88.
10. The expectation of personal impact or organizational gain is based on individual perception, of course. See Daryl R. Conner, *Managing at the Speed of Change* (New York: Villard, 1992).

CHAPTER NINE

1. See Malcolm Gladwell, *The Tipping Point* (New York: Little, Brown, 2000).
2. Thomas A. Stewart, "Architects of Change," *Harvard Business Review*, Apr. 2006, p. 10.

3. See Michael Beer, Russell A. Eisenstat, and Bert Spector, "Why Change Programs Don't Produce Change," *Harvard Business Review*, Nov.–Dec. 1990, p. 159. The authors correctly argue that because culture changes last, it is backward to attempt to change attitudes first. The correct approach, they hold, is to impose new roles, responsibilities, and relationships, allowing behavior and attitudes to follow over time.

4. Joseph Bower and Donald K. David, "Is This the End of Corporate Strategy?" *Financial Times*, Mar. 6, 2006; retrieved May 23, 2007, from http://www.ft.com/cms/s/68534436-ac64-11 da-8226-0000779e2340.html.

5. John D. Durrett, "Recovering from Crisis: An Interview with the CEO of McKesson," *McKinsey Quarterly*, no. 2, 2006; retrieved May 29, 2007, from http://www.mckinseyquarterly.com/article_page.aspx?ar=1742.

6. Louis V. Gerstner Jr., *Who Says Elephants Can't Dance?* (New York: HarperBusiness, 2002), p. 177. Gerstner refers to the challenge as the "rigor mortis that sets in around values and behaviors." Another example of culture being at the root of performance problems is Ford Motor Company. See Jeffrey McCracken, "'Way Forward,' Requires Shift at Ford," *Wall Street Journal*, Jan. 23, 2005, p. B1. The writer states, "The central challenge at Ford is fixing the company's culture, which past and present employees describe with words like 'cautious,' 'toxic,' 'cliquish,' and 'hierarchical.' "

7. See Rosabeth Moss Kanter, *The Change Masters* (New York: Simon & Schuster, 1984).

8. John R. Ehrenfeld, "The Roots of Sustainability," *MIT Sloan Management Review*, Winter 2005, p. 25.

9. Kurt Lewin, "Group Decision and Social Change," in T. M. Newcomb and E. L. Hartley (eds.), *Readings in Social Psychology* (Austin, Tex.: Holt, 1958). See also Kurt Lewin, *Field Theory in Social Science* (New York: HarperCollins, 1951).

10. Based on social network analysis, Rob Cross, Wayne Baker, and Andrew Parker put forward strong evidence that individuals tend to be energizers or de-energizers in a change effort. Identifying both and promoting the energizers while neutralizing the de-energizers is an important part of the consolidation process. See Rob Cross, Wayne Baker, and Andrew Parker, "What Creates Energy in Organizations?" *MIT Sloan Management Review*, 2003, 44(4), 51–56.

Chapter Ten

1. *Edelman Trust Barometer 2007* (Jan. 22, 2007), p. 10; retrieved May 2, 2007, from http://www.edelman.com/trust/2007/.
2. *Edelman Trust Barometer 2007*, p. 25.
3. Quoted in David McCullough, *Truman* (New York: Simon & Schuster, 2001), p. 560.
4. The fundamental tenet of culture is nowhere advanced more powerfully than in the work of the political scientist Samuel P. Huntington. See Samuel P. Huntington, "The Coming Clash of Civilizations?" *Foreign Affairs*, Summer 1993, pp. 22–49.
5. Stephanie Quappe, David Samso-Aparici, and Jon Warshawsky, *Corporate Culture Is Serious Business—How Building It Can Build Your Bottom Line* (New York: Deloitte, Nov. 30, 2006), p. 6; retrieved Mar. 7, 2007, from http://www.deloitte.com/dtt/article/0,1002, sid%253D26554%2526cid%253D123644,00.html.
6. Jim Collins comes to the same conclusion in his study of "good to great" companies. His summary statement on the issue is: "Enduring great companies preserve their core values and purpose while their business strategies and operating practices endlessly adapt to a changing world. This is the magical combination of 'preserve the core and stimulate progress.' " My analysis would take it a step further to say that organizations must now be willing to abandon even their core purpose, leaving values as the sole intact element of the organization. See Jim Collins, *Good to Great* (New York: HarperCollins, 2001), p. 195.

ABOUT THE AUTHOR

Timothy R. Clark is founder and chairman of TR Clark Associates, LLC, an international consulting and training organization that specializes in strategy, leadership development, and organizational change. He advises leaders and organizations around the world, helping them navigate change and develop the competencies they need to compete in the global age.

Clark earned a doctorate in politics and social science from Oxford University and was both a Fulbright and a British Research Scholar. He earned a master's degree from the University of Utah and a bachelor's degree from Brigham Young University, where he was named a first-team academic all-American football player.

INDEX